W9-BFT-813

THE ILLUSTRATED ENCYCLOPEDIA OF
WILDLIFE

VOLUME 9

Reptiles
and
Amphibians

MEDIA CENTER
EDEN PRAIRIE HIGH SCHOOL
17185 VALLEY VIEW ROAD
EDEN PRAIRIE, MN 55346

REFERENCE-- NOT TO BE
TAKEN FROM THIS ROOM

WITHDRAWN

Wildlife Consultant

MARY CORLISS PEARL, Ph. D.

Distributed by Encyclopaedia Britannica
Educational Corporation

Grey Castle Press

Published by Grey Castle Press, 1991

Distributed by Encyclopaedia Britannica Educational Corporation, 1991

All rights reserved. No part of this book may be reproduced or transmitted in any form or by any means electronic or mechanical, including photocopying, recording or by any information storage and retrieval system, without permission in writing from the Proprietor.

THE ILLUSTRATED ENCYCLOPEDIA OF WILDLIFE
Volume 9: REPTILES AND AMPHIBIANS

Copyright © EPIDEM-Istituto Geographico De Agostini S.p.A., Novara, Italy

Copyright © Orbis Publishing Ltd., London, England 1988/89

Organization and Americanization © Grey Castle Press, Inc., Lakeville, CT 06039

Library of Congress Cataloging-in-Publication Data
The Illustrated encyclopedia of wildlife.
    p.   cm.
      Contents: v. 1 – 5. The mammals — v. 6 – 8. The birds —
v. 9. Reptiles and amphibians — v. 10. The fishes —
v. 11 – 14. The invertebrates — v. 15. The invertebrates
and index.
    ISBN 1 – 55905 – 052 – 7
    1. Zoology.
QL45.2.I44 1991   90 – 3750
591—dc20   CIP

ISBN 1 – 55905 – 052 – 7 (complete set)
     1 – 55905 – 045 – 4 (Volume 9)

Printed in Spain

Photo Credits
Photographs were supplied by: *Heather Angel*: 1559; *Ardea*: (P. Morris) 1501; (H. & Y. Beste) 1608; (J. Daniels) 1759r; (Jean-Paul Ferraro) 1623; (K. Fink) 1694; (F. Gohier) 1576, 1741b; (H. Reinhard) 1688; *C. Bevilacqua*: 1752; *Bruce Coleman*: 1514l, 1570, 1586; (Andrada) 1513; 1737; (E. & P. Bauer) 1528t; (J. & D. Bartlett) 1656, 1678b, 1782l; (S.C. Bisserot) 1675b, 1723, 1740, 1791l; (M. Boulton) 1632; (M. Burnley) 1749; (J. Burton) 1521, 1540, 1562, 1566, 1603t, 1605b, 1632, 1675c, 1698t, 1700r, 1705, 1714, 1766, 1767, 1784, 1788, 1797, 1758, 1759l; (B. & C. Calhoun) 1789; (A. Compost) 1648, 1650; (S. Dalton) 1696, 1697p; (L.R. Dawson) 1539; (J. Dermid) 1533, 1556, 1702, 1720, 1743, 1751; (F. Erize) 1601; (J. Fennel) 1727; (K.W. Fink) 1610, 1611; (M.P. Fogden) 1520, 1582r, 1652, 1655r, 1660b, 1707, 1726, 1769b, 1794, 1797, 1798; (J. Foott) 1573tr; (D. Freeman) 1674; (M. Freeman) 1531; (C.B. Frith) 1588, 1649, 1665; (C.B. & W.D. Frith) 1519, 1592, 1609; (S. Halvorsen) 1561; (U. Hirsch) 1544, 1575b, 1619, 1735, 1761; (A.J. Hobbs) 1719; (D. Hughes) 1551, 1552, 1662, 1757; (P. Jackson) 1664, 1695c; (F. Lanting) 1525, 1575t; (J. Markham) 1558, 1636; (A.J. Mobbs) 1786, 1791b; (N. Myers) 1509, 1618, 1620b, 1635; (M.T. O'Keefe) 1547b; (Oxford Scientific Films) 1709; (G. Pizzey) 1687; (D. & M. Plage) 1523; (M.P. Price) 1511, 1682; (H. Reinhard) 1536, 1542, 1564r, 1584, 1596b, 1628, 1630, 1631, 1651r, 1659b, 1700c, 1703, 1711, 1713, 1725, 1728, 1736, 1771, 1777, 1787; (H. Rivarola) 1692t, 1800; (L. Lee Rue) 1679t; (L. Lee Rue III) 1535, 1744; (F. Saver) 1613; (R. Schroeder) 1550b; (J. Shaw) 1581, 1643; (J. Simon) 1545, 1553, 1693; (M.F. Soper) 1557; (L.M. Stone) 1538, 1739; (K. Taylor) 1605t, 1654; (N. Tomalin) 1537b, 1555, 1661; (F. Vollmer) 1543; (J. Wallis) 1670, 1671; (R. Williams) 1580, 1582l, 1597r; (G. Ziesler) 1681; *D. Hosking*: 1634, 1639, 1672; *E. Hosking*: 1508, 1512t, 1568b, 1600, 1614t, 1657, 1663, 1676, 1677, 1680, 1689; *E. & D. Hosking*: 1704; *Jacana*: (G. Annunziata) 1504, 1505; (A. Bertrand) 1583b; (J. Champroux) 1660t; (Devez-CNRS) 1529, 1769t; (J.L. Dubois) 1530, 1547t, 1573tl, 1616, 1773; (Fiore) 1673; (Gillon) 1739, 1782r; (J. Hervey) 1691t; (R. Konig) 1528b, 1548, 1549, 1569, 1587t, 1659t, 1666, 1667, 1675t, 1706, 1799; (J.M. Labat) 1690, 1698b, 1755; (P. Laboute) 1554, 1669; (C. & M. Mioton) 1796b; (M. Moisnard) 1527; (C. Nardin) 1665l; (Pecolatto) 1792; (F. Petter) 1572, 1596t; (Pilloud) 1541; (A. Rainon) 1537t; (J. Robert) 1612, 1683; (B. Stegler) 1585, 1620t, 1653; (J.P. Varin) 1508b, 1534, 1578, 1691b, 1695t, 1717b; (Varin-Visage) 1518, 1532, 1550t, 1560, 1576, 1589, 1692b; (J. Vasserot) 1730, 1753; (Y. Vial) 1512b, 1564b, 1615l; (R. Volot) 1516, 1522t, 1522b; (Zeni/Vendal) 1678t; (Ziesler) 1599, 1705; *M. Leigheb*: 1617, 1640, 1641; *A. Margiocco*: 1779; *G. Mazza*: 1754; *NHPA*: (A.N.T.) 1503; (A. Bannister) 1785; (L. Campbell) 1515; (J. Cann) 1614b; (J. Carmichael) 1502; (S. Dalton) 1590, 1591, 1638, 1679b, 1721, 1775, 1797t; (M. Leach) 1699; (M. Marcombe) 1587cr; (J. Sauvanet) 1765, 1780, 1781; (B. Wood) 1546; *Planet Earth Pictures*: (K. Lucas) 1615r, 1717t, 1731, 1738; *A. Pozzi*: 1762, 1763, 1779, 1774, 1776, 1783, 1793; *J.H. Tashjian*: 1517, 1567, 1571, 1597, 1621, 1626, 1627, 1646, 1647, 1651l, 1658; *OSFB/B. & B. Wells*: 1568t; (Z. Leszczynski) 1583t, 1603b.

FRONT COVER: A White's tree frog (Bruce Coleman/ A. Purcell)

CONTENTS

REPTILES
AND
AMPHIBIANS

INTRODUCTION

The origins of the reptiles and amphibians can be traced much further back in time than the origins of the mammals and birds. Amphibians had been in existence for some 200 million years before the first birds appeared. But despite their early ancestry, it is wrong to regard the reptiles and amphibians as primitive. They have evolved some extraordinary habits and physical features to suit their environments, and some are able to survive under conditions that no mammal can tolerate, such as the baking, arid climates of the world's driest deserts.

The main reason that reptiles and amphibians can thrive in harsh conditions is that they are cold-blooded—a misleading term since, when they are active, their blood is often as hot as that of humans. However, the way humans and the reptiles and amphibians heat their blood is different. In the case of humans, we heat ourselves from within by burning up a large proportion of the energy we gain from food. By contrast, reptiles and amphibians absorb heat from their surroundings by basking in the sun or swimming in warm water. In this way, they do not need to eat simply to keep warm. They can therefore survive on a fraction of the food needed by a mammal of comparable size, and live in places where food is scarce—provided they can absorb enough heat to stay active.

Amphibians

Of the two groups, the amphibians—which include the frogs, toads, newts and salamanders—were the earliest to evolve and were the first vertebrates (animals with backbones) able to live on land. They developed from the fishes, and have retained the fishes' characteristic of laying their eggs in water (or in damp places on the land). Their eggs do not have waterproof shells, and would dry out and die if laid in a dry place. Adult amphibians face the same problem—their skin does not stop water evaporating from their bodies, and the danger of drying out forces them to live in or near water or wet vegetation.

In many of the 4015 species of amphibians alive today, the young live entirely in the water—the tadpoles of frogs are an example—and absorb oxygen through gills, in the same way as fish. To become adults, they undergo dramatic changes in their body shape (a process known as metamorphosis) and acquire lungs that enable them to breathe air.

Reptiles

Reptiles—which include the turtles, tortoises, snakes, lizards and crocodiles—have one crucial difference from amphibians: their skin is waterproof. Their bodies are covered in a tough layer of scales that stops them from losing body moisture, and their eggs have water-retaining

LEFT Like all tree frogs, the red-eyed tree frog of Central America climbs branches and leaves with ease, gripping the smooth surfaces of leaves with the adhesive pads on its fingers and toes.
ABOVE The deserts of Australia are home to a huge variety of reptiles, including the bearded dragon. It fans out the loose collar of skin around its neck to ward off enemies.
PAGE 1501 White's tree frog of Australia commonly ventures into houses, favoring damp places such as lavatories and water tanks.

shells. These adaptations mean that reptiles are not forced to live near water, and can live in a much greater range of habitats than amphibians, including deserts, mountains, grassland and forests, as well as freshwater and marine habitats.

When they lost their dependence on water, the reptiles were ideally placed to exploit the resources of the land, for when they first appeared there were no mammals and birds to compete with them. An "Age of Reptiles" began, which lasted from about 280 to 65 million years ago. During this great stretch of time, the reptiles evolved into a multitude of forms. Some could swim, fly or run, while others crawled or burrowed. They ranged in size from tiny, lizard-like creatures to the great dinosaurs, the awe-inspiring remains of which tower over visitors to the natural-history museums of the world.

Some 65 million years ago, at the end of the Cretaceous period, the dinosaurs vanished, possibly because of a dramatic change of climate. Most of the reptiles that survived the catastrophe were, in general, the smaller, less spectacular animals such as the lizards and snakes. These animals flourished, and make up the bulk of the 6547 reptiles that exist today.

THE
REPTILES

THE REPTILES: CONQUERORS OF DRY LAND

Reptiles are the third major group of vertebrates (animals with backbones) after the mammals and the birds. They include the turtles, tortoises, terrapins, lizards, snakes, crocodiles and alligators.

Origins and evolution

Reptiles have a long history; the most primitive examples discovered so far date from the mid-Carboniferous period, about 315 million years ago. Found within fossil tree stumps, their remains show that they were small creatures, similar to lizards in shape.

Though these early reptiles had evolved from primitive amphibians, they were able to do something that no amphibian could—they laid their eggs on dry land. An amphibian's egg has to be laid in a permanently moist place to stop it from drying out, but a reptile's egg is enclosed in a waterproof shell that prevents the loss of fluid. When it is laid, the reptile's egg has its own internal water supply contained in a fluid-filled sac surrounding the embryo (the developing young). The embryo is nourished by the food supply in the yolk, and a network of blood capillaries surrounding the embryo provides it with oxygen that enters the blood through pores in the shell. Such an egg is almost completely self-sufficient—whether laid on a beach, under a rock or in the desert sand, it will develop and hatch by itself, provided it is kept sufficiently warm.

The second important development for the reptiles was the replacement of the soft amphibian skin for a hard, water-resistant skin. As with the eggs, the new protective layer prevented the bodies of the early reptiles from drying out and enabled them to survive in most kinds of habitats, including the driest, hottest deserts of the world.

Flourishing on dry land

For several million years, the primitive reptiles appear to have been small in number, but from the beginning of the Permian period (about 280 million years ago), they began to flourish.

One group in particular, the pelycosaurs, advanced in spectacular fashion, both in variety of species and in actual numbers. They had few rivals on land, and in the absence of competition they spread into a wide range of habitats and took on a variety of life-styles. Like their amphibian ancestors, they were "cold-blooded" or ectothermic—they maintained their body temperature by absorbing heat from their surroundings instead of generating it from within in the manner of birds and mammals. Some had large, fin-like structures on their backs, containing blood vessels. These were probably temperature regulators. They could act as solar panels for heating up the blood, or as surfaces from which heat could escape if the animals needed to warm up or cool down quickly.

Early offshoot

The turtles and tortoises appear to have evolved separately from the other reptiles at an early stage. Though their skulls are similar in some respects to those of the earliest fossils, they do not match up with the skulls of other reptiles that developed later. It seems that they branched off on their own about 250 million years ago, but since no fossil turtles from this period have been found, the precise details of their early development are unknown. The first turtles appear very suddenly in the fossil record at about 215 million years ago.

During the Permian period (about 280 million years ago) another group of reptiles had been developing. Known as the therapsids, they were the distant ancestors of the mammals. In due course, they displaced the pelycosaurs as the dominant reptiles, until they in turn were ousted by another group called the thecodonts, about 200 million years ago.

These developments occurred over millions of years, and the rise of one group over another probably resulted from long-term climatic changes that favored one type of animal at the expense of another. It is possible, for example, that the therapsids were better able to cope with a period of cold conditions than other reptiles. As the ancestors of the mammals, they may have been partly "warm-blooded" themselves, not relying entirely on gaining warmth from their surroundings. Their eventual decline may have resulted from an improvement in the climate in the middle

RIGHT The chart shows the evolution of the various reptile groups, from their origins among the early amphibians to the orders that exist today.

PAGES 1504-1505 The crocodiles and their relatives have changed little since the period when dinosaurs dominated the Earth over 65 million years ago.

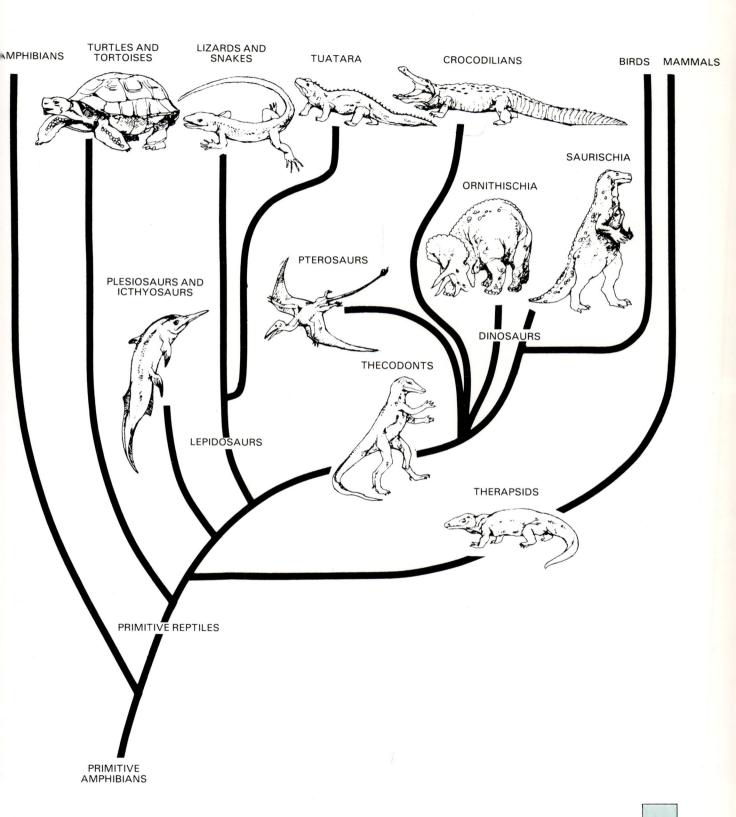

AMPHIBIANS

TURTLES AND
TORTOISES

LIZARDS AND
SNAKES

TUATARA

CROCODILIANS

BIRDS   MAMMALS

SAURISCHIA

ORNITHISCHIA

PTEROSAURS

PLESIOSAURS AND
ICTHYOSAURS

DINOSAURS

THECODONTS

LEPIDOSAURS

THERAPSIDS

PRIMITIVE REPTILES

PRIMITIVE
AMPHIBIANS

1507

Triassic period. They did not entirely disappear, however, and the mammal descendants were to flourish anew almost 140 million years later.

Ruling reptiles

The reptiles that evolved from the thecodonts were known as the archosaurs, which literally means the "ruling reptiles." The most successful of these animals were the dinosaurs, which flourished for over 125 million years—an enormous stretch of time considering that human beings have only existed for about 500,000 years. Most people think of dinosaurs as vast, lumbering creatures, but not all dinosaurs were giants. Many were small, agile animals that ran about on two legs rather like ostriches. The smallest discovered so far was about the size of a chicken.

There were two great orders of dinosaurs, the Ornithischia and the Saurischia, both of which contained dinosaurs that walked on two legs, and those that moved about on all fours. All the Ornithischians, or "bird-hipped dinosaurs," such as *Iguanodon* and the horned *Triceratops*, were herbivores (plant eaters). The Saurischia, or "lizard-hipped dinosaurs," included some of the largest herbivores, such as the huge 55.5-ton *Brachiosaurus*, as well as giant carnivores (meat eaters) like the 49-ft. long *Tyrannosaurus*, which stalked its prey on two legs.

Two other groups of reptiles were included among the archosaurs—the pterosaurs, or flying reptiles, and the early crocodilians (that survive today as the crocodiles, the alligators and the gharial). Like modern-day bats, the pterosaurs flew on membranes of skin supported by the greatly extended and strengthened fourth fingers of each hand. Their flight muscles were attached to keeled breastbones, and their skeletons were lightened by air spaces within many of the bones. Both these features are shared by

TOP LEFT The iguana's scaly skin protects it from cuts and also from parasites, but its most important role is in stopping the reptile's body from drying out. The skin of amphibians is not as waterproof, and prevents them living in dry habitats where their body fluids would evaporate.

LEFT The thick, high-arched shell of the Galapagos giant tortoise can reach up to 47 in. in length in the largest individuals. Though the shells of tortoises provide excellent protection from would-be predators, their weight greatly limits the animals' speed and agility in moving around.

birds, but the pterosaurs formed an entirely separate line of development from the birds, and played no part in their evolution.

Surviving to the present

The dinosaurs and the pterosaurs died out at the end of the Cretaceous period about 65 million years ago, but the crocodilians have persisted to the present day. We still do not know why they survived the catastrophe that overwhelmed their fellow archosaurs, but whatever their secret, they shared it with the lizards and snakes.

The ancestors of the lizards and snakes developed separately from the archosaurs, and represent a further line of reptile evolution. They outlived the dinosaurs, and have proved to be the best equipped reptiles for modern conditions. Having survived the rigors of the ice ages that gripped the Earth as recently as 10,000 years ago, lizards and snakes flourished to rank among the most diverse and highly adapted of all land animals.

Scaly skin

As mentioned earlier, one of the most important factors in the evolution of reptiles was the development of strong, impermeable skin, which prevented them from drying out on land. As in other vertebrates, a reptile's skin consists of two layers, with the inner layer, the dermis, covered and protected by an outer layer, the epidermis.

The outside of the epidermis is made of a tough material called keratin, and in a reptile this is thickened into a series of plates or scales. The scales are often folded over each other, overlapping like tiles on a roof to provide extra protection. Although similar in appearance to the scales of a fish, they are quite different in structure. Whereas fish scales are separate, glassy flakes loosely attached to the skin, reptile scales are part of the skin itself, and are all connected to each other by flexible hinges of skin.

The connections between the scales are revealed when the outer keratin layer is discarded (molted) and replaced, as it is several times a year among young snakes. In such cases, the snake slides out of its old skin, leaving the scaly outer layer in one piece, and in such perfect condition that the species can be identified from its discarded skin alone. The keratin layer usually starts to come away at the animal's head,

ABOVE All reptiles shed their outer layer of skin at regular intervals. In some reptiles, it comes away in small flakes, but snakes discard all of their skin at once. The cobra (above) has just stripped off its old skin, which remains in one piece with each scale attached to the next by a hinge of soft skin. The snake emerges from the old, tattered skin with a glossy new coat that is in perfect condition.

beginning at its mouth. The animal immediately starts scratching its head against the ground or rocks to remove the rest of the loosened skin. With lizards, the skin comes away in large pieces rather than all at once, and in the case of tortoises and crocodiles, small pieces of skin are shed continually, similar to dandruff.

The frequency of molting varies. Young reptiles shed their skin more often than adults, and if the skin is damaged, it may be discarded sooner than usual. Conversely, if the animal is unhealthy, or if the conditions of temperature and humidity are wrong, the molt may be delayed by weeks or even months.

Plates and studs

Reptiles have several types of scales. Some are small, plate-like, and partly overlapping; their borders may be rounded like fish scales, angular or even extended into spines. Other scales form rounded or sharp-edged studs as on crocodile skin. Lizards and snakes may also have large, interlocking plates encasing their heads. The scales on the underside of a snake are enlarged, overlapping plates that protrude downward to give the animal grip when it moves.

Some reptiles have fine bristles on their skin that are basically filaments formed from modified scales. Geckos have clumps of these bristles on their toe pads, giving them an extraordinary gripping power and enabling them to climb up surfaces as smooth as glass, and to cling upside down to ceilings.

The claws of tortoises and crocodiles have horny layers on both the uppersides and the undersides, whereas the claws of lizards and the tuatara are hard and horny on the topside only. As these animals scuttle about, the parts of the claws that touch the ground are continually worn away, keeping the claws sharp.

Skin deep

The inner layer of the skin, the dermis, carries blood vessels, nerves and, in most reptiles, small plate-like, bony formations called osteoderms. These originate deep within the dermis and grow outward, reinforcing the scales. Among lizards, osteoderms occur all over the body, but in other reptiles, they are restricted to certain parts: on the tuatara, for example, the bony plates are found on the upper part of the tail, while on crocodilians bony plates grow on the heads, backs and tails, producing the characteristic ridged effect of crocodile skin.

REPTILES CLASSIFICATION

There are 6547 species of reptiles distributed throughout the world. They are classified in four orders. The order Chelonia consists of the 244 species of turtles, terrapins and tortoises. The order Rhynchocephalia is represented by only one species, the tuatara. By contrast, the largest order, the Squamata, contains no fewer than 6280 species of lizards, worm lizards (or amphisbaenans) and snakes. The fourth order is the Crocodylia, which comprises the 22 species of crocodiles, alligators and their allies (collectively known as the crocodilians).

In turtles and tortoises, the osteoderms have become greatly enlarged and fused together to form the bony foundations of the shell. The glossy plates that cover the shell are essentially modified scales.

Despite their scaly armor, reptiles have quite sensitive skins. The dermis is well supplied with nerve endings, which are often clustered together into specialized areas to act as highly sensitive, tactile organs, rather like human fingertips. The scales on such areas are generally small or absent.

The dermis contains most of the pigment cells that give the animal its color (called the chromatophores). In some reptiles, the pigment in each cell can be concentrated or dispersed by hormones or nerve signals. By increasing the strength of one type of pigment cell at the expense of another, the animal can change its color. The most well-known reptiles to change their color are the chameleons. They change their body color to match their surroundings as a means of camouflage, making them less visible both to predators and prey alike.

Reptiles have few skin glands, unlike the amphibians whose skin is pitted with glands that produce mucus to protect them from drying out (some species also have poison-producing glands). A reptile has no need of mucus, since its scales are protection enough, but several nonvenomous snakes can produce an irritant secretion from the glands on their backs in order to deter predators. In many lizards and in some turtles, glands on or near their hind limbs produce scent that appears to be used as a sexual signal; secretions of the musk glands on the throats of crocodiles are also thought to play a role in sexual behavior.

Skeleton and the nervous system

The backbones of reptilian skeletons are composed of strong, flexible vertebrae like those of mammals. The limbs of most reptiles are also similar in structure to those of mammals, but are positioned differently: their legs are attached to the sides of their bodies, and their feet face outward instead of forward, giving many reptiles an awkward, sprawling gait. There are some exceptions—crocodiles, for example, can raise their bodies well clear of the ground and run surprisingly fast.

The skeletons of several groups of reptiles have become highly modified. In turtles and tortoises, for example, the backbone and ribs are fused to the bony,

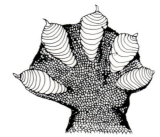 

ABOVE The skin of crocodiles is reinforced by bony plates beneath the scales, and studs and sharp-edged projections run along the animals' backs. The armor is so tough that even bites from rival crocodiles do not inflict much damage.

RIGHT In many of the geckos (a family of lizards) the scales on the feet have been modified into rigid pads with tiny bristles that can provide a grip on almost any surface including sheets of glass. Two types of toe pads are shown here.

inner part of the upper shell (the carapace), while some of the shoulder bones and abdominal ribs form the basis of the lower shell.

The limbs of marine turtles have evolved into flippers, while the limbs of many other reptiles have become reduced, or lost altogether. The most extreme examples of this are the snakes, which in most cases have lost not only their external limbs, but also the pelvic and shoulder bones that once supported them. Instead, snakes have a greatly increased number of vertebrae—over 400 in some species—each attached to a pair of ribs that form a tubular cagework protecting the internal organs.

An egg-eating feat

Snakes are notable for the extremely wide gape of their jaws, seen at its most spectacular in the egg-eating snake that can engulf an egg twice as wide as its head. The two halves of both the upper and lower jaws are only loosely attached, both to one another and to the skull, by muscles and ligaments.

Reptilian teeth are generally peg-like structures that eventually fall out, and are replaced by others. In the crocodile, the teeth have a ragged, gappy appearance, since each jaw is equipped with a random collection of large, old teeth and small, new ones. Not all reptiles have teeth: turtles and tortoises have horny beaks; and venomous snakes are equipped with long, hollow fangs attached to poison glands.

Reptiles are not noted for their intelligence, and their brains are much smaller than those of mammals of similar size and weight (the brain of an 8-ft.-long crocodile is only about the size of a large walnut). The forebrain (the part associated with reasoning and

learning), is particularly poorly developed, and most reptiles are slow to learn in comparison with mammals. Nearly all their actions are governed by instinct.

Superb senses

A large proportion of a reptile's brain is devoted to decoding messages received from its sense organs. These provide the animal with an accurate picture of its surroundings, possible dangers and potential prey. Reptiles do not have external ears like mammals. Sounds are registered by the eardrum, which passes the vibrations on to a small, connecting earbone that ends in a tube coated with sensory nerve cells. These cells pass the vibratory signals to the brain for analysis.

In some reptiles, the earbone is attached to a small muscle that acts as a shock absorber, suppressing sounds that are too intense. The uncovered eardrum is often clearly visible, although in some cases it is protected by a scaly covering. Snakes have no eardrums, and since the earbone is linked to the jaw, it is unlikely that they hear sounds in the usual way. Instead, they pick up vibrations from the ground.

Heat sensors

The heads of some snakes—for example, pit vipers, most pythons and most boas—are equipped with heat-sensitive organs or "pits" that enable them to detect minute variations in heat and, in particular, the change in air temperature caused by the presence of warm-blooded prey. These pits are visible as simple hollows at the end of the snout, and they vary in number and arrangement. Pit vipers have two such heat receptors, located between the eyes and nostrils; in pythons and boas, they occur on the snakes' lips. Each pit consists of an external chamber open to the air, and a deep inner chamber. A thin membrane of skin, well supplied with blood vessels and nerve endings, divides the two chambers. The nerve endings transmit the heat signals to the brain.

Since these heat-sensitive organs can detect temperature changes of less than $0.002°F$, a snake will often detect traces of potential prey, such as a mouse or a small bird, well before it sees or hears its victim. Because the pits are paired, they allow the snake to focus on the prey with extreme accuracy, determining both its direction and its distance. With such sensory equipment, the snake can home in on its victim in complete darkness, and kill it with one strike.

TOP Some reptiles have senses that are quite unfamiliar to humans. The pits between the eyes and nostrils of a rattlesnake detect body heat and allow the snake to stalk its prey in complete darkness.

ABOVE Lizards track their prey by using their eyesight, and the vertically elongated pupils in the large eyes of a gecko improve its night vision. The ears, by contrast, are simple apertures in the side of the head.

Organs of smell

As with mammals, the reptile's nose has a double function: it enables the animal to breathe and serves as a sense organ. The nasal chamber connects to the outside via a filter of leaves made of cartilage, and the walls of the chamber are lined with cells that detect scent. The nerve endings of these cells are attached to a large lobe at the front of the brain that interprets the signals from the nerves and recognizes smells.

In many reptiles, the basic sense of smell is enhanced by Jacobson's organ, a region of chemically sensitive nerve endings in the roof of the mouth that connects to a secondary lobe in the brain. In the tuatara, Jacobson's organ picks up scent on the air as the animal breathes, but among snakes and lizards the scent is carried to the organ by the long, flexible tongue. When the animal moves forward, flicking its tongue in all directions, it collects chemical molecules in the air and transfers them to the Jacobson's organ for analysis. Snakes and lizards also appear to use the Jacobson's organ to detect the presence of water.

Adjustable sights

A reptile's eye is similar to that of other vertebrates, but lizards, the tuatara and turtles have a number of small, bony plates inside their eyes that enable them to

ABOVE The eyes of a chameleon are mounted in scaly turrets and can move independently of one another in all directions, giving the animal a large field of view without the need for it to move its head. Such eyes are extremely valuable, for the chameleon's hunting technique is either to stay still and wait for prey to come within range, or to stalk its victims very slowly, with the minimum of body movement. By keeping its head still and searching with its eyes, it goes unnoticed by its prey until the moment it strikes with its long tongue.

focus. By distorting the shape of their eyes, the animals adjust the distance between the lens and the retina, which picks up the visual signals and transmits them to the brain. Snakes have a slightly different system; their eyes do not have bones within them, and they focus in much the same way as a camera by moving the lens forward and backward.

A transparent disk called the "brille" covers the snake's eyes, which are permanently open. The brille is a part of the outer skin layer that is renewed whenever the animal sheds its skin. Eyelids protect the eyes of most other reptiles; these eyelids often include a nictitating membrane or "third eyelid" (similar to those found in birds), which moves sideways across the eye. Tear glands offer additional protection to the

oxygenated blood from the lungs back around the body. However, in most reptiles, the two sides are not fully separated. The upper chambers of the heart (the atria) are separate, but the main pumping chambers (the ventricles) are divided by an incomplete partition that allows the blood carried in the arteries and veins to come into contact. In practice, there is very little mixing. When the ventricles contract at each heartbeat, the two types of blood are propelled down the correct blood vessels.

The heart of a crocodile is more advanced. Here, the division between the ventricles is almost complete, which makes mixing of the two types of blood virtually impossible. It also ensures that blood being pumped to the muscles and internal organs carries as much oxygen as possible.

Breathe in, breathe out

All reptiles—even marine turtles—obtain their oxygen from the air, using lungs similar to those of mammals (though some modifications to the basic pattern have evolved). In most legless lizards and snakes, the left lung tends to be reduced or even completely absent—an adaptation to their long, slim shape. To compensate for this, the right lungs of these creatures are greatly elongated.

The lungs of some marine turtles are enclosed in bony chambers to prevent them from being damaged by excessive pressure while the animals are submerged in the water. Since the shell-clad body of a turtle cannot expand when it breathes in, its lungs are so arranged that they are full of air when at rest; when the turtle breathes out it has to compress its lungs with special muscles.

Styles of reproduction

When reptiles abandoned the aquatic breeding habits of their amphibian ancestors to breed on land, they had to modify their method of reproduction. Eggs laid in water can be fertilized externally, by covering them with sperm; many frogs fertilize their spawn like this. On land, however, this is rarely possible, since sperm need a moist environment to complete the job of fertilization. Among land animals, the female solves this problem by retaining the eggs (ova) inside her body where conditions are moist and warm. The male then places his sperm in the birth canal so that they can find their own way to the eggs.

ABOVE Reptiles usually abandon their nests immediately after laying their eggs. Some snakes, such as the carpet python, are exceptions, brooding their eggs by entwining their bodies around them and raising the temperature by contracting their muscles to give off heat (in the same way that muscular activity in humans generates heat). Crocodilians keep a close watch on both their eggs and their young at all times to defend them from predators.

eyes. These grow to enormous size in sea turtles, since they have to clear the excess salt deposited on the eye surface by the seawater.

The shape of the pupil is usually a good guide to the life-style of a reptile. Round pupils are characteristic of reptiles that are active during the day, whereas vertical pupils are typical of nocturnal species. Lizards tend to have good eyesight because colors are an important guide in mating and hunting (chameleons, for example, hunt largely by sight). Most snakes have rather poor eyesight, since they rely on taste and smell to track their prey.

The heart of a reptile

In mammals, the heart is divided into two separate pumping units—one to send deoxygenated blood from the body to the lungs, and another to send

In the tuatara, one of the most primitive of surviving reptiles, the sex organs of both the male and female consist simply of a cloaca (an opening used for both reproduction and excretion). To mate, the male tuatara passes his sperm into the female merely by placing his cloaca against hers. In the case of turtles, tortoises and crocodilians, males have extended cloacas that protrude, and are used to place the sperm inside the female.

Among lizards and snakes, the males possess paired sex organs known as hemipenes, although only one is used at a time during mating. Each hemipenis consists of a pouch that the male turns outward through the cloaca during mating. Its shape varies from species to species, and it often has crests, nodules or spines to grip the inside of the female's cloaca and stop the organ slipping out if the animals move. In some snakes, turtles and tortoises, the female may retain the sperm for a long period before fertilization takes place. In some species, odd individuals in captivity have laid fertilized eggs up to six years after mating.

The females of a few reptile species, such as the whiptail lizard of the USA and the rock lizard of the USSR, can reproduce without mating. In these cases, the vast majority of newly born reptiles are females—males are occasionally born, but rarely survive. The problem with single-sex reproduction is that since no mating takes place, there is no mixing of the genes. Without variation of genes, evolution of the species is almost impossible.

Most reptiles lay eggs, although some give birth to fully formed young. They lay their eggs in sheltered positions, either beneath stones or bark, or in holes in the ground. The eggs vary in type: those of many snakes and lizards have parchment-like shells, while the eggs of crocodiles and tortoises have brittle, chalky shells like those of birds.

Once she has laid the eggs, the female leaves them to hatch, and the young have to fend for themselves from the moment they are born. In some cases, however, the parents look after the nests—crocodilians care for both their eggs and the young. The Great Plains skink looks after its eggs throughout the incubation period, and not only helps the young to hatch out by freeing them from their fetal membranes but also stays with them for about 10 days. During this period, the Great Plains skink defends its offspring and cleans them with its tongue.

ABOVE The viviparous or common lizard is unusual among reptiles in that it lives as far north as the Arctic Circle in Scandinavia. The female avoids the problem of finding a warm nest site for her eggs by retaining them inside her body. The baby lizards hatch inside her and are born live, like the young of a mammal. Viviparous lizards hibernate during the long winters at high latitudes, when food is hard to find and the air temperature is too low for them to be active.

Dependent on the climate

Reptiles are found in all the continents except the Antarctic, but the number of species decreases gradually from the tropics toward the poles. The reduction in species results from the lower than average temperatures and wide seasonal variations that occur toward the far north and far south.

In the tropics, reptiles that absorb their body heat from the surroundings can be active all year round. However, in the high latitudes, the temperature in winter rarely rises high enough to heat the reptiles, making it impossible for them to move around and hunt. The lower temperatures mean that they have to remain dormant (inactive) for part of the year, to ensure that their breeding cycle takes place during the summer.

The reptiles' reliance on warm conditions has prevented their spread to the colder parts of the world.

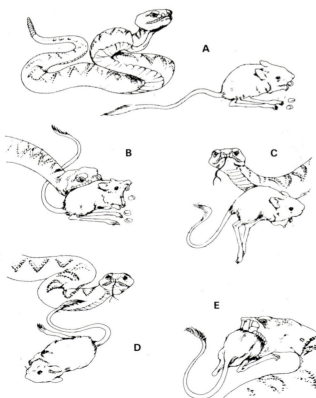

ABOVE Snakes are meat eaters, and will tackle many kinds of prey. Here, a viper swallows a fish head first so that the scales do not catch in its gullet. Once inside the snake's mouth, the fish will be pushed along by strong muscles until it reaches the stomach where it is slowly digested.
LEFT A rattlesnake pursues a jumping mouse (A), bites it with its poison fangs (B), and then releases it (C). Within minutes the mouse falls dead from the venom (D), and the rattlesnake begins to swallow its prey (E).

Snakes, for example, are widespread, with well over 2000 species occurring worldwide, but only 6 of these occur in northern Europe, where the cold winters force them into dormancy for several months each year.

Hatched in the body

Species adapted to cold climates tend to reproduce only once every two or three years. The females produce young by hatching their eggs within the body. In such species, the young develop in the womb within the egg membranes, drawing nourishment from the egg's yolk sac. After hatching, the young are born fully formed and active. Some species have gone one step further. In addition to using the yolk sac, the embryo has developed a way of absorbing nutrients directly from the mother's bloodstream.

Reptiles that give birth to live young do not have to rely on a steady air temperature to keep their unborn young warm (unlike reptiles that lay eggs). Since they stay inside the mother's body, the young are protected from the elements and develop at a steady rate, enabling them to be born in good time before the winter. Two examples of reptiles bearing live young are the European adder and the viviparous lizard (found as far north as Arctic Norway). Similar adaptations are also found among reptiles living at high altitudes in the Himalayas and the Andes mountain ranges.

The reptile's menu

Most reptiles are meat eaters (carnivorous), though some eat only plants (herbivorous) and others feed on both animal and plant foods (omnivorous). As with mammals, some species are flexible in their diet, while others have become specialists and are highly adapted to a particular food source.

Lizards eat mainly insects, but many species, such as the ocellated green lizard, supplement their diets with small mammals or nestlings. By contrast, the slowworm is a specialized feeder, eating mostly slugs and earthworms. The moloch, an Australian lizard, eats only ants—perhaps up to 1500 at one sitting.

The marine iguana of the Galapagos Islands is one of the few plant-eating lizards, feeding on marine algae collected from the seabed near the shore. The large monitor lizards are active predators, although they also eat the remains of dead animals (carrion). The biggest lizard of all, the Komodo dragon, will kill animals as large as deer and even water buffalo.

Snakes prey only on living animals, and many are equipped with poison fangs to immobilize or kill their victims. Each snake species has its own specialty; some prey only on birds, others only on small mammals. Some snakes prefer eating eggs that they steal from birds' nests. On rare occasions, some will eat plant matter such as fruit. The diet of snakes often changes with the seasons, depending on the availability of prey, but it rarely includes carrion.

Turtles and tortoises are usually too slow to hunt animal prey, and consequently most are herbivores. Those that do eat animal matter prey on sluggish animals such as worms and mollusks.

The hunting tactics of reptiles vary. Lizards are usually active hunters, moving after their prey, but they may also lurk in one place, immobile, waiting for

ABOVE The slender, elongated shape of a tree-dwelling vine snake is an extreme example of the body plan that has made the snakes among the most successful of all the vertebrates. With up to 400 bones making up their spines, no trace of limbs, and internal organs that are streamlined to fit their shape, snakes have changed a great deal from their scuttling, lizard-like ancestors.

suitable prey to come within range. Chameleons freeze in one place for long periods, only moving their eyes as they watch for prey. When an insect alights nearby, the chameleon takes aim and shoots out its long, sticky tongue to capture the victim. Snakes, some turtles and many crocodiles ambush their victims, creeping up on them and striking suddenly.

Down the hatch

Reptiles generally swallow their food in large lumps, since their teeth are not adapted for chewing. Tortoises and turtles may shred their food, pulling it apart with their sharp beaks and strong claws, but they do not pulp it in their mouths. Snakes swallow their prey whole, always beginning with the head, since if the prey were swallowed tail first, against the direction of its fur or feathers, it might not pass down into the snake's stomach, and would have to be ejected.

A snake's digestive system is affected by its body temperature. The colder the snake is, the longer the food takes to digest: if a captive snake is not given the opportunity to warm up, its digestion may cease altogether. The food inside the animal will then rot in the stomach, causing the snake to die.

The energy needs of a reptile are low, largely because it keeps warm by absorbing heat from its surroundings, rather than burning energy internally to provide its body heat (as mammals do). A viper hunts by ambush and swallows large prey, so it expends a minimum of energy in actually finding food. However, it uses up a surprising amount of energy digesting its prey. A lizard, by contrast, hunts actively and feeds on small prey; it therefore requires less energy for digestion and more for movement.

It is not certain how much food a reptile needs to survive. The Egyptian cobra has to eat six percent of its body weight a week, although it normally eats twice that amount. Although this amounts to over 200 small mammals and lizards a year, it is little when compared

LEFT Armed with a battery of sharp-edged scales, a spiny lizard raises its body clear of a hot rock to cool its body temperature. In the tropics, reptiles can easily become too hot as well as too cold.
BELOW Adjusting body temperature in the desert: a beaded lizard (A) basks on a rock to gain heat; a horned lizard (B), a rattlesnake (C) and a desert tortoise (D) cool off underground; and a chuckwalla (E) keeps its temperature constant by lying on the sand beneath a shady stone.

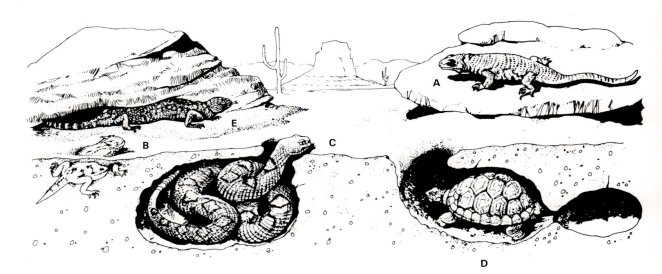

RIGHT Camouflage is an important means of defense for reptiles, because they often have to bask for long periods in the open to raise their body temperature. Without camouflage, they would be spotted easily by predators. The skin of the northern leaf-tailed gecko matches the lichen-covered bark of the tree so well that the animal is only visible at close range.

with a small, insectivorous mammal like the pgymy shrew, which eats it own weight in food every day. Few snakes eat more than once a week, and many species eat only 10 times a year. Some, like the large python, can do without food for over a year or more.

Temperature regulation

Each day, a reptile's body temperature has to warm up to a certain level before the animal becomes completely active. In temperate regions, in winter, the air and ground temperature never reaches a sufficient level and the animal is forced to stay dormant until better weather arrives in the spring.

During the reptile's dormant period, all its bodily functions are reduced to a minimum. Its metabolic rate (the rate at which the animal uses energy) slows down and the only signs of life that the animal shows are weak respiration and a very slow heart rate. Some days before the reptile becomes dormant, it stops eating, since the digestive juices stop flowing as the body systems slow down.

Reptiles may undergo periods of dormancy, either alone or in company. Many gather to spend the winter in single-species groups, and it is not uncommon to find several species gathered in one place. A burrow uncovered in North America contained over 260 snakes of different species that belonged to three separate genera. Such winter shelters are usually located over one and a half feet below the surface where they escape the worst of the winter cold.

Reptiles do not only suffer from the cold. In hot regions, they have to prevent themselves from overheating. In extreme cases, they may retreat into a burrow and lower their metabolic rate, in much the same way as when dormant. More often, reptiles living in hot areas avoid daytime heat by hiding in the shade, and foraging for food by night. Some species vary their habits according to the season; the horned viper, for example, is most active by night in the summer, but in winter it hunts by day.

Some like it hot

Most desert reptiles function more effectively at high temperatures than species found in temperate regions. Reptiles generally have a fixed body temperature at which they operate best, but they will still remain active if they heat up or cool down to within five to seven degrees of the optimum temperature.

If a lizard becomes too cold, it moves to a warm spot and basks in the sun until it has absorbed enough heat to raise its body temperature. By lying flat on its stomach on a sun-heated rock, it is also able to absorb heat from the ground. If it overheats, it will rest in the shade to cool down before continuing. But when the surrounding temperature falls too low—at the end of the day, for example—the animal retreats to its lair before its falling body temperature prevents it from moving, and it becomes a sitting target for predators.

Reptiles are able to make small adjustments to their body temperature by contracting their muscles to

generate heat. In this way, the larger snakes can raise their body temperatures by five to nine degrees. The female python, for example, incubates her eggs by coiling around them; if necessary, she contracts her muscles to keep them warm. Since a snake has no hair or feathers to provide insulation, the small amount of heat generated in this way quickly disperses.

To cool its body temperature, a reptile may open its mouth and increase its respiration rate, in the same way that a dog pants to lose heat. Under such circumstances, a viviparous lizard has been known to increase its breathing rate from a normal 31 breaths per minute to 114 per minute.

Defense techniques

Many reptiles use camouflage for defense, as well as to conceal themselves from their prey. Water turtles, such as the matamata and snappers, are colored to match the debris at the bottom of ponds, enabling them to lie in wait for unsuspecting fish. Many snakes and lizards that live in the grass or trees are colored green to match the foliage. Desert-living species are often yellow or gray in color, and are patterned to resemble stones and sand. Reptiles that live in the undergrowth are often brightly colored and are patterned with lines or bars to disguise their shape.

TOP The sidewinder rattlesnake is unusual among snakes in that it moves at right angles to the way it is facing. It skims along the ground sideways, leaving telltale tracks in the desert sand.
ABOVE An Indian krait uses rocks as firm objects to push against in order to slide forward.

FAR RIGHT A grass snake feigns death as a final attempt to ward off an attacker, holding its head limp and its jaws open. The snake keeps its body so rigid that it does not stir even if someone picks it up; if turned over, however, the snake will immediately flip back to its original pose.

Reptiles do not only rely on color for camouflage. The shape of their bodies may play an important part as well. The tree-dwelling boomslang, for example, is so long and slender that it can easily be mistaken for a branch. The body outlines of many desert lizards are made irregular by their spines or crests, which also break up their shadows.

The colors and markings on reptiles not only serve as camouflage; on some species they are used to warn or frighten other creatures. When the cobra adopts its threat posture—raising itself up and spreading its hood—the neck markings look like two huge eyes, making it very intimidating to its enemies. Other species, such as the poisonous eastern coral snake of the southern USA, are brightly colored as a warning to potential enemies not to interfere with them. The coloration of the eastern coral snake is such an effective deterrent that many harmless snakes mimic its red, yellow and black colors in order to avoid being attacked. Many lizards make themselves appear larger and fiercer by suddenly displaying brightly colored parts of their bodies that are normally hidden underneath folds of skin.

Flight or fight?

Coloring and shape are passive means of defense, but reptiles can also use active defense mechanisms. Running away is the simplest method, and many lizards have developed a refinement of this: they voluntarily discard the ends of their tails if attacked. The severed end twitches vigorously as it lies on the ground, distracting the predator while its quarry steals away to safety. Eventually the lizard will grow a new tail. Turtles and tortoises protect themselves by retreating into their shells.

Spitting venom

Some snakes and lizards pretend to be dead if attacked, becoming rigid and lifeless. To add to the effect, they may open their mouths to produce foamy saliva and they discharge a strong, rotting smell. The most dramatic and effective way of subduing prey comes from the venomous and often fatal bite of the snake. Reptiles do not always have to attack a predator in order to defend themselves: the mere threat of an attack is often enough to frighten away the enemy. If the threat posture fails, some poisonous snakes spit venom aggressively at their enemies.

TOP Though the cobra's bite is lethal, it usually avoids struggles with its enemies—its threat display alone will persuade them to retreat. It raises its head and spreads the "hood" of skin on either side of its neck.

ABOVE If a box turtle is overturned, it draws its legs, head and tail into its shell and closes up the gaps behind them. The defense is effective against small predators, but larger animals can just smash the shell open.

ENCASED IN ARMOR

Turtles and tortoises have evolved one of the most effective defenses in the animal kingdom—a thick and virtually impregnable shell into which they can withdraw their heads and limbs when danger threatens

Desert tortoise

Snake-necked turtle

Leatherback sea turtle

Argentinian snake-necked turtle

African mud turtle

American box turtle

Leopard tortoise

Big-headed turtle

Spiny softshell

No one knows how turtles came to evolve their shells. Fossils of the ancestors of present-day turtles appear for the first time in rocks laid down about 215 million years ago, during the early reign of the dinosaurs. Even then the shell was fully formed, giving no clue as to how or why this unique feature evolved. Whatever the reason, it serves as a highly effective piece of protective armor.

The shell consists of flattened bones welded together to form a strong box made up of two parts: the carapace, covering the upper part of the body, and the plastron beneath, protecting the animal's stomach. The two parts are joined by bridges of bone or elastic ligaments. The carapace is fused to the animal's backbone and ribs, while the plastron is a highly modified extension of the collarbones and the abdominal ribs (the rearrangement of the tortoise's anatomy has meant that its shoulder blades and hips have shifted inside the ribs). The whole shell is covered by strong, horny plates (called scutes). The familiar "tortoiseshell," used for jewelry and ornaments since the Roman times, comes from the shell of the hawksbill turtle.

The shell has two openings—one for the head and forelimbs, and one for the tail and hind limbs. Several species can withdraw the head and limbs inside the shell, but because they are exposed at the openings, they are armored with thick, horny skin. Some turtles, such as the mud turtles and box turtles, have hinged

BELOW When young leatherback turtles hatch from their eggs on tropical beaches, they face a hazardous crawl down to the sea. Many are killed by sea birds and crabs on the way, and predatory fish await them when they reach the water.

PAGE 1523 The Indian star tortoise takes its name from the striking markings on its shell. It is common in sandy terrain in parts of India, and though it is usually active in the twilight hours, it is often seen in the daytime during the monsoon.

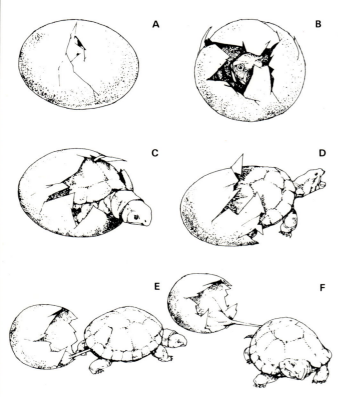

plastrons that can move to close the openings, enabling the animals to seal themselves within their shells. Sealed inside, they have an even better defense against predators and are better able to conserve their body moisture.

Reduced shells

Although the shell provides excellent protection, it is both bulky and heavy. In several species that live entirely underwater, the shell is reduced in size, giving the animal a more streamlined shape and freeing its legs for swimming. The shell of the leatherback sea turtle has virtually disappeared, having become merely a mosaic of small bones covered by a thick, oily hide.

Turtles do not have teeth, but they do have horny beaks rather like the bills of birds. Most species have sharp, blade-like beaks that they use to tear food apart. The legs of most ground-dwelling tortoises are stout

LEFT A hatching tortoise cracks open its egg with the aid of a horny "tooth" on its snout (A and B). It then breaks its way through the shell, emerging head first (C and D), with its body still attached to the egg by a cord (E and F).
BELOW The map shows the geographical distribution of some of the turtles and tortoises.

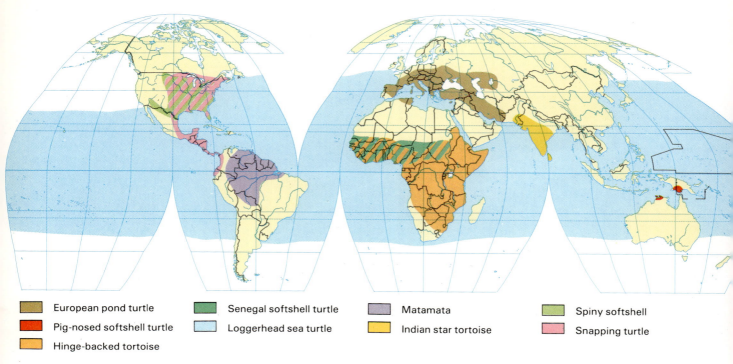

▨ European pond turtle	▨ Senegal softshell turtle	▨ Matamata	▨ Spiny softshell
▨ Pig-nosed softshell turtle	▨ Loggerhead sea turtle	▨ Indian star tortoise	▨ Snapping turtle
▨ Hinge-backed tortoise			

and cylindrical, with thick claws. Aquatic species, such as terrapins, have webbed feet, while the limbs of sea turtles have evolved into flattened flippers.

Underwater breathing

Since a turtle cannot expand its chest like a normal reptile it has had to develop its own technique of breathing. Its muscles compress the lungs to expel air, then relax to allow the lungs to fill again. The lungs are full of air when at rest, enabling the turtles to hold their breath underwater. Most species can also absorb oxygen through their skin, or through the thin lining of the throat. Turtles absorb most of their oxygen in this way, allowing the animals to stay underwater almost indefinitely; several species spend the entire winter in a dormant state underwater, relying on air in the water passing through the skin to keep them alive.

Turtles and tortoises have limited color vision. They make few sounds, except during mating, and many are thought to be almost deaf by our standards. However, experiments show that the green turtle is able to distinguish low to medium-pitched sounds between 60 and 1000 Hz, the frequency range of many sounds that are transmitted through water.

Despite their small brains, turtles and tortoises have quite good memories and learn reasonably quickly. In laboratory experiments, they have been able to find their way out of simple mazes and to solve straightforward problems.

Armored dances

All turtles and tortoises—even those turtle species that spend most of their lives in the open ocean—lay eggs on land. The eggs are fertilized inside the body following courtship and mating. Land-dwelling species have a brisk courtship ritual. The male is usually bigger than the female, enabling him to overcome any reluctance on her part. He follows her about and strikes her repeatedly with his head and shell, often biting at her limbs until she retracts them. When she stops walking the male moves behind her and raises himself onto her carapace so that his hind legs remain on the ground and his forelegs grip her back. The male produces a variety of grunting and mewing sounds during mating, and among giant tortoises, the noise can be considerable.

Aquatic species are more subtle in their courtship approaches, particularly in those species in which the

ABOVE Sea turtles, such as the green turtle, have become highly adapted for swimming. They propel themselves through the water with their long, flattened front limbs, and use their much shorter hind limbs for steering. Green turtles spend almost all their lives at sea, coming ashore only to lay their eggs. Passengers on oceangoing ships may see them basking on the water.

male is smaller than his partner. Several pond and river turtles perform a dance in the water, in which the male swims backward with his nose resting on the female's nose as she follows him. He strokes his partner's throat several times with his feet until she is ready to cooperate, and then the two animals mate.

Sea turtle species swim into coastal waters and mate near the beach where the female later lays her eggs. The green turtle regularly undertakes migrations of over 2800 miles to return to the nesting grounds where it hatched. It leaves its feeding grounds long before the breeding season, and returns to the same beach to nest throughout its life—an average of once every three years over about 20 years.

Green turtles migrate to their breeding grounds in such large numbers that up to 40,000 egg-laying females have been counted on a single beach within the space of a few days.

Side-necked turtles

The turtles and tortoises are classified in two suborders, distinguished by the way they bend their necks when retracting their heads into their shells. Turtles of the smaller of the two suborders are known as the side-necked turtles, because they retract their heads sideways, stowing them to one side within the shell. These turtles are basically Southern Hemisphere species: one family is found in northern South America and southern Africa, while the other occurs in much of South America and Australia.

The family of Afro-American side-necked turtles are aquatic or semiaquatic and generally small, although the Arrau or South American river turtle of the Amazon and Orinoco rivers is one of the largest known freshwater turtles, often growing to over three feet long and weighing up to 198 lbs. It feeds on water plants and the fruit that falls into the water from bankside trees.

During the breeding season, the Arrau turtles may migrate over a distance of 93 miles to reach their favorite sandbanks for egg-laying. They make the journey in the rainy season, and when they arrive at the nesting grounds, the sandbanks are still covered by the waters from the swollen river. As soon as the level drops, exposing the sand, the turtles leave the water together to dig their nests and lay their eggs—from 80 to 200 in each nest.

The Amazonian Indians take advantage of this ritual egg-laying to capture the turtles and gather the eggs. As long ago as the mid-19th century, the naturalist Henry Walter Bates calculated that over 48 million eggs were taken each year, and the Arrau turtle is now an endangered species. All turtles are vulnerable to predators as they always return to the same nesting grounds and have little defense against man.

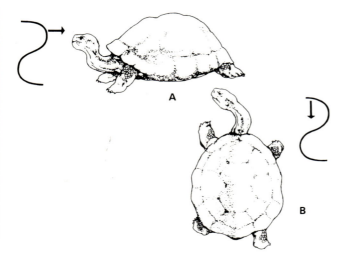

A

B

TOP, CENTER AND BOTTOM Turtles and tortoises fall into two main categories. The majority of species, including the loggerhead turtle (top), are so-called hidden-necked turtles, while the remaining species, such as the West African mud turtle (center), are known as the side-necked turtles. The former pull their necks into a vertical S-shape when they draw their heads into their shells (A), while the latter pull their necks back by twisting them to the side (B).
RIGHT The helmeted turtle is a common species in many parts of Africa, from the river Nile to the shallow, salty waters of Etosha Pan in Namibia.

TURTLES AND TORTOISES CLASSIFICATION: 1

The turtles, tortoises and terrapins all belong to the order Chelonia (also known as the Testudinata or Testudines). The order is divided into two suborders: the Pleurodira or side-necked turtles, and the Cryptodira, or hidden-necked turtles and tortoises.

Side-necked turtles

The suborder Pleurodira consists of the Afro-American side-necked turtles of the family Pelomedusidae, and the Australo-American side-necked turtles of the family Chelidae. Both families contain both aquatic and semiaquatic species. The family Pelomedusidae contains 24 species in five genera, distributed over tropical South America and sub-Saharan Africa. They include the Arrau or South American river turtle, *Podocnemis expansa*, of the Amazon and Orinoco basins; the helmeted turtle, *Pelomedusa subrufa*, of Amazonia; and the West African mud turtle, *Pelusios castaneus*.

The family Chelidae contains 37 species grouped in nine genera, ranging over South America, Australia and New Guinea. They include the snake-necked turtle, *Chelodina longicollis*, of southeast Australia; the matamata, *Chelus fimbriatus*, of Amazonia; and the carranchina, *Betrachemys dahli*, of Colombia.

ABOVE Reaching 35 in. in length, the Arrau turtle is one of the biggest of all the freshwater turtles. Like its large marine relatives, it travels huge distances to lay its eggs at traditional breeding grounds. Many hundreds of turtles congregate at these sandy sites every year, and the predictability of the event makes the animals vulnerable to local hunters who kill the adults and harvest their eggs. As a result, the Arrau turtle is now an endangered species.

The closely related mud turtles of Africa are much smaller than the Arrau turtle—from 5 to 18 in. long. They have hinged lower shells, enabling them to seal themselves inside for protection. Another member of this family, the helmeted turtle of Africa, has an unusual habit of becoming dormant during the dry season. It buries itself in the mud and remains dormant until the following rainy season. It is an excellent swimmer, but often comes out onto land to search for food, including fly larvae.

Vulnerable heads

The other family in the suborder contains the Australo-American side-necked turtles. These are long-necked creatures, and only a few of the 37 species can withdraw their heads into their shells. The snake-necked turtles of Australia are typical. They are agile, aggressive animals with, as their name suggests, particularly long necks. The sexes appear to be identical: on one occasion, a researcher marked all the females (identified during egg-laying) but, despite knowing which were the males and which the females, he was unable to spot any visible differences.

The snake-necked turtles lay their eggs in holes dug in the hard ground, leaving them to incubate for a long time; the young may not appear for six months or more after the eggs have been laid. Some species spend their dormant periods on dry land and some underwater, on the riverbed.

The western swamp turtle of southern Australia is the smallest of the Australian turtles, measuring just under 5 in. It has a short neck covered in large,

cone-shaped bumps or tubercles. It lives in pools of water that often dry up, forcing it to adapt to difficult conditions. It is now an endangered species, and its chances of survival are not helped by the fact that it only lays three to five eggs a year. However, the Australian government has taken steps to preserve their natural habitat in order to encourage breeding.

Lurking in the riverbed

The South American species in the Australo-American family are varied and normally larger than their Australian cousins. One of the most distinctive species is the matamata, which lives in murky pools and rivers in Amazonia, South America. Its carapace (the top of the shell) may be up to 18 in. long, and has a rough surface with three central ridges along its back. Its head and neck are broad and flat and are covered in numerous protrusions and tubercles, and its snout is elongated, enabling it to breathe air from the surface, even when fully submerged.

The predatory matamata catches its prey by lying in wait on the river or seabed, almost invisible due to its irregular outline and camouflage—it blends in with the dead leaves on the riverbed. When prey approaches, the matamata suddenly opens its mouth wide: the water rushes in, carrying the turtle's prey with it.

ABOVE With a ragged outline and a coloring that resembles dead leaves, the matamata is superbly camouflaged as it lies motionless at the bottom of a stream or pool. To complete the disguise, its shell is often coated in a layer of green algae. The matamata waits on the stream bed to ambush its prey. When a fish swims within range, the turtle suddenly opens its huge, yawning mouth and expands its throat. The surrounding water floods in, carrying the unfortunate fish right into the turtle's stomach.

Argentinian snake-necked turtles feed in a similar way to the matamata. They lurk on the sea or riverbed and when their prey swims by, they quickly shoot out their long necks and grasp the fish or insect between their jaws. Although these turtles cannot retract their necks into their shells, the related twist-necked turtle can—it has an extension on the front of its shell into which it fits its extremely long neck.

The carranchina lives in shallow ponds and lakes in Colombia. Like many turtles, it is only semiaquatic, and can move more swiftly over ground—it is often seen in the early morning and at dusk. It has a broad head and an unusually small lower shell (narrower in the males). When threatened, it uses its large, webbed feet to propel itself quickly through the water. Carranchinas eat snails, insects, tadpoles, frogs and some plants.

ABOVE The small head and sinuous neck of the snake-necked turtle make it one of the most easily recognized of all the Australian turtles. By poking its head above the surface, it can breathe in shallow water while resting on the bottom. It captures unwary fish and other small water animals by throwing out its neck to its full extent and snapping them up in its mouth. However, it is unable to draw its head right back into its shell.

Hidden-necked turtles and tortoises

The larger suborder of turtles and tortoises includes all the species that bend their necks into an upright S-shape when they retract their heads. They are known as the Cryptodira—literally "hidden-necked" turtles—and include the sea turtles and the tortoises.

Four of the 11 families in the suborder have only one species each: creatures that are so individual that they appear to have no close relatives. The Central American river turtle is one of these: it lives in the rivers of Mexico, Honduras and Guatemala.

The river turtle spends much of its time submerged on the riverbed in search of fallen fruit, leaves and aquatic plants. It rarely comes to the surface to breathe, taking most of the oxygen it needs for respiration by diffusion (it extracts the oxygen from the water through its skin). The river turtle also takes oxygen through the throat lining—taking water in through the mouth then expelling it through the nose. It rarely leaves the water, and when placed on dry land it moves clumsily and has to rest its large, heavy head on the ground. Like all aquatic turtles, its toes are webbed for swimming, and its limbs, neck, head and tail can all be retracted into the shell if danger threatens.

Musky and muddy

The American mud and musk turtles family contains 20 species of small turtles found in both North and South America. They live in rivers and ponds, where they forage on the riverbed for food such as shellfish, insects, worms, small fish and aquatic plants. In the coldest parts that they inhabit (they are found as far north as Canada), the mud and musk turtles lay eggs that undergo a period of dormancy, delaying the hatching of the young until the spring when plenty of food is available.

Mud turtles have flattened shells, webbed feet and often strong claws. The lower shell has two hinges that move shell lobes at the front and rear, enabling the animal to retract its head, tail and limbs and close the shell after them so that it becomes virtually impregnable. They inhabit parts of North, Central

and South America, preferring stagnant inland waters and the slightly salty water of estuaries.

The musk turtles are so-called because of the strong smelling, musky liquid they produce from their scent glands, in between the carapace and plastron. Their lower shells are much smaller than those of the mud turtles, and are not hinged, although parts of the shell are flexible.

Stinkpot

One of the more widespread species of musk turtles, the stinkpot, derives its name from its particularly pungent smell. It occurs throughout eastern and central North America, from Canada to the Gulf of Mexico. Measuring about 5 in. long over its shell, it only leaves the water to lay its eggs. It prefers slow-running rivers, ponds and luxuriant swamps, where it feeds mainly on animal remains, usually carrion, and the odd plant. It normally lays one to five eggs in natural holes among tree roots or in the abandoned burrows of other animals; occasionally clusters of up to 60 eggs have been found, and it appears that several females may lay their eggs in the same nest if it is a particularly good site.

The three species of Mexican musk turtles form a separate family. The narrow-bridged musk turtle has

ABOVE The stinkpot or "stinking jim" is one of the American musk turtles, a group notorious for the strong, musky smell produced by the scent glands on their flanks. A strictly aquatic turtle, it feeds on fish, insects and plants, emerging from the water only to lay its eggs under decaying vegetation.

a comparatively restricted distribution between Mexico and Central America. It has a three-keeled carapace and a very small plastron (lower shell) without flexible joints. It measures up to 14 in. long, and has strong, muscular feet and a large head. By contrast, the two species of cross-breasted turtles have short heads and legs and short slender tails, and the front section of the cross-shaped plastron is mobile.

Aquatic predators

The snapping turtles of North and Central America are powerful predators. There are two species: the snapping turtle and the alligator snapping turtle, and between them they use a variety of ways to catch food. Concealed by their cryptic coloration and rough carapace, they may lie passively on the bottom, waiting for prey to swim within range, securing it with a rapid strike of their sharp, beak-like jaws. The more active of the two, the snapping turtle, will also chase its quarry, often right out of the water—for it is agile and

ABOVE The snapping turtle of North and Central America is an aggressive predator that will raid henhouses in search of eggs, chicks and even adult birds. It occasionally eats other turtles if the chance arises.

BELOW For a snapping turtle, a snake is a potential meal. Here a turtle confronts a large snake (A), grips it behind the neck with its powerful jaws (B), and rolls over with the snake in its mouth (C and D) until the victim finally succumbs.

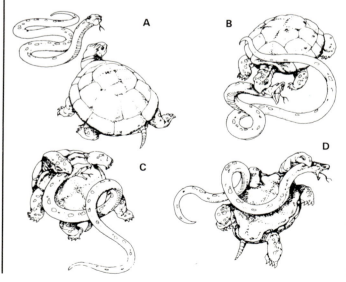

surprisingly swift over the ground.

The snapping turtle is the most widespread turtle in North America. It forages by day in the more northerly parts of its range, but prefers to hunt by night in the southern states where the nighttime temperatures are high enough for reptiles to be active. It measures about 18 in. long, much of which is its head and tail. Its lower shell is comparatively small to make movement easier, and can be moved in relation to the carapace, enabling the animal to withdraw its large head when danger threatens—although it keeps its powerful jaws wide open.

The snapping turtle is extremely bold and aggressive. It will attack fish, amphibians, reptiles, birds and small mammals, and will even raid farms to carry off geese and hens. It supplements its diet with plant matter, and will also feed on carrion; tales are told of snapping turtles being used to find the corpses of drowned men in swamps and lakes.

If disturbed, it will snap violently and is much feared by bathers in the areas it inhabits. If attacked from the front it leans forward onto its forelegs, raises its hind legs, hides its tail under its shell and withdraws its head as far as possible under its carapace, with its sharp jaws gaping wide. It snorts and hisses, blinking its eyes and attempting to bite whenever it gets the chance. If the attack comes from behind, the turtle bends its hind legs, keeping its tail under its belly, and raises its forelegs. If attacked from the side, it raises the legs on the opposite side to lean over toward its enemy, always taking care to shield the softer parts of its body behind its shell.

Snapping turtles mate between April and October. The female then digs a nest in the ground where she lays 20 to 30 eggs, and these hatch out after three months. However, there are records of the young spending all winter in their shells, only emerging in the warm spring weather.

The alligator snapping turtle is the largest of the freshwater turtles, measuring 5 ft. long—although only half of this is accounted for by the shell—and it may weigh up to 220 lbs. It has a large, triangular head and widely spaced eyes. The shell is three-ridged, extremely rough and often covered in algae, with the result that the turtle looks more like a rock than an animal, as it lurks motionless on the bottom. Though aggressive, it is less agile than the snapping turtle and, like the matamata, it relies on passive techniques to catch its food, waiting for prey such as fish, to swim into range, rather than actively pursuing it through the water.

ABOVE At 198 lbs. in weight, the alligator snapping turtle of the USA is the largest freshwater turtle. It catches fish by lurking on the bottom of a lake or river and luring the unsuspecting prey toward its open mouth by means of a fleshy appendage attached to its tongue. The bait becomes bright pink when it fills with blood, and the turtle wriggles it in its mouth so that it resembles a worm.

TURTLES AND TORTOISES
CLASSIFICATION: 2

Most species within the order Chelonia belong to the suborder Crypdodira, the hidden-necked turtles and tortoises. The suborder itself is divided into 11 families.

Musk turtles and the Central American river turtle

The American musk and mud turtles of the family Kinosternidae consist of 20 species grouped into two genera. They are confined to aquatic habitats in the New World, and include the stinkpot, *Sternotherus odoratus*, which ranges throughout North America. The Mexican musk turtles form a separate family, the Staurotypidae. The family numbers three species in two genera, including the narrow-bridged musk turtle, *Claudius angustatus*, and the Mexican cross-breasted turtle, *Staurotypus triporcatus*. They live in freshwater habitats in Mexico and Central America. The only member of the family Dermatemydidae is the Central American river turtle, *Dermatemys mawei*, which inhabits rivers and lakes in Mexico, Honduras and Guatemala.

Snapping turtles and the big-headed turtle

The family Chelydridae contains two fresh-water species: the snapping turtle, *Chelydra serpentina*, of much of lowland North America, Central America and northwest South America, and the alligator snapping turtle, *Macroclemys temminckii*, of the southwestern USA. There is only one species in the family Platysternidae: the big-headed turtle, *Platysternon megacephalum*, which inhabits mountain streams in Southeast Asia.

MEDIA CENTER 27072
EDEN PRAIRIE HIGH SCHOOL
17185 VALLEY VIEW ROAD
EDEN PRAIRIE, MN 55346

Attached to its tongue, the alligator snapping turtle has a bright red, sinuous, worm-like growth that it moves with special muscles. The turtle uses this as a lure: it lies motionless on the river bottom with its mouth open, twitching the lure to tempt fish. When a fish approaches, the turtle snaps its jaws shut. A small fish may be completely engulfed, but it has to pierce and grip large fish in its hooked jaws, and then tear them apart with its powerfully clawed forefeet.

A big-headed climber

The big-headed turtle of Southeast Asia is another unusual species, so unlike any other that it has been classified in a family of its own. It is well named, for its head is massive and appears to be quite out of proportion to the rest of its body. It also has an extremely long tail for a turtle, armored with horny rings. Its carapace is flat, with a hollow at the front and a slight ridge at the rear, and it is joined to the lower shell by elastic ligaments that allow the upper and lower parts of the shell to move slightly further apart or closer together. Despite this, its head is too large to be withdrawn into its shell, so it is covered by a horny plate for protection. Its jaws have sharp, converging tips that make its mouth look rather like the beak of a parrot, and its webbed feet are equipped with strong claws that allow the animal to climb well.

Big-headed turtles live in mountain streams in China, Thailand and Burma, where they feed largely on shellfish, crunching through their shells with their strong jaws. They will also leave the water to forage on land, usually at night, even climbing trees in search of food, gripping the bark with their sharp claws and supporting themselves with their tails. The females lay only one or two eggs in each clutch, a comparatively low reproductive rate for a reptile.

A numerous family

The largest family in the order consists of the 85 species of pond and river turtles. Found in the Americas, Europe, Asia and northwest Africa, they include many of the more familiar species such as the terrapins, which are often kept as pets. The painted turtle is a North American species found in lakes, ponds and rivers. It is well named, for it has yellow stripes on its head, neck, legs and tail, while its shell is decorated with red. The shell shape and patterning varies according to the region the turtles inhabit.

ABOVE The European pond turtle spends much of the time on land basking in the sun, but it will dive into the water as soon as it senses danger. It has broad tastes in food, and will eat almost anything that it can catch.

BELOW During courtship, the male European pond turtle swims backward in front of the larger female (A). Afterward, he caresses her with his forefeet until she sinks to the bottom (B) and allows him to mate with her.

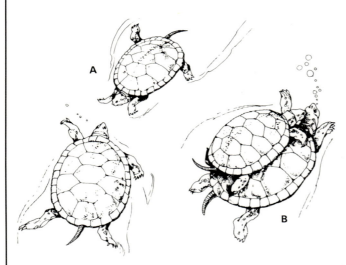

ABOVE Several small species of turtles are captured in the wild or bred in captivity for sale as pets. The demand for the North American slider is so great that millions of the animals are reared on farms.

RIGHT The painted turtle is a common and adaptable species that inhabits lakes and ponds over much of North America. It can live in stagnant, weed-covered water and has even colonized ponds in cities.

The map turtles are brightly colored animals that take their name from the patterns on their shells and bodies that resemble the contours on a map. They are of average size, measuring up to 12 in. long, and live mainly in the eastern United States, although some species have settled in the lakes and rivers of Mexico. In recent years, several populations throughout the continent have dwindled, partly as a result of pollution and partly because many of their home rivers have been made into canals—involving straightening, dredging and channeling through with concrete.

Most members of the family have flattened shells, since the streamlining improves their mobility in the water. However, the box turtles, found in central and eastern parts of the USA and northern Mexico, have domed shells like tortoises. Many species, such as the eastern box turtle, have in fact left the water, but

they still have the webbed feet typical of turtles, and they prefer to live in wet areas.

All box turtles are small animals, rarely exceeding 6-8 in. long. They are named for the precision with which the front and rear sections of the lower shell close on the carapace to form a sealed box if the turtle senses danger. They are omnivorous animals, eating insects, spiders, worms and snails, or green plants, fruit and fungi. Like many turtles, they are long-lived, and there are records of box turtles surviving to ages of 60 or more.

The diamondback terrapin is one of the better-known species. It was once widely hunted for its meat, until it neared the point of extinction at the end of the 19th century. Now it is a protected species in many areas. The diamondback terrapin takes its name from its distinctive shell—each plate on its back is raised in concentric rings to form a series of ridged mounds. The turtles live on seacoasts, salt marshes and estuaries, rarely straying from these areas, and quickly falling prey to fungal infections if kept in fresh water. They feed on crustaceans, mollusks and sometimes fish.

Stopping the trade

One group of turtles from the New World measure about 8-16 in. in length, and usually have striped heads, necks and limbs. The group includes species that are an important food source to people in South America, as well as species that are widely kept as pets. The red-eared turtle used to be one of the most popular of all turtles in captivity, but conservation measures in recent years have made a serious impact on the turtle trade.

The yellow-bellied turtle takes its name from its yellow plastron. It grows to about 9 in. in length (although some have been found up to 12 in., near the Savannah River Atomic Energy project) and has a strong, thick shell. The yellow-bellied turtle's range overlaps that of the alligator, and its strong shell may protect it from the powerful jaws of the larger reptile.

ABOVE LEFT The eastern box turtle can seal itself entirely within its colorful shell. When it draws in its head, tail and limbs, it closes up hinged plates of the shell behind them.

LEFT Despite their clumsy appearance, most turtles are surprisingly agile in the water. Here a diamondback terrapin snatches a crab (A) and a European pond turtle grabs hold of an eel (B).

ABOVE Caspian stripe-necked terrapins live mainly in dry terrain in southeast Europe and southwest Asia. They collect around almost any available stretch of water, from small ponds and marshes to slow-flowing rivers and lakes, and can tolerate salty or even polluted water. If all the water in one area dries up, the terrapins become dormant until the next rains come.

It is an omnivore, eating both meat and vegetation, feeding on aquatic plants and small animals, and can be found in a variety of freshwater habitats from deep springs to streams and ponds.

The wood turtle is easily recognized by its rough, ridged, flat shell, orange throat and legs and jet black head. It has often been kept as a pet—though it is now protected in most of the areas where it is found—and is thought to be one of the more intelligent turtles. It is adaptable and lives in a range of habitats, though it is not particularly aquatic and will only come to water for mating and periods of dormancy, spending the winter in the mud and slime of the riverbed.

The Spanish turtle will live in the filthiest water, where it often becomes infected with a variety of parasites and fungal diseases. Since the effects of these include the shell breaking up, its Latin name—*Mauremys leprosa*—is well justified (the disease leprosy in humans causes parts of the body to rot away).

TURTLES AND TORTOISES — CLASSIFICATION: 3 —

Pond and river turtles

The largest family within the order Chelonia is the Emydidae, the pond and river turtles. It contains some 85 species grouped in at least 30 genera (zoologists differ over the precise details of classification). These occur in parts of Europe, North Africa, Asia and the Americas, in freshwater, coastal and terrestrial habitats.

Members of the family in the New World include the map turtles of the genus *Graptemys* and the box turtles of the genus *Terrapene*, both from the USA and Mexico; and the slider turtle, *Pseudemys scripta*, of North, Central and South America (two races of which are the yellow-bellied turtle and the red-eared turtle).

Among the Old World species are the Caspian stripe-necked terrapin, *Mauremys caspica*, of southeast Europe, the Middle East and east to Iran and Armenia; the snake-eating turtle, *Cuora flavomarginata*, of southern China, Taiwan and the nearby Ryuku Islands; and the common batagur or tuntong, *Batagur baska*, of Southeast Asia.

ABOVE In the past, hundreds of thousands of Mediterranean spur-thighed tortoises were brought into Britain every year for sale as pets. The trade seriously depleted the wild population, particularly in North Africa. Fortunately, it is now illegal to import these animals, and the trade has stopped. If all the other importing countries enforce bans too, the tortoises will have a chance to regain their numbers in the wild.

The spiny turtle of Southwest Asia is a vegetarian turtle found in streams, often in the mountains. It has a spiny carapace, and the scutes at the edge are drawn out into sharp points, resembling a cogwheel. In the young turtles, the carapace is flat, but as the animal matures, the spines at the edges turn upward. The spines are probably there to deter predators.

Reeves' turtle is common in eastern Asia, and has been introduced to many places outside its natural habitat because it is considered a useful food source. Often only about 4 in. long, it can reach up to 14 in. It is easily identified by the three ridges on its shell.

Many temples in Thailand, especially in Bangkok, keep turtles in the ponds in their grounds. One such species is commonly known as the temple turtle. Buddhists release the turtles into the canals and ponds in the temple, as they believe that by "saving" the turtle, they will improve their lot in the next life. A herbivorous turtle, it inhabits slow-moving rivers, swamps and marshland. It has a dark brown or blackish carapace and a yellow and black plastron—a frequent color pattern in members of the family. Many Thais keep these turtles as domestic pets.

The Asian leaf turtle develops a partial hinge across the plastron when it reaches maturity, probably to allow their extra-large, brittle-shelled eggs to be laid without being cracked against the shell. Several turtles have similar flexible plastrons, and the movement this allows enables the animals to retract their heads inside the shell with their jaws still gaping open—a good defense against predators and drought.

All of the Asiatic box turtles have hinged plastrons. Three of the five species have shells specially shaped so that they can be shut tightly. These include the 7-in.-long snake-eating turtle, a species found in ponds and paddy fields.

The Indian roofed turtle, with its high-sided, tall carapace, is a common species in India. It reaches about 7 in. in length, but its relative, the Burmese roofed turtle, reaches nearly 24 in. in the female. The male, as in many turtles, is smaller, reaching about 18 in.

Scientists consider the long-tailed, edible Taiwan turtle to be one of the more primitive turtles in the pond and river turtle family. It flourishes in ponds and slow-moving water, reaching about 10 in. when fully grown, and is eaten for food in parts of China. The head and other soft parts are marked with attractive, greenish stripes.

The common batagur or tuntong has a smooth brown shell and is the largest species in the pond and river turtle family, reaching up to 24 in. in length and weighing up to about 55 lbs. Found through much of Southeast Asia, it lives in brackish and salt water. Local people collect the eggs; in recent years this has led to the common batagur's decline.

The tortoises

Tortoises have hard shells with convex, high-vaulted carapaces (upper shells), and are all terrestrial. Strong scales cover their stout limbs, their toes are short and have no webbing, unlike the aquatic species of turtle. With their hefty shells, tortoises move slowly, and as a result feed mainly on vegetable matter (though they will eat carrion, waste and invertebrates). They can withdraw their head, legs and tail into the

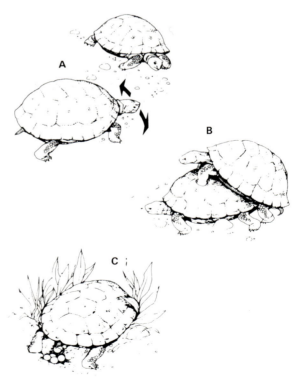

ABOVE **Hermann's tortoise lives in southern Europe, where it often raids garbage dumps, foraging through them for edible scraps such as rotting grapes and potato chips.** RIGHT **A male Hermann's tortoise courts a female by wagging his head from side to side (A). He also** bites her legs and butts her with the front end of his shell. To mate, the male must climb onto her smooth, slippery shell (B), often falling off in the process. The female lays her eggs in a hole in the soil (C), where they will be incubated by the warmth of the sun.

shell, and this adaptation, together with the high-vaulted shape of the shell, provides a good defense from most predators, whether birds or mammals. Tortoises occur on both sides of the Equator in both the Old and New worlds. They range from tropical to warm temperate climates, occurring around the Mediterranean, in the Middle East, Central Africa, Madagascar, Southeast Asia and the Americas.

The Mediterranean spur-thighed tortoise, which grows to about 10 in., is found around the northern shores of the Mediterranean. Its shell tends to be shades of yellow, brown or green with black markings. In Britain it has always been a favorite pet, but recent conservation measures there have put a stop to the sale of tortoises, giving the wild populations a better chance to recover. Hermann's tortoise, measuring about

ABOVE The colorful red-footed tortoise lives in forests and grassland in northern South America and the West Indies. In some parts of its range, its meat is highly prized by local people. When mating, the male utters a strange "clucking" call similar to that of a hen.

FAR RIGHT The Galapagos giant tortoise is active during the day, though it often shelters in pools to escape the full midday heat. It will eat almost any vegetable material that is available, including manzanilla fruit, which is poisonous to most other animals.

8 in. long, is the other widespread European tortoise. It lacks thigh spurs, but has a large scale on the tip of the tail. The little Egyptian tortoise is smaller still, reaching only 5 in., although the males average 4 in.

The marginated tortoise is a larger animal, reaching 12 in. in length. Its shell is flared at the back. The top shell is usually black, though each of the larger scutes has a yellow or orange patch. The Afghan tortoise has a rounded, rather flattened shell. It lives at altitudes of up to 8200 ft. in Pakistan and tolerates arid conditions and extremes of temperature across much of its range. In the summer heat, it comes out to feed only in the cool of morning and evening, and during the cold winter months, it can survive temperatures below freezing as it has "anti-freeze" chemicals in its blood.

These tortoises all show a similar pattern when mating and courting, which usually takes place in late spring. The male launches himself against the female's shell, butting her with his own shell. He bites her repeatedly, sometimes causing injury, and then climbs onto her back, hanging on with his strong front claws. While copulation takes place, the male utters a sound similar to that produced by a toy trumpet, along with panting and whining sounds. The number of eggs that a female lays varies according to her size, but may be as little as one or more than a dozen. She lays them in sand or soft soil and the young hatch after about three months (although some species take up to a year to hatch). The young resemble the adults, but their shells are rounded and more clearly patterned.

The largest tortoises occur on oceanic islands. Their size seems to be related to the lack of competition for food from other herbivores, and the absence of predators on the islands.

Lumbering giants

The giant tortoises of the Galapagos Islands in the Pacific Ocean are among the best known of all the reptiles. They reach over 3 feet in length and can weigh over 507 lbs. Once abundant on the islands, they have undergone a drastic decline in population, particularly during the last hundred years. They first started to fall in number in the 16th century, when the Spaniards discovered the Galapagos Islands. Sailors soon realized that the slow-moving tortoises were easy to capture and that they provided a ready source of food and oil (turtle oil was used for many products, including soap). The sailors collected the animals in large numbers, both to slaughter and eat on the spot, and also to load live onto ships to provide a constant supply of fresh meat.

Rats, goats and pigs, brought to the Galapagos Islands by sailors, added to the tortoises' problems by eating the eggs and young and destroying the natural vegetation. Today, several subspecies of the Galapagos giant tortoise are nearing extinction and others are under great threat. Fortunately, conservation measures, including the rearing of young in protected areas and the extermination of pigs and goats, give some hope for the species' future.

Although the Galapagos giant tortoises all belong to one species, they are divided into two distinct groups: those with "saddle-backed" shells and those with

LEFT The different races of the Galapagos giant tortoise evolved on different islands in the Galapagos achipelago or, in the case of the largest island, Albemarle, in areas separated by fresh lava flows. Here, members of the Volcan Alcedo race, which live on one of Albemarle's volcanoes, congregate at a waterhole. As well as keeping the tortoises cool, bathing probably gets rid of biting insects from their bodies.

"dome-backed" shells. Saddle-backed subspecies have the carapace (the top part of the shell) raised at the front, allowing the tortoises' long necks to stretch as high as possible—a useful aid to browsing for scarce food. Moreover, on the smaller, more arid islands of the Galapagos, the prickly pear cactus is an important source of food and water. On these islands the cactus grows upright, making it necessary for the tortoises to reach up to browse. Subspecies with dome-backed shells live on larger islands with more lush vegetation, where the evolution of saddle-shaped shells would not have had any obvious advantages.

Size varies greatly between the different subspecies of the Galapagos giant tortoise. Adults on the island of Pinzon (or Duncan) reach about 26 in. in length in the males and 24 in. in the females (Galapagos giant tortoises are unusual in that the males are larger than the females). Male Pinzon tortoises weigh up to about 121 lbs. On the large, neighboring island of Santa Cruz (or Indefatigable), however, the male tortoises can weigh up to 550 lbs. or more and measure 47 in. in length.

Boosting the numbers

Pinzon is one island on which the tortoise population has been boosted by conservation measures. The eggs have been incubated artificially and the young reared in safety, away from the feral rats that have overrun the island. Santa Cruz is recommended to visitors as the best island for watching giant tortoises—it has a nature reserve especially for the animals.

The tortoises on Santa Cruz breed in areas known as "campos," which have soft, fine soil into which the females can lay their eggs. The animals walk to the campos along tracks that have been worn smooth by thousands of tortoises in the past. The same track may have been in use for centuries. When a female reaches the nesting site, she chooses an unshaded patch of earth, urinates on the spot to make it muddy, digs a hole in the softened ground and lays her eggs in the cavity. She then covers the eggs and may smooth the

TURTLES AND TORTOISES — CLASSIFICATION: 4 —

Tortoises

The tortoises make up the family Testudinae, with 41 species in 10 genera. They are terrestrial animals, and range over southern Eurasia, Africa, South America and some parts of North America. Members of the genus *Testudo* include the Mediterranean spur-thighed tortoise, *T. graeca*, of southern Europe, North Africa and the Middle East; Hermann's tortoise, *T. hermanni*, which is restricted to southern Europe; and the Afghan tortoise, *T. horsfieldi*, of Afghanistan, Pakistan, the central Asian USSR and Iran.

One of the largest genera, *Geochelone*, includes species such as the leopard tortoise, *G. pardalis*, of much of southern and East Africa; the Indian star tortoise, *G. elegans*, of India and Sri Lanka; the Galapagos giant tortoise, *G. elephantopus*, of the Galapagos Islands; and the Aldabra giant tortoise, *G. gigantea*, of the islands of Aldabra in the Indian Ocean. The spider tortoise, *Pyxis arachnoides*, occurs in Madagascar, and the geometric tortoise, *Psammobates geometricus*, lives in South Africa.

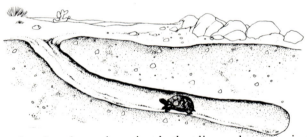

ABOVE The Florida gopher tortoise lives in dry, sandy places, where it spends the nights and the whole of the winter hidden away in a deep burrow. Other creatures, including venomous rattlesnakes, often share the tortoise's burrow.

RIGHT The Florida gopher tortoise's burrow can be up to 33 feet long and may penetrate as deep as 13 feet below the surface. The tortoise starts on the burrow when it is young and gradually deepens and widens it during its lifetime.

mud down over them by pressing it with her plastron (the underside of the shell). The sun bakes the mud into a hard layer that stops the eggs from being broken by the feet of other tortoises and helps prevent the eggs from drying out.

Low turnover

The biggest tortoises of all live on Aldabra—a large coral reef, or atoll, about 404 mi. off the coast of East Africa in the Indian Ocean. The males reach 4 ft. 6 in. in length, while the females grow to 31.5 in. The Aldabra giant tortoise is the only surviving member of a group of species that once inhabited Madagascar and the Seychelles, and it, too, is endangered. At present, breeding activity seems to be dangerously low in the wild, possibly because the tortoises' diet has recently become inadequate. Although population fluctuations

are hard to detect in animals that live as long as giant tortoises (captive Aldabra giant tortoises have lived for over 100 years), researchers have noted a lack of young on the island.

The giant tortoises of the Indian Ocean once included a group of species from the Mascarene Islands— Mauritius, Reunion and Rodriguez. These became extinct by the early 19th century, having been completely wiped out by hunting. A relative of the giant tortoises, the radiated tortoise, is native to Madagascar. It reaches about 16 in. in length, and has a black and yellow head, yellow legs and an attractive black and yellow patterned shell. People who have captured radiated tortoises have noted that the animals release high-pitched cries that can continue for over an hour. Afterward, however, the sound is rarely uttered again, even during a lifetime of captivity.

Spider's web

Madagascar is also the home of the spider tortoise, which takes its name from the yellow-on-black pattern on its domed shell that looks similar to a spider's web. A small tortoise, reaching about 6 in. in length, it is the only species that has a hinged, movable flap at the front of the plastron.

Kenya and Tanzania are the home of the pancake tortoise, a species quite unlike any other. It takes its name from its flattened shell that is soft to the touch and quite pliable. It lives on dry mountains, preferring rocky areas that offer plenty of hiding places. The pancake tortoise deals with threats in a completely different way from most other tortoises. Instead of withdrawing into its shell, it runs away. If danger threatens, it scampers toward a rock crevice and slides inside. Once there, it puffs its body up until it is firmly wedged into its shelter, making it virtually impossible for a predator to pull out.

Hinges on the top

Several tortoises have hinged parts on their plastrons, but the hinge-backed tortoises of Africa are unusual in that they have a hinged carapace. The movement allowed by the hinge may close the shell more completely for defense or open it to make egg-laying

ABOVE Local people hunt green turtles in many parts of the world for the delicate flavor of their flesh. They catch females on the nesting beaches and capture males in the water offshore, often by harpooning them. In recent times, the pressures of hunting have become so great that they now threaten the survival of the species. On many of the beaches where it nested in the past, the green turtle has been driven to extinction.

easier. Young animals do not show a trace of the hinge, but as they grow older, the hard tissue between a pair of scutes on each side of the carapace is replaced by more flexible tissue. Gradually the flexible tissue spreads across the shell, forming the complete hinge. Schweigger's hinge-back tortoise is the largest of these species, with a shell measuring up to 12.5 in. long. It lives in damp, well-vegetated habitats.

The geometric tortoise is a very rare tortoise of South Africa, and is disappearing as its evergreen shrub and grassland habitat is plowed up for agriculture. Fortunately, some of the areas in which it lives are protected, so that at least a remnant population should be preserved. The species is 6 in. in length, and has a starred pattern on the shell. There are more females than males in the population, but zoologists have yet to discover why this should be so.

ABOVE AND RIGHT Loggerhead turtles lay their eggs in holes on beaches, and then cover the hole with sand. The temperature of the sand affects not only the incubation time of the eggs, but also the sex of the hatchlings. Eggs raised at 82.4°F all hatch as males. At 86°F the sex ratio is approximately half-and-half, and at 89.6°F all the young turn out to be females.

PAGES 1548-1549 Some races of the Galapagos giant tortoise—those of the smaller, more arid islands—have "saddlebacked" shells, with a high arched front. They also have longer legs than their "dome-backed" relatives. These features allow the animals to reach higher for food in areas where the population is dense and competition for food is great.

Sea turtles

Sea turtles spend most of their lives in the ocean, and barnacles and seaweed often cover their bodies. In adapting to a marine life-style, sea turtles' legs have evolved into long, broad and powerful flippers that enable the creatures to move through the water with an elegant, flying motion. To propel itself forward, the turtle beats its fore flippers up and down, in the same way as a bird, and uses the hind flippers mainly as rudders for steering. Sea turtles only leave the ocean to lay their eggs, swimming great distances to reach the beaches where they breed.

THE GREEN TURTLE
— THE HAZARDS OF BREEDING —

The dense, underwater weed pastures where the green turtle feeds are usually a great distance from their traditional breeding grounds. Many green turtles live off the coast of Brazil, where they feed in the shallow coastal waters on turtle weed. Some will migrate westward along the Brazilian coast for hundreds of miles to the coasts of the Guianas, where they breed. Others set off eastward and swim more than 1200 miles to Ascension Island in the mid-Atlantic. It is not known how they find their way across such distances to the small island.

Nesting occurs all year round in many green turtle breeding sites. Mating takes place offshore, the males seizing the females at the front of their carapace (the top shell) with the claws on their front flippers. The males often wound the females with their claws as they mate. The females then make their way slowly up the beach, bleeding from their wounds, to where the sand is dry and they can dig their nest.

The female uses her front and rear flippers to dig a pit in the sand, into which she fits comfortably. She then begins to dig a smaller hole at the back of the pit, deftly using her rear flippers to shovel the sand out. She lays her eggs—usually about 100—in the hole, and fills it in, moving herself a little further up the beach as she does so. By the time she turns back to return to the sea, she has flattened the ground around the eggs, making the nest difficult for predators to detect. Despite this, predators (human or animal) often find the nest and steal the eggs.

Eggs by the thousand

The female may return six or more times, laying as many as a thousand eggs before leaving the breeding grounds. The males rarely emerge from the sea—they are aggressive throughout the breeding season, often fighting rivals for a female. The competition among males for females may be intensified by the fact that so many females become prey to predators when they leave the water to nest on the beach. Green turtles are nimble in the water, but on land, their heavy shells restrict their movement.

Once all the eggs have been laid, the turtles return to their feeding grounds and abandon their nests. Several months later the hatchlings emerge, working their way up through the sand. They hatch all at once and head straight for the area of brightest light—the sea (which reflects the light of the sun or moon). On tourist beaches, the green turtles are sometimes confused by the lights of discos and hotels, and head off in the wrong direction. Only a handful of young are likely to survive the predators who await them as they return to the sea. Those that do survive will return years later to the same beach to breed as mature animals.

Adult green turtles, however, also face serious problems. Their flesh is used to make turtle soup, and because of this the green turtle has been overhunted, wiping out many of their populations and bringing others to the edge of extinction. It is protected in some places, but the future of the turtle depends on strict conservation measures.

BELOW LEFT On hatching from its egg, the young green turtle is dark blue and white in color. As it grows older, its back will become greenish, brown, buff or black, and its underparts yellowish.

RIGHT The green turtle is a powerful underwater swimmer, using its long front flippers like wings to "fly" through the water. The rear flippers act mainly as rudders.

BELOW A female green turtle digs a nesting pit with her flippers (A), and lays her eggs in the hole (B). When the young turtles hatch, they work their way up to the surface of the sand (C). Once there, they risk the danger of waiting predators—such as rats, coyotes, gulls and crabs—as they crawl down the beach to the sea.

BELOW RIGHT To protect her eyes from flying sand while digging and covering the nest, the female green turtle produces "tears" of mucus that run from her eyes down her cheeks and wash the sand away.

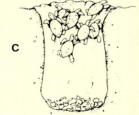

A

B

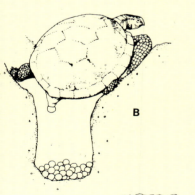

C

ABOVE **Female Pacific ridley turtles emerge from the sea in large numbers to nest at their breeding sites on sandy shores. In contrast to the laborious progress of other species, such as the green turtle, Pacific ridleys crawl their way quickly up the beach with only brief moments of rest. They shovel the sand from their nesting pit, drop 50-160 eggs in the hole, smooth over the hole and return to the sea, the whole process usually taking no more than 50 minutes. In contrast, a green turtle may be out of the water for three hours.**

For centuries, the flesh and eggs of sea turtles have been valued as food, and the creatures have played an important part in the local economies of people living along tropical coasts. However, almost all sea turtles are now endangered as a result of uncontrolled hunting and egg collection. In addition, the growth of tourism has seriously reduced the number of beaches where the turtles can breed undisturbed.

The sea turtles comprise seven species: six of them belong to one family, and are characterized by the turtles' usual covering of horny plates, or scutes; the seventh species, the leatherback sea turtle, stands in a family of its own, and has a carapace composed of many small, bony plates covered with a thick, smooth, leathery skin.

Of the six hard-shelled sea turtle species, the largest is the green turtle, an inhabitant of tropical waters. It measures about 39-51 in. long, and weighs about 330 lbs., though the heaviest specimen on record weighed 650 lbs. As with many turtles, the male green turtle can be distinguished from the female by its longer, thicker tail. In mature animals, the carapace may be olive-green, brown, gray or black, and is usually patterned in a darker shade.

The loggerhead turtle is larger than the green turtle and occurs in the temperate and subtropical waters of the Atlantic, Pacific and Indian Oceans. Because it tolerates low temperatures, it is sometimes seen in more northerly latitudes—as far as Nova Scotia (Canada) and Scotland. These northern seas are well beyond its breeding range, and turtles that swim in such cold waters during winter rarely survive.

Anti-shark shell

The loggerhead has a large head and a distinctive red-brown carapace that weighs about 220 lbs. and grows to over 3 feet long. The shell is particularly thick, and may provide protection from the teeth of sharks. Like the green turtle, the loggerhead migrates to its nesting grounds each year—although it rarely travels anything like as far and tends to nest more than once a season. Loggerhead turtles generally nest along warm coasts outside the tropics. In the

TURTLES AND TORTOISES — CLASSIFICATION: 5 —

Sea turtles

The sea turtles are divided into two families, and between them they range over the oceans of the world, from tropical to temperate waters. The leatherback sea turtle or leathery turtle, *Dermochelys coriacea*, is the sole member of the family Dermochelyidae. It occurs in most tropical and temperate stretches of the Atlantic, Pacific and Indian Oceans.

The second family, the Cheloniidae, contains the other six species of sea turtles, which are grouped into four genera. The hawksbill turtle, *Eretmochelys imbricata*, and the loggerhead turtle, *Caretta caretta*, both range through the Atlantic, Indian and Pacific Oceans. The green turtle, *Chelonia mydas*, is similarly widespread, but the flatback turtle, *C. depressa*, is more restricted, nesting only around the northern coast of Australia. The Pacific or olive ridley turtle, *L. olivacea*, is a species from tropical parts of the Pacific and Indian Oceans and the South Atlantic, while Kemp's or Atlantic ridley turtle, *Lepidochelys kempi*, lives in the Gulf of Mexico and the North Atlantic.

Softshell turtles

The family Trionychidae contains the softshell turtles, which live in freshwater habitats in parts of North America, Africa, southern and northeast Asia, Indonesia and the Philippines. There are 22 species grouped in six genera. They include the Indian flapshell turtle *Lissemys punctata* of India and Bangladesh; the Zambezi softshell turtle *Cycloderma frenatum* of parts of East and southern Africa; the Senegal softshell turtle *Cyclanorbis senegalensis* of West Africa; the narrow-headed softshell turtle *Chitra indica*, which ranges from Pakistan through India to Thailand and Malaysia; the antipa *Pelochelys bibroni* of southern China and Southeast Asia; and the spiny softshell turtle *Trionyx spinifer*, which ranges from Canada to northern Mexico.

The pig-nosed softshell turtle (or Fly River turtle or minowa) *Carettochelys insculpta* is the sole member of the family Carettochelyidae. It lives in rivers in the south of New Guinea and in the Daly River in northern Australia.

ABOVE Kemp's ridley has only one known nesting site in the world—a beach near the village of Rancho Nuevo on the Gulf of Mexico. The females emerge from the sea together in large numbers, sometimes several hundred at a time. In the past, however, nesting Kemp's ridleys were counted in the tens of thousands. Egg collecting and the killing of adult turtles by local people are largely responsible for a drastic decline in the turtle's population over the last 40 years.

ABOVE **Hawksbill turtles roam throughout the tropical seas of the world, with different subspecies living in different oceans. Those from the Atlantic are renowned for laying more eggs on average than any other turtles, the largest clutch on record being 221. The hawksbill turtle is greatly threatened because it is the source of tortoiseshell — a material used to make brooches, ornaments and spectacle frames. Though widely protected, it is still hunted freely in many areas.**

Mediterranean, the loggerhead still nests on the Italian, Turkish and Israeli coasts, though it is threatened almost everywhere by holiday developments. It is probably less threatened on the North African coasts.

As with other sea turtles, the temperature at which the loggerhead's eggs incubate in the sand determines both the sex of the young, and the length of the incubation period. Higher incubation temperatures produce more female than male young. In the temperate regions where the loggerheads nest, the eggs incubate for about two months, whereas the eggs of tropical species may remain in the ground for a year or more. Although it eats water plants, the loggerhead turtle is mainly a carnivore, using its powerful, crushing jaws to feed on squid, jellyfish, fish, crabs and shellfish.

Smallest of sea turtles

Ridley turtles are close relatives of the loggerhead, and are the smallest of the sea turtles. Kemp's ridley turtle rarely grows more than 27 in. long, and weighs about 110 lbs. Its carapace is gray or olive-green, and round in shape (in juveniles, the carapace may even be broader than it is long).

Kemp's ridley turtles nest on only one remote stretch of beach in Mexico. They used to gather here in great numbers during the summer in order to breed—in 1947, an estimated 40,000 were counted at one mass nesting. By 1973, only about 1000 Kemp's ridley turtles could be seen nesting at the same time. Their numbers have been reduced by local people who slaughter the animals as they lie on the beach, and then collect their eggs. Adult turtles occasionally drown accidentally in trawlers' nets.

The Pacific or olive ridley turtle is roughly the same size as Kemp's ridley turtle, but differs in having a narrower, usually darker, shell, and weaker jaws. However, it is also a carnivore, and feeds on shrimps, fish and jellyfish. As with other marine turtles, mature individuals migrate to traditional breeding beaches.

The hawksbill turtle is another relatively small sea turtle: adults do not grow more than 36 in. long, and usually weigh 99-154 lbs. These sea turtles prefer the tropical waters of the Atlantic, Pacific and Indian Oceans, and seldom travel north into temperate European waters. The hawksbill is mainly carnivorous, and feeds on a wide array of creatures, especially sponges, shellfish and fish. Its narrow head probably enables it to probe intricate coral reefs for food.

Although the hawksbill is hunted for its flesh, for example in Guyana, South America, it has been exploited to a far greater extent for another commodity—tortoiseshell. In the wild, seaweed and barnacles often mask the hawksbill's mottled carapace, but its thick, overlapping, yellowish brown scutes are extremely attractive when polished. The scutes are removed from live or dead animals by applying heat. They are then shaped and welded together to produce the final tortoiseshell product, such as a comb or spectacles. Each shell provides about 11 lbs. of tortoiseshell.

The largest turtle in the world

The leatherback sea turtle is the largest turtle in the world—its shell measures over 70 in. long, and the animal weighs 827 lbs. on average. It differs from the other marine turtles in having no hard external features: the upper shell is leathery and the lower shell is soft; the skin has no scales; and the jaw lacks horny plates. The front flippers are very long, spanning as much as 71 in., while the rear flippers are broad and joined to the tail by skin. The leatherback's streamlined carapace is dark brown or black, with a scattering of white spots in varying density, and there are five or seven distinctive, sometimes notched, ridges running along the length of its back.

ABOVE It was only in the 1960s that zoologists discovered the pig-nosed softshell turtle living in a few rivers in northern Australia. Up to that time, the rare and secretive animal was known only in New Guinea. Since the species often wanders offshore from the coast of New Guinea, it may have swum across the sea to Australia, though it is also possible that people carried it across.

The leatherback inhabits the open ocean, and seldom enters coastal waters. It feeds mainly on tiny, free-swimming invertebrates known as salps, as well as on jellyfish. The leatherback's jaws are not particularly strong (hence its diet of jellyfish), but both the upper and lower jaw end in a sharp hook at the front. Although it has been recorded swimming high up in the North Atlantic, the leatherback is mainly a turtle of tropical and warm waters, breeding on the shores of the Indian, Pacific and Atlantic Oceans, and the Mediterranean Sea. The female leatherback nests at night, and probably does so several times in one season, on each occasion laying up to 100 eggs.

A New Guinean oddity

The pignosed softshell turtle (also known as the minowa or Fly River turtle) of New Guinea has been placed in a family of its own. Measuring 22 in. or

ABOVE With its flattened body and sandy coloration, the spiny softshell turtle of North America can lie invisible in the silt on river beds. It is a fast and agile swimmer that preys on aquatic insects, crawfish, fish and, in some cases, mollusks. Large individuals may even catch ducks by snapping at their feet and pulling them beneath the water surface.

more in length, it is closer in shape to the sea turtles—especially the leatherback—than to other freshwater turtles. There are no horny plates (scutes) on the shell, which is covered instead with skin, and its forelimbs have evolved into flippers. The turtle's carapace is gray, and it has a thick extension to the snout that is probably an adaptation for breathing.

The softshell turtles

Softshell turtles are widely distributed through the world, occurring in warm temperate and tropical regions. Their flat, flexible shells lack scutes, and they have three claws on each foot, unlike most other turtles that have four or five claws (sea turtles have one or none). Their streamlined shape enables them to move through the water quickly, and they can also move surprisingly fast on land.

The snouts of softshell turtles are either elongated or blunt, and the animals' beaks are equipped with fleshy lips that conceal jaws designed to cut or crush their food. The turtles probably breathe mainly through the skin, which is well supplied with capillaries and almost devoid of scales (a few are found only on the limbs). These aggressive turtles are unafraid of humans and will not hesitate to bite anyone who disturbs them.

One group of the softshells, the flapshell turtles, have flaps at the back of the plastron that cover the hind limbs after they have been withdrawn inside the

shell. The Indian flapshell turtle is one of the smaller softshells—males reach about 6 in. long and females about 10 in. Its dark gray-green carapace, marked with yellow spots, is unusually domed for a softshell. It lives in slow-moving and still waters, and feeds on aquatic invertebrates, fish and amphibians.

The 14-in.-long Senegal softshell turtle is another flapshell species. It ranges from Senegal in West Africa across to southern Sudan where Bari tribespeople eat its flesh and use the shell as a bowl. In some parts of Africa, people put the turtle in wells, so that it can keep the water clear of rotting matter.

The remaining softshells lack the plastron flaps. The narrow-headed softshell turtle of Asia measures over three feet long, and is one of the oddest-looking of all turtles. Inhabiting rivers with sandy beds, it has a long, pointed skull, and an olive-green carapace marked with a complex, dark gray pattern that gives the turtle a mottled appearance from above. The patterning provides good camouflage in the water, but it becomes less distinct as the turtle ages. The narrow-headed softshell catches its prey by ambush, waiting on the river bottom and striking out at its unsuspecting victims.

One species of softshell turtle, known by its Philippine name, antipa, reaches as much as 49 in. long. It has an olive shell and head, and the back may be speckled with black, white or yellow. The turtle inhabits all aquatic environments, from wide, slow-moving, muddy rivers to clear streams.

The spiny softshell turtle of North America takes its name from the small spines that run along the front of its sandy-colored, spotted carapace. Some specimens reach over 15 in. in length, and the females are generally larger than the males. It is both a carnivore, eating shellfish and invertebrates, and a scavenger.

A LIVING RELIC

The only surviving member of an ancient order, the tuatara has changed little since the age of the dinosaurs; it haunts islands off the coast of New Zealand, where it rests by day and hunts by night

The tuatara is a unique reptile, similar in shape to a lizard, but belonging to an entirely separate order. Members of that order were numerous and widespread millions of years ago, but today the tuatara is the sole surviving species. It lives only in New Zealand, and its range there has been severely reduced in recent times. Its last remaining strongholds are 30 small islands and islets that lie off the mainland, having high cliffs, low forest and scrub vegetation and pebble-strewn beaches.

Little changed

Zoologists believe that, like the lizards and snakes, the tuatara is descended from an ancient group of reptiles known as the diapsids. The diapsids had two oval openings in each side of the skull just behind the eyes. In lizards and snakes, the bars of bone beneath the lower openings no longer exist, but the skull of the tuatara still has two pairs of holes completely surrounded by bone. Since it retains the primitive skull structure, the tuatara can be regarded as a "living fossil." Animals similar to it are known to have appeared in the late Triassic period over 200 million years ago, and the tuatara has changed little since then; its skeleton is virtually identical to that of a fossil that has been dated at 140 million years old.

The tuatara has a number of features that distinguish it from the lizards, in addition to the shape of its skull. Its teeth, for example, are merely pointed extensions of the jawbone, rather than separate structures that slot into the jaw. The bones that make up its spine are hollow at each end, unlike those of lizards, and its heart is the most simple in structure of all the reptiles.

Crested males

Male tuataras grow to just under 24 in. in length from the nose to the tip of the tail, and weigh over 2 pounds. The smaller females reach 18 in. and weigh

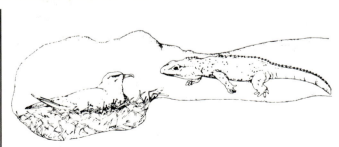

ABOVE LEFT The tuatara finds much of its food on the forest floor, foraging for beetles, slugs, snails, earthworms and spiders. It may also steal the eggs and chicks of birds, and sometimes catches lizards. On occasion, it even eats the young of its own species.

LEFT Tuataras sometimes share their burrows with nesting sea birds.
PAGES 1557 AND 1559 Tuataras once lived on mainland New Zealand, but they now survive only on some offshore islands where their natural habitat still exists and where they are not preyed on by rats.

ABOVE Tuataras are slow to develop, young animals not becoming sexually mature until they are 20 years old. They compensate for their slow growth rate by being extremely long-lived. Those that survive life's natural hazards may reach more than 120 years of age.

about 1 lb. Tuataras are olive-green or slate-gray in background color, with fine, yellowish white speckles over most of their skin. The word "tuatara" is the Maori name for the animal and means "peaks on the back" (the Maoris are the original inhabitants of New Zealand). "Peaks" refers to the triangular folds of skin that form a crest along the back and tail of the male. The male holds the crest erect when he is excited during courtship or when he is alarmed.

One of the tuatara's strangest features is the parietal body or "third eye," a structure in the roof of the skull just below the skin. In young tuataras, it can be seen lying under a transparent scale. Although common to all reptiles, the parietal body is particularly associated with the tuatara, since it was on this animal that research on the structure was first conducted. The parietal body measures 0.2 in. in diameter and has a lens and a retina. Nerves connect it to a gland in the animal's brain, known as the pineal body. Mystery still surrounds the purpose of the parietal body: it is sensitive to light but is unable to recognize objects like a real eye.

Tuataras are nocturnal animals, but on warm days they often emerge to bask in the sunshine. They feed mainly on invertebrates, though they also eat small lizards, chicks and birds' eggs, and find most of their food at ground level in the forests. They spend the day in underground burrows, either those they have dug themselves, or holes they have taken over from nesting sea birds, such as shearwaters and petrels, that dig their burrows in the soft soil of the cliff tops. Large populations of tuataras occur only on islands where there are high densities of sea birds. Not only do the birds provide convenient burrows, but they also produce abundant droppings that enrich the forest soil and support a greater concentration of small invertebrates.

Slow progress

Tuataras mate in January, which is summertime in the Southern Hemisphere. The females lay 6-15 eggs in October or November (spring in the Southern Hemisphere), placing them in shallow depressions or small burrows that they have dug in the soil. The oval eggs, each about one inch in length, are covered with earth and do not hatch for a further 15 months—the longest incubation period known for any reptile.

Before hatching, the eggs absorb moisture and their leathery shells become swollen. The young tuatara is equipped with a horny egg tooth that it uses to break open the shell. About two weeks after hatching, the egg tooth disappears. The young are immediately active, foraging for food and even digging their own small burrows for shelter during the day. Growth in tuataras is a long, slow process. They are usually 20 years old before they can breed, and they may continue to grow in size for another 60 years. Not surprisingly, they are some of the longest-lived of all the vertebrates.

Tuataras are severely threatened in the wild, only surviving in healthy numbers on islands where they have remained undisturbed by human settlement and where their haunts have not been overrun by non-native animals. The introduced animal that has proved to be the most harmful is the Polynesian rat or kiore, which eats both the eggs and young of tuataras.

TUATARA CLASSIFICATION

The tuatara *Sphenodon punctatus* of New Zealand is the only living member of the order Rhynchocephalia (and therefore the only member of its family, the Sphenodontidae). It lives on small islands and rock stacks off the northern and eastern coasts of the North Island, New Zealand, and in Cook strait, which separates the North Island from the South Island.

SPINES, CRESTS AND FRILLS

Lizards have evolved a spectacular variety of scales for decoration and defense—they range from the spiky crests of the marine iguana to the flared ruff of the frilled lizard and the thorny devil's razor-sharp armor

LIZARDS CLASSIFICATION: 1

The lizards make up the suborder Sauria, part of the large reptile order Squamata (which also contains the worm-lizards and the snakes). At least 3750 species of lizards exist, and are distributed throughout the tropical and temperate regions of the world. They are divided into 16 families, among the largest of which are the Gekkonidae, the geckos; the Iguanidae, the iguanas; the Scinicidae, the skinks; and the Lacertidae, the wall and sand lizards.

LEFT The Moorish gecko has large eyes that enable it to hunt insects in the dark. Many geckos are nocturnal, but most other lizards are active during the daytime.

PAGE 1561 Marine iguanas spend many hours basking beside the sea, raising their body temperature so that they can survive the chill of the water when diving for food.

Lizards, snakes and worm-lizards belong to the largest order of reptiles, the Squamata. The lizards, the oldest members of the order, evolved 200 million years ago during the Triassic period, and there are now some 3750 different species. The snakes (covered in the next chapter) did not evolve until the Lower Cretaceous, 135 million years ago, while the worm-lizards, the youngest members of the order, number some 140 different species, and their fossil remains date from 65 million years ago. Worm-lizards are the only true burrowing reptiles, living underground in tunnels that they dig themselves. The majority of lizards, snakes and worm-lizards live in the tropical and temperate regions of the world.

The members of this order all share several features in common. For example, they all possess a pair of sensory organs in the head known as Jacobson's organs. These are hollow, domed structures that lie just above the roof of the mouth and open into the mouth through slender ducts (see volume 26, page 1513). Lizards, snakes and worm-lizards use these extremely sensitive organs to follow the trails left by their prey and to detect other members of the same species for mating. Their flickering tongues sense the outside air and transfer "molecules of smell" to the ducts of the Jacobson's organ.

The lizards

Lizards show a greater variety of size and form than any of the other reptiles. They range from the smallest geckos, measuring just over an inch long, to the Komodo dragon, a monitor lizard that can reach 10 feet in length. Although most lizards have four well-defined limbs, some species have lost one or both pairs of legs during their evolutionary development, making them more snake-like in appearance. In such cases, positive identification can only be made by examining the skeleton. Unlike snakes, all lizards show some evidence of bones in the chest region, such as a ribcage and breastbones.

Lizards are particularly well adapted to living in deserts and on oceanic islands. It has been suggested that they have been so successful because they excrete semisolid uric acid rather than watery urine, and so do not face the problem of having to conserve water.

Many desert-dwelling species have flattened bodies that allow them to squeeze into rock crevices, while others are streamlined to burrow into the sand. Desert lizards often have expanded feet, either in the form of pads or with a fringe of scales that increase their surface area and enable them to scamper over the surface of loose sand without sinking in. Tree-living lizards have feet that are specially adapted to climbing.

Green iguana

Meller's chameleon

Fischer's chameleon

Sail-fin lizard

Common snake lizard

Island night lizard

Tokay gecko

Yellow-headed gecko

Common agama

1563

The tree-living chameleons, for example, have toes that face in opposite directions, an adaptation that, together with their long tails, enables them to grip firmly onto branches as they hunt for food.

Geckos are agile climbers that also have specially adapted feet. Many live in rocky areas in the tropics, and have become adapted to hunting insects in and around buildings. In many species, the foot is divided into a series of ridges that a microscope reveals to be made up of clumps of fine, hair-like processes (setae), each subdivided into even more delicate projections (bristles), ending in a minute suction-like disk or plate.

Lizards have well-developed muscles, and many are capable of rapid bursts of speed as they dart out at prey or escape from predators. The race runners of the United States live in open country, and some can achieve quite remarkable bursts of speed of up to 15 miles per hour, but generally only for short periods. Some of the larger land iguanas run fast on two legs, and the basilisks of Central America can even scurry on their hind legs across the surface of the water.

Some lizards—notably the flying dragons, chisel-teeth lizards and the flying geckos—have flaps of skin along the side of their bodies that enable them to parachute down from the high branches of trees to make a soft landing.

Styles of reproduction

Most of the lizards, worm-lizards and snakes reproduce using internal fertilization. The males have paired reproductive organs, called hemipenes, that vary in form from species to species, and so can be used as a reliable means of identification.

The majority of lizards are egg-layers (oviparous). Their leathery-shelled, porous eggs expand by absorbing moisture as the embryo grows. Although anole lizards tend to lay a single egg, and geckos usually only two, some members of the iguana family can lay up to 50 eggs at a time. Other lizards, such as some species of skink, give birth to live young (viviparity). They inhabit colder environments where there is insufficient heat to incubate the eggs.

Another form of reproduction, called ovoviviparity, also occurs among lizards. The female produces eggs, but they remain in the female's oviduct, the young hatching out within her body.

Lizards do not usually care for their young, except by finding a suitable site for egg-laying. However,

TOP AND ABOVE When confronted by predators, many lizards voluntarily break off their own tails—a remarkable tactic that is intended to distract attackers and allow the lizards to escape. The Moorish gecko (top) has regrown a new tail to replace the one it has lost, but unlike the old version, the new tail is supported by a rod of cartilage rather than a series of bones. Snakes cannot shed their tails—one obvious way in which they differ from the many legless species of lizards (above).

there are some exceptions. The female five-lined skink of the United States, for example, remains with her eggs for six weeks until they hatch, turning them so that they receive maximum heat from the sun. The females of the Great Plains skink and California alligator lizard free their offspring from their fetal membranes and stay with their young to protect them from predators.

Disposable tails

Lizards have developed a variety of methods of defense. Most species are able to discard their tails when threatened. They sever the tail from their body by contracting their muscles. Once it has been detached, the tail may twitch independently for a short time, distracting the predator and enabling the lizard to make its escape.

Some species have developed more specialized ways of defending themselves. The Australian frilled lizard, for example, extends its broad, shield-like neck fan when disturbed, at the same time opening its mouth wide and baring its teeth. Some skinks have brightly colored tongues and linings to their mouths that give a sudden, dramatic flash of color and scare off their enemies. A number of spiny-tailed lizards hide headfirst in crevices, exposing only their barbed tails. The African armadillo lizard goes one step further and rolls into a ball, holding its spiny tail in its mouth with its forefeet, presenting a totally armor-plated body. Horned lizards (popularly known as horned toads, although they are, in fact, reptiles and not amphibians) spurt blood from the corners of their eyes, and some geckos can emit a brown, sticky substance from their tails to trap their predators.

Most lizards feed on insects and other small invertebrates, catching them by dashing forward quickly and securing them in their jaws. Chameleons, however, with their camouflaged body markings and their ability to change color to blend in with their environment, rely mainly on stealth. Once the prey is within range, the chameleon shoots out its long tongue and snares the prey on its sticky end. Monitor lizards are strong, active predators that take a variety of animal prey, ranging from hatchling crocodiles to ground-nesting birds and small mammals. The Komodo dragon takes even larger mammal prey, including small deer, pigs and even adult water buffalo. In contrast, most iguanas usually have a strictly vegetarian diet.

BELOW The map shows the ranges of two common species of geckos, two species of chameleons, the green iguana, the snake lizards and the agamas.

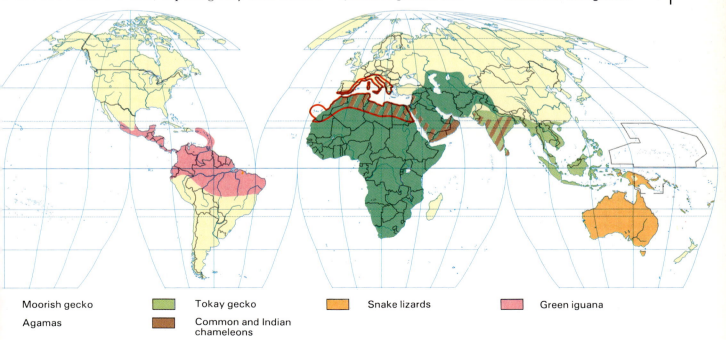

Moorish gecko

Agamas

Tokay gecko

Common and Indian chameleons

Snake lizards

Green iguana

TOP AND ABOVE The flying geckos are a group of Southeast Asian lizards with folds of skin running from their heads to their hind legs. When leaping from one tree to another, the geckos stretch these folds out so that they act as parachutes. The webbed feet of flying geckos help to break their fall. Suction pads on the toes of most geckos allow them to climb surfaces as smooth as glass.
BELOW A leaf-toed gecko adopts a defensive posture to protect its eggs from an approaching predator.

The geckos

Geckos are notable among lizards for their loud call and their ability to climb vertical surfaces. These nocturnal creatures originate from a large and ancient family of lizards, and fossils of geckos have been found dating from the Eocene times, some 50 million years ago. Most of the 800 species of gecko are small, stoutly built creatures with short, fleshy tails. Commonly thought of as climbing forest lizards, geckos also inhabit areas of drought. Many geckos live in rocky terrain and can adapt to survive in houses, where they hunt insects that are lured to the lights. Species of geckos flourish in both the Old and New Worlds and on oceanic islands, and they are especially diverse in the tropics.

The largest gecko is the 12-in.-long tokay, which inhabits Southeast Asia. It commonly takes up residence in houses in Malaysia where it hunts insects, birds and even mammals. If the prey is too bulky to kill by biting, the tokay will clamp it firmly in its jaws and beat it against the ground or wall. The smallest gecko comes from tropical America and measures some two inches in length. It belongs to a group of ground-living geckos in which the females lay only a single egg.

Patterns and color changes

Geckos naturally have subdued coloration due to their nighttime activities. However, they may display a broad range of body markings. These include spots, blotches and intricate marbled or banded patterns, all of which allow geckos to merge with their natural habitat. The few species that are active during the daytime tend to be more brightly colored and share the ability of chameleons and green anole lizards to change color. Kotschy's gecko, a slender Mediterranean species, can alter its background color from black to various shades of brown.

The Madagascar day gecko enjoys sunlight in moderate amounts, and has particularly intense body colors and patterns. Scattered over its green body, it has streaks and spots of scarlet. It also has rounded pupils and an elongated head. As a tree-living species, it feeds on both insects and nectar. Madagascar is also the home of the leaf-tailed gecko. It has a broad, flat tail and a fringe of scales around the body that provide excellent camouflage when it rests on a branch or against a tree trunk.

Geckos characteristically have a hard, unblinking stare like that of a snake. Most geckos have eyes that lack movable eyelids. Instead, the lids usually fuse to form a transparent "spectacle," or covering, over the cornea. The reptile cleans its eye with its large, flat, fleshy tongue, and the spectacle itself is shed when the gecko molts its skin.

Nocturnal geckos have large, cat-like eyes. The shape of the pupil alters according to different light intensities. When exposed to strong sunlight, the pupil either reduces to a vertical slit or closes to four pinhole openings. In the latter case, each pinhole can focus a superimposed image on the retina at the back of the eyeball, giving an extremely efficient method of focusing. Banded geckos are unusual in having movable eyelids, enabling them to close their eyes.

Walking up walls

Clinging pads on the undersides of their feet make geckos formidable climbers; these pads differ according to the species. The tokay gecko has rows of horizontal scales that consist of 150,000 or more individual hair-like projections called setae. Each seta ends in a minute saucer-like endplate or spatula measuring approximately 0.2 micrometer in diameter.

The large surface area that the four feet, 20 toes, the rows of scales and the setae offer the tokay enable it to climb almost any surface. Blood-filled cavities push the endplates against any irregularities in the climbing surface, giving a suction-like grip. In addition to their clinging pads, geckos have large claws at the ends of their toes. In order to use the pads, the gecko has to curl its toes upward at every step. Ground-living geckos do not require these special modifications and tend to have just claws. The web-footed gecko of South Africa, inhabiting the shifting dunes of the Namib desert, has expanded toes that function in a similar way to snowshoes.

Several tree-dwelling geckos have gripping or prehensile tails to aid their climbing. The undersurface of the tip of the tail is further modified into rows of hair-like projections similar to those on the toes. Most tails are slightly flattened, allowing them to press against the climbing surface. The largest Central American species, for example, has a tail shaped like a turnip, and another Australian gecko has a knob at the end of its turnip-shaped tail. When a gecko sheds its tail, the dragging skin makes a grating sound that

ABOVE The tokay gecko often lives in and around houses in tropical Asia. It is a welcome resident because it eats insects, and some people believe that it brings good luck to the occupants.

BELOW A tokay gecko uses its tongue to clean the clear protective covering of its eye (A). Tokay geckos prey on a variety of flying insects (B) and will even tackle small vertebrates such as half-grown mice.

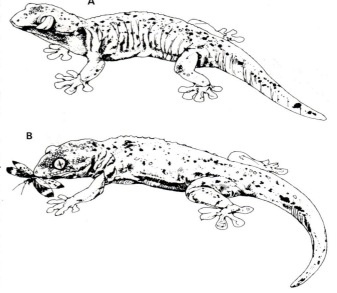

A

B

confuses predators and enables the gecko to escape. Indeed, it is not uncommon to see a gecko with two or three tails that have regrown from the original stump.

A mean tail

The tail forms one of the few means of defense available to the gecko to ward off predators. Australian geckos deter foes by ejecting a viscous fluid from cavities located in the upper surface of the tail. The fluid travels several inches, and the sticky substance can trap such predators as lycosid spiders and snake lizards. The pinkish yellow Texas banded gecko, a particularly attractive species from the deserts of the USA, issues from rock crevices at dusk to prowl in search of insect prey. When hunting, it raises its body off the ground, cocks its head and twitches its tail. In courtship, the male waves his tail and licks the female, striking her lightly on the sides before mating.

The flying gecko of Southeast Asia has an expanded flap of skin that stretches from the head to the hind legs. If the creature has to travel quickly, the flap opens out like a parachute to soften its descent as it leaps from tree to tree. By gliding to a distant perch, the gecko can escape its predators. When at rest, the reptile flattens its body against the tree surface, effecting perfect camouflage. The common house gecko defends itself by shedding large portions of skin, even if lightly grasped. It then regenerates the regions of lost skin.

Unlike the great majority of other reptiles, geckos have developed a wide range of calls for communicating, as a result of their nocturnal habits. They range from chirps, cackles and croaks to plaintive mewing sounds and large barks. Some sounds are thought to be produced by the animal clicking its broad tongue against the roof of its mouth. Geckos also have well-developed vocal cords. The name "gecko" derives from the call of a common North African species that utters a repetitive series of geck-geck, chik-chik and tock-tock noises. Certain Asian species of geckos can produce a sound similar to a rattlesnake by rubbing their tail scales together.

Most geckos lay one or two spherical eggs with hard, chalky shells. Their incubation period is long, and the toughness of their shells, laid under tree bark for protection, enables them to colonize many environments. Newborn geckos escape from their shells by piercing it with sharply pointed egg teeth on the snout

TOP Like all lizards, Bynoe's geckos of Australia periodically shed their old skin to reveal a fresh covering of scales beneath. ABOVE Unlike most geckos, the fan-footed gecko of the Seychelles is active during the day. It hunts for insects in trees and also feeds on the nectar that oozes from flowers. Sometimes fan-footed geckos accompany the large tortoises of the Seychelles, sheltering beneath their shells and darting out to capture insects disturbed from the undergrowth.

ABOVE LEFT The delicate markings of the Madagascan leaf-tailed gecko provide excellent camouflage when it rests with its body flat against a lichen-covered branch.

ABOVE The Turkish gecko is another well-camouflaged species. It is native to the Mediterranean region and southwest Asia, and has been introduced into the Americas.

that drop off soon after birth. Communal laying sites are typical of many species. Geckos often increase their range by lodging eggs in driftwood, particularly in the islands of the South Pacific. Indeed, the African house gecko and the Asian horse gecko have crossed continents by laying their eggs on driftwood.

Most geckos are insectivores, although a few will eat small mammals and birds. Others eat nectar and the sweet substances that some trees exude from their bark. Many also eat their shed skin.

Snake lizards

Snake lizards are found mainly in Australia, with two species living in New Guinea. Although most live above ground, some have adapted to living underground and are known as the burrowing snake lizards.

Snake lizards, as their name suggests, closely resemble snakes, both in appearance and in the way they move across the ground. Although they all lack forelimbs, some evidence of the shoulder or pectoral girdle, and remnants of the hind limbs, remain. In many species, the hind limbs appear as scaly flaps that contain several small bones. These flaps are generally held close to the body, near the cloacal opening, the vent through which both the excretory and reproductive fluids pass. Scalyfoots—one group of snake lizards— possess the largest of these flaps, which contain a complete set of miniature leg bones and four-toed feet. When handled, scalyfoots hold their flaps out at right angles to the body, rather like tiny wings.

The snake lizard's head is covered with large, symmetrical scales, with rectangular, shield-shaped scales on the underside. In most species, the eyelids are fused to form a transparent covering, and the ear opening is visible (except in burrowing species).

LIZARDS CLASSIFICATION: 2

Geckos

The geckos form the large family Gekkonidae, with some 800 species in 85 genera. They are widespread in Africa, southern and Central Asia, Australasia and South America, and also occur in warmer parts of North America and Europe. Members of the family include the Western banded gecko, *Coleonyx variegatus*, of the southwestern USA; the Moorish gecko, *Tarentola mauritanica*, which occurs in the Mediterranean regions of the southern Europe and North Africa; the Turkish gecko, *Hemidactylus turcicus*, which ranges from southern Europe and North Africa through southwest Asia to India (and has been introduced to parts of North and Central America); the European leaf-toed gecko, *Phyllodactylus europaeus*, which occurs on Corsica, Sardinia and a number of smaller Mediterranean islands, and in a few places on the Italian mainland; the tokay gecko, *Gekko gecko*, of southern Asia; the flying gecko, *Ptychozoon homalocephalum*, of Southeast Asia; the Australian leaf-tailed gecko, *Phyllurus cornatus*, of Australia; and the web-footed gecko, *Palmotagecko rangei*, of Namibia.

ABOVE **Burton's snake lizard occurs in a variety of habitats across mainland Australia. It has no forelimbs at all, and only small spurs in place of the** hind legs. It is active both at night and during the day, hunting other, smaller lizards, such as skinks and geckos — the victim shown here is a gecko.

LIZARDS CLASSIFICATION: 3

Snake lizards, night lizards and blind lizards

The 31 species and eight genera of snake lizards make up the family Pygopodidae. They are confined to Australia, New Guinea and a few islands nearby. Burton's snake lizard, *Lialis burtoni*, occurs in central Australia, Queensland and New Guinea, while the hooded scalyfoot, *Pygopus nigriceps*, lives in Western Australia.

The night lizards of the New World form the family Xantusiidae. There are 16 species grouped in four genera, including the desert night lizard, *Xantusia vigilis*, of the southwestern USA and Mexico; the Cuban night lizard, *Cricosaura typica*, of Cuba; and the Middle American night lizard, *Lepiodophyma flavimaculatum*, of Central America.

There are only four species in the family Dibamidae, the blind lizards. The three Asian blind lizards of the genus *Dibamus* range from Southeast Asia to New Guinea. The fourth species, the Mexican blind lizard, *Anelytropsis papillosus*, occurs in eastern Mexico.

Most snake lizards lay two long, oval eggs with parchment-like shells.

A warning to predators

Most snake lizards have a long tail, usually about three times the length of the head and body combined, which can be shed as a means of defense. They can also flex their tails into coils in a similar way to snakes. Some species of scalyfoot imitate the defensive behavior of venomous snakes when threatened. If confronted by a predator, the scalyfoot raises its head off the ground, bending its neck into an S-shape. At the same time, the scalyfoot puffs out its body, making it seem larger than it actually is. If the predator closes in, the lizard will strike at its enemy.

Snake lizards have muted coloration in shades of browns, grays or black to blend in with the ground. Burton's snake lizard, for example, has brown and cream stripes that run from the back of its head to its tail (although variations in its coloration do occur throughout its range). Most snake lizards feed on insects and other invertebrates, although some of the larger species are active hunters of smaller lizards.

Little is known of the behavior of most species of snake lizard. Indeed, one species (*Ophidiocephalus taeniatus*) discovered in Australia in 1896, has only recently been rediscovered.

Night lizards

The night lizards are a small, exclusively American family containing 16 species spread throughout the western USA, Mexico and Central America, with one species living in Cuba. They measure 1.5-5 in. in length, have long tails and legs, and are covered with granular scales that resemble pimples. Night lizards, like most of the geckos, do not have movable eyelids; instead, the eyelids are fused and transparent, forming a kind of "spectacle" over each eye to protect it from the sand. The tongue is fleshy and either covered with small bumps (papillae) or lined with narrow folds. They are secretive and generally nocturnal—hiding during the day and emerging to forage at night.

Night lizards give birth to live young. Up to three eggs (ova) develop inside the female; as they develop, they receive their nutrients and rid themselves of waste via the tissues of the mother in an arrangement similar to that of the placenta in a mammal.

The night lizards occupy four types of habitat: rock outcrops, deserts, pebble beaches, and tropical forests. The granite night lizard of southern California and Mexico lives in rocky canyons, where its flat, soft-skinned body enables it to hide in crevices. Its back is marked with large, dark spots that contrast with the pale yellow background, camouflaging the animal as it crawls across the speckled, granite rocks. The desert night lizard often shelters from the heat of the day beneath the fallen branches and leaves of the Joshua tree (a species of yucca whose stem grows more than 33 ft. high). Joshua trees form a microhabitat within the desert environment.

The island night lizard is a rare species that occurs only on certain small islands off the coast of southern California. It is less secretive than other night lizard species, being active during the day, and although it eats some invertebrates, it feeds mainly on plant matter. The night lizards include one of the rarest lizards in the world—the Cuban night lizard—described for the first time in 1860. It is confined to a

ABOVE The Middle American night lizard lives in the humid coastal forests of Central America. It shelters by day in tree trunks and among dense vegetation, emerging at night to hunt for small insects and spiders. In some parts of the species' range, the population consists solely of females, with each new generation of female young developing from unfertilized egg cells. This remarkable feat, known as parthenogenesis or "virgin birth," occurs in several kinds of lizards.

ABOVE The short-horned lizard ranges from Mexico as far north as Canada, inhabiting mainly dry terrain where it feeds on ants. The scales on its back are modified to form sharp spines designed to deter predators.

ABOVE RIGHT Horned lizards occasionally display a strange form of defensive behavior. They squirt blood from spaces behind their eyes through a pore in each eyelid to produce a fine stream that may shoot out for about three feet.

small coastal area of eastern Cuba, where it lives among loose limestone rocks.

The four species of blind lizards are little-known lizards that live in Asia and the New World. Their eel-shaped bodies are covered with rounded scales, and their heads are small (about the same diameter as their trunks) with flattened snouts, enabling them to slip easily into crevices in the ground. All species of blind lizards are secretive, and burrow into the leaf litter, soil, sand or rotten logs of wet tropical and pine and oak forests.

Blind lizards have pointed tongues, and the teeth are small and bent slightly backward to give them a better grip on worms and other invertebrate prey. Female blind lizards lack limbs, but the males bear remnants of the hind limbs on either side of the cloaca (the excretory and reproductive cavity) that are thought to be used to clasp the female during mating.

Blind lizards are unusually colored, with tones ranging from flesh-colored to purplish brown. The Mexican blind lizard, a limbless reptile found in central and eastern Mexico, is the only species of blind lizard that lives in the New World.

The iguanas

Iguanas are a family of 650 species of lizards comprising 55 genera that are confined mainly to the New World. Many species have the word "iguana" in the name, but others do not, and these include such genera as the spiny lizards, horned lizards, basilisks and anoles. Iguanas range in size from the Texas horned lizard, that may measure as little as 2 inches long, to the green iguana that reaches 6 ft. 6 in. or more in length. Most iguanas, however, are medium-sized and strongly built; the hind limbs of many are especially well developed, giving the animals remarkable power for running or leaping. All iguanas have movable eyelids, and the animals grow new teeth after the old ones have been worn down.

The smaller iguanas tend to be insect eaters, while the larger ones are mainly plant eaters. Iguanas occupy all kinds of habitats, from tropical forests to deserts, and in the Andes, some are found up to 16,400 ft. above sea level. Iguanas have two main shapes: in tree-living types, such as the helmeted iguana, the body is flattened from side to side; in ground dwellers, such as the North American earless lizards and horned lizards, the bodies are flattened from top to bottom. Small, bony, knob-like projections (tubercles), spines and crests often decorate the iguanas' heads; in males, these crests are especially well developed and the iguanas use them in territorial displays.

Running on water

Iguanas use their generally long tails for various purposes: the green and marine iguanas use their muscular tails to propel themselves through the water when swimming, and the green iguana will defend itself by lashing its tail like a whip. Both the basilisks and the collared lizard can run on their two hindlegs along the ground, using their tail as a counterbalance. The basilisk lizard can even continue its two-legged

run over water, prevented from sinking by its speed, light weight and widely spread, long toes equipped with tiny lobes.

Tree-climbing iguanas have developed their own style of moving about, gripping the branches with their hind feet and using their forelimbs and tail as a balance. The tree lizards of the United States have sharp claws that give them a firm hold on the branches, and pointed scales on the tail that the animal presses against the bark for a secure grip.

Spiny fence sitters

The spiny lizards are a group of iguanas that include many of the lizard species found in the southern United States. All are moderately sized, measuring up to 10 in. long, with overlapping scales each bearing a ridge (or keel) topped by a sharp spine, from which the lizards take their family name. Most spiny lizards are ground dwellers, but others live on rocks and around treestumps.

The most common members of the spiny lizard group are the eastern and western fence lizards— named after their habit of sunning themselves on fences. During his courtship display, the male eastern fence lizard bobs his body up and down, exposing patches of blue on the throat and belly. If the female is unwilling to mate, she raises her body high off the ground, arches her back, and makes small sideways jumps. The female eastern fence lizard lays 4-17 eggs in a hole in the ground, and the young hatch after about 10 weeks.

The horned lizards occur throughout the dry, hot areas of the western USA and Mexico. They have squat, flattened bodies with short tails that, in males, swell at the base when the animals are ready to breed.

ABOVE LEFT When it confronts a rival, a male green iguana erects the crest of spines along its back in an effort to appear more fearsome. In spite of its appearance, the animal is harmless to people and feeds only on plants.

ABOVE The collared lizard lives in canyons and gullies, and among rocky outcrops in Mexico and the arid southwest of the USA. It is an agile lizard, leaping between rocks and running quickly on its hind legs in pursuit of prey.

Sharp, projecting scales cover the body, and the head is armored with 6-10 dagger-like spines (most obvious in the flat-tailed horned lizard). Horned lizards are generally light gray or brown with spotted markings—a coloration that camouflages them when they stand stock-still against rocks and sand. These lizards are remarkably fast burrowers, disappearing into loose soil by tilting alternate sides of their bodies down into the ground and shoveling the soil up until they have entirely covered themselves.

The seven species of horned lizard in the United States live in a range of similar habitats. In the southwest, the flat-tailed horned lizard prefers areas of fine, wind-blown sand; the desert horned lizard lives on sandy flats; and the regal horned lizard lives mainly in regions of rock and gravel.

Blood from the eye

All horned lizards have the unusual ability to defend themselves by shooting a fine stream of blood from the inner corner of each eye for a distance of up to 3 feet or more. The blood actually comes from inside the "third eyelid," the nictitating membrane that slides protectively across the eye from the inner corner, and is forced out when the animal increases the blood pressure in its head. Most horned lizards feed mainly on ants, though they also eat other insects,

THE MARINE IGUANA
— A LIFE BESIDE THE SEA —

The marine iguana lives on the Galapagos Islands in the Pacific Ocean, 620 miles west of Ecuador, and is the only lizard adapted for a life spent partly in the sea. It is a heavy animal with a spiky crest running from its head to the tip of the tail, a short, blunt snout, thick legs and long claws.

Marine iguanas spend most of the day gathered in tight groups, basking in the sun on the coastal lava fields in order to raise their body temperature before venturing into the cold water. As soon as the tide falls, the iguanas clamber down the cliffs to feed on the exposed algae growing on the rocks— gripping the strands of algae in the sides of their jaws and wrenching them off with a twist of their powerful necks. While some cling onto the rocks with their massive claws, others take to the water, swimming out to deeper areas and diving down to forage on seaweed growing on the seabed.

The marine iguanas are at home in the water, staying below the surface for 20 minutes or more. Their tails are flattened sideways and the iguanas use them like oars, moving them from side to side to propel themselves forward.

They hold their limbs close to their bodies for more streamlined movement. The large amount of salt that the iguanas absorb from their seaweed diet (and from the seawater) collects in glands lying between the eyes and the nose on each side of the head. The iguanas then expel the salt through their noses in a jet of water vapor.

Keeping in heat

The aquatic habits of the marine iguana were noted by the great naturalist Charles Darwin, when he visited the Galapagos Islands in 1835. He wrote in his diary: "When in the water this lizard swims with perfect ease and quickness, by a serpentine movement of its body and flattened tail—the legs being motionless...."

The iguanas have a further adaptation to feeding in the sea. In the cold water, the iguanas keep their body heat in by tightening the arteries near the skin. The blood is then forced to stay closer to the center of their bodies, allowing the blood to remain warmer for a longer time. After feeding (and before they lose too much heat), the marine iguanas return to land to continue their sunbathing on the cliffs.

LEFT Ritual combat in marine iguanas: a male with a group of females (A) is confronted by an intruder that he rushes toward and head-butts (B), forcing the intruder to retreat (C).
TOP RIGHT A male marine iguana (center) surrounded by smaller females on Espanola in the Galapagos archipelago. Iguanas from other islands of the Galapagos are dark gray but those on the island of Espanola have orange and red on their flanks.
RIGHT The marine iguana is the only lizard that finds its food in the sea, sometimes diving to a depth of 33 feet to forage on the seabed.

Head-butting trials

During the breeding season, the male marine iguana adopts an aggressive posture to show off his strength. He first lowers his head and opens his mouth slightly, then raises his body off the ground. The males may fight by head-butting their rivals, their conical head scales preventing real damage from being done.

Both male and female marine iguanas will mate with more than one partner, the females wandering from one male's territory to another. Before they lay their eggs, they gather on a sandy beach, aggressively jostling for the best nesting sites. Here, each female spends up to four hours digging a 12 in. long burrow in which to lay two or three leathery-shelled eggs. She covers the hole with sand and leaves the eggs to be incubated by the warm equatorial sun. The young, measuring about 9 in. long, emerge after about 112 days.

ABOVE Green iguanas are most common in trees along the banks of rivers. Though adults climb high into the topmost branches of trees, reaching up to 66 ft. above the ground, young iguanas, such as the juvenile here, usually keep to lower levels.
LEFT In ritual confrontations between male South American iguanas, the two animals face each other sideways on and slap their tails together.

spiders and wood lice.

Spiny and horned lizards can change the color of their skin from light to dark and back again according to the air temperature. At cooler temperatures, their bodies darken to absorb heat more quickly.

A disappearing act

The fringe-toed lizard has a fringe of scales on the feet that expand when the lizard presses down on the sand, thereby increasing the surface area of the feet which prevents the animal from sinking in. When they are disturbed, they dive into the sand and by making rapid "swimming" movements with their limbs, they quickly disappear below ground. As protection against the sand, valves cover their nostrils and ear openings, and fringed eyelids surround the eyes.

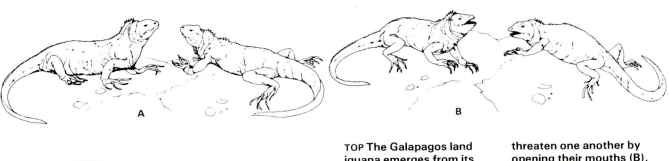

TOP The Galapagos land iguana emerges from its burrow in the morning to search for a variety of plant foods, including sharp-spined cacti.

LEFT AND ABOVE Two rival male land iguanas face each other with their heads raised (A) and then threaten one another by opening their mouths (B). Suddenly the dominant male lunges at his opponent and grips his head in his mouth (C). The fighting usually ends without injury, and the less powerful of the animals moves off in defeat.

1577

ABOVE Like all lizards, chuckwallas need to bask in the sun to raise their body temperature. In the early morning, they often lie on warm rocks, waiting for their bodies to reach a working temperature before they can go off to forage for leaves, buds and flowers. When threatened, chuckwallas slip into crevices between rocks and inflate their bodies, wedging themselves so tightly in the cracks that they are impossible to remove.

Spiky crests

True iguanas are the largest and most primitive members of the iguana family. Distinctive dorsal crests ornament their back, running from behind the head to the middle of their heavy tail. Most of them live in Central America, although some appear in South and North America and on the islands of the Galapagos, Fiji and Tonga.

The 6 ft. 6 in. long green iguana is one of the most impressive of the iguanas in appearance. The male's pronounced crest of comb-like spines can reach up to 3 in. high (slightly smaller in females), and is orange and yellow in color. Both sexes have large, permanently visible throat sacs. The green iguana grows at a steady rate throughout its life. However, when seasonal variations limit food supplies, growth is intermittent. During dry seasons, adult iguanas suffer severe weight loss. They survive by living off large reserves of fat that they build up when food is plentiful, and store in the angle of the lower jaw and around the neck.

The green iguana is an agile tree climber that inhabits the sunny, upper foliage of trees during the day (particularly along the banks of rivers). At night, and in times of danger, it retreats to long burrows that it has dug in the ground. Young green iguanas particularly fall prey to the common basilisk lizard that catches both hatchlings and juveniles between two and three months of age.

When in danger, green iguanas rely on their rapid reflexes and speed to escape. They readily jump to the ground from a height of 20 feet, sprinting into the undergrowth as soon as they land. If necessary, they will dive into the water and swim, both on the surface and underwater, by propelling themselves with their tail—they can remain submerged for considerable periods. During a fight, green iguanas defend themselves by biting with their sharp teeth, scratching with their strong claws and using the whiplash power of their muscular tail.

Inhabiting islands

The Galapagos Islands, that straddle the Equator about 620 miles west of Ecuador in South America, are the home of three species of plant-eating iguanas. Two of these are land-dwelling reptiles, while the third is the famous marine iguana that inhabits the rocky coasts of the islands (see pp. 1574-1575). Each island has its own subspecies, similar in appearance and behavior.

Marine iguanas usually grow to a length of 69 in., and feed on tidal and subtidal algae. Males tend to grow larger than females, but the different subspecies vary in size from one island to the next. They have a crest of spiny scales along their backs, and knobs or tubercles decorate their blunt, flattened heads.

Mating colors

The marine iguana normally has gray-brown skin, but develops red spots during the mating period (in one species, the male develops green crests and red flanks). The male gathers a number of females around him and fiercely defends his territory against other males. During their ritualized displays, the two rivals confront each other and bare their teeth. If neither retreats, the rival males test their strength by butting their heads together, attempting to force the other

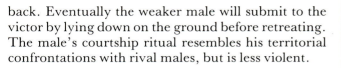

back. Eventually the weaker male will submit to the victor by lying down on the ground before retreating. The male's courtship ritual resembles his territorial confrontations with rival males, but is less violent.

Aggressive land iguanas

The Galapagos land iguana has a heavy, compact yellow and brown body, with a crest that begins at the nape and extends right down its back. Older individuals also have rolls of fat around their necks. Like their marine relatives, they feed on plants, especially cacti, and display similar breeding behavior. However, land iguanas are noticeably more aggressive toward each other than marine iguanas. Territorial intruders will attack resident males with their teeth, biting viciously until they draw blood.

Despite rivalry among males and predation from the Galapagos buzzard, the land iguanas once flourished on the islands—until the arrival of man. Hunters drastically reduced their numbers, not only by shooting the reptiles for sport and food, but also by introducing predators such as cats and rats. Today, domestic goats are systematically destroying the scrub vegetation in which the land iguana takes shelter. They are becoming increasingly scarce, and have even become extinct on some of the islands.

The Fiji banded iguana inhabits woodland areas of the islands of Fiji and Tonga in the Pacific. In appearance it resembles a slender green iguana, but has a smaller crest. The male is banded with light green, while the female is uniformly green in color. Its long fingers and toes, ending in sharp claws, enable it to cling on to branches and trunks when climbing. When food is scarce, it stores fat in its tail and saves water in lymph glands in the folds of skin along its sides. The chuckwalla, a closely related species, appears in semiarid, rocky areas in the southwest USA.

Running power

Basilisks are largely tree-dwelling iguanas that have long, powerful hind limbs and long tails, enabling them to run on two legs. The leafy plum-tree basilisk, whose toes are lobed to increase their surface area, is even able to run for short stretches across the surface of smooth water. As it runs, it gradually lifts up its front legs until its body is leaning forward at an angle of about 40 degrees to the ground. It uses its long tail as a counterweight. While running, it takes long,

LIZARDS CLASSIFICATION: 4

Iguanas

The family Iguanidae contains the 650 species of iguanas and their relatives. Grouped into 55 genera, they are distributed over much of North and South America, with a few species from the islands of Madagascar, Fiji and Tonga.

The largest of the iguanas, the green or common iguana, *Iguana iguana*, lives in Central and northern South America. Both the marine iguana, *Amblyrhynchus cristatus*, and the land iguana, *Conolophus subcristatus*, are confined to the Galapagos Islands. The Fiji banded iguana, *Brachylophus fasciatus*, occurs in Fiji and Tonga, and the rhinoceros iguana, *Cyclura cornuta*, is an inhabitant of Haiti and other islands of the Lesser Antilles in the Caribbean.

North American members of the family include the spiny lizards of the genus *Sceloporus*; the horned lizards of the genus *Phrynosoma*; the collared lizard, *Crotaphytus collaris*; and the zebra-tailed lizard, *Callisaurus draconoides*. The basilisks of the genus *Basiliscus* range over southern Mexico, Central America and northern South America, and the anoles of the large genus *Anolis* range from Central America to Bolivia and Paraguay.

powerful strides, increasing the thrust of its hind feet by twisting its whole body from side to side with each step. Basilisks can reach speeds of up to 7 mph.

The male basilisk grows to 31 in. in length and has a "casque" on its head that resembles a tall, narrow helmet. A dorsal crest runs along its back, supported in some species by bony plates. The casques are of limited value as a means of identification, since females and immature males do not develop them.

Basilisks eat mainly fruit and small animals, particularly insects and invertebrates. They often populate branches overhanging water. If danger threatens, they take to the water and lie on the bottom. The helmeted lizard, an inhabitant of the forests of Central America, uses a different technique—it will stay on its branch and intimidate an attacker by inflating its throat sac, opening its eyes wide and lowering its head to display its neck frill.

THE GREEN ANOLE
— QUICK-CHANGE ARTISTS —

The green anole, a medium-sized lizard that measures up to 7 in. in length, belongs to the iguana family. Common throughout tropical and subtropical areas of the Americas, from the United States to Brazil, it is popularly named the "false chameleon" after the true chameleons of the Old World, with whom it shares the ability to change body color.

The green anole has a triangular head with elongated jaws. Like the gecko, the light, slender feet of the green anole have enlarged finger and toe pads. A dense mat of microscopic hooks covers these clinging pads which, together with sharp claws, enables it to clamber over even the smoothest surfaces with speed.

The green anole becomes active at first light. Emerging from its resting place, it scuttles to the high branches of the leaf canopy to bask in the direct sunlight. Its skin is dark at first, since dark skin absorbs a greater degree of radiant heat. While still dark, it is conspicuous against the green leaves of foliage. Although this makes it more vulnerable to predators, it has to balance the danger of being seen against the need to keep warm. If the anole is cold, it retains its dark coloration regardless of the color of its surroundings. When it reaches its optimum body temperature, the green anole reverts to pale green and descends beneath the leaf canopy to begin hunting for insects.

Usually, the green anole alters color in response to changes in stimuli, such as temperature, light intensity and its mood. As the anole's eyes and skin react to the stimuli, the color change takes place. The response of the eyes to light seems to be the dominant factor in color change. If a dark brown anole is blindfolded with a dark cap and exposed to the light, it maintains its dark color, while others around it turn green. During the hottest part of the day, the anole is usually green in color, matching the forest foliage.

Once the anole's brain has gathered information from the stimuli, it passes signals to the pigment cells in the skin, resulting in the reptile's color change. Some of these cells, the melanophores, contain the dark pigment melanin, while others have red, yellow and white pigments. Triggered by the action of hormones in the bloodstream, the pigment cells expand and contract. If the dark cells expand and the pale cells contract, the animal becomes darker. But if the pale cells expand at the expense of the dark, the anole grows paler.

Colorful display
The green anole is highly territorial, and usually stays within a relatively small area. However, during the breeding season, the territory of a breeding male can expand twenty-fold. The resident male defends his territory fiercely against other trespassing males. If he discovers an intruder, he will confront it and, when provoked, will inflate a reddish throat sac. The sudden display of bright color often startles the aggressor. The green anole will also raise his dorsal crest and inflate his body so that it appears much larger than it is.

If the intruder persists, the ritualized confrontation may end in combat, although this is uncommon. During a fight, the two animals bite and scratch at one another, sometimes causing severe damage. Certain species of the anole bristle up a crest on their neck or spine, and increase their body size, at the same time inflating their throat sacs—all actions that make them appear larger and more intimidating. Some species also produce loud noises to add to the effect of their displays. During the mating ritual, the male will exhibit his crest and throat sac in order to impress a female or mark his territory.

When threatened by a predator, the green anole will sometimes inflate its body to discourage attack. More often it will flee and may even take to the water in an attempt to escape. If the enemy is too close for flight, the lizard freezes and feigns death, a ploy that can often deter a predator that catches only live prey.

The "freezing" reaction has been induced experimentally by scaring captive lizards with stuffed hawks (birds of prey are their main enemies) but, curiously enough, a stuffed hawk with the eyes removed seems to be much less alarming. The suggestion is that lizards are most alarmed by the large, forward-facing eyes of a hawk, whereas small birds react to the outline of the predator in the sky.

TOP LEFT During territorial disputes with rival males, and in his courtship displays, the male green anole inflates his throat sac to reveal the red and blue skin that is normally concealed. BOTTOM LEFT Two male green anoles threaten one another by displaying their throat sacs and raising their tails. RIGHT For much of the day, when the green anole is out hunting, it is colored green to blend in with the predominant color of the forest foliage. When basking in the sun, however, it turns brown, the darker color absorbing more heat. It can change its color in seconds.

ABOVE AND ABOVE RIGHT
Helmeted lizards (left) and basilisks (right) are closely related tree-dwelling lizards. The males of both species make spirited displays when threatened, raising the bony projection on the back of their heads and puffing out the flap of skin behind their necks. As a result, the head of the animal appears greatly enlarged.

The anoles of America

Anoles are the largest group of iguanas, inhabiting tropical and subtropical areas of America. Certain species, such as the green anole, have adhesive pads (similar to those of the geckos) on the underparts of their toes, enabling them to climb up smooth walls.

By exploiting different layers of vegetation, different species of anole are able to live in the same area without competing with one another for food. On Cuba, for example, three species coexist—one species lives and hunts in the treetops, another species inhabits tree trunks and a third prefers grassland scattered with bushes.

Anoles are often colorful reptiles. Many species have a throat sac beneath their chins that they can stretch out like a fan to reveal bright colors that would otherwise be concealed. The throat sac is usually larger in the male, and frills and fringes often adorn its head and back. Anoles use the color signals, together with rhythmic head movements and loud calls, in territorial displays and courtship rituals.

The chisel-teeth lizards

The family of chisel-teeth lizards, also known as dragon lizards, differ from the iguanas in that their teeth are fused at the base on the ridge of the upper and lower jawbones. The teeth of reptiles are usually fixed in sockets, or rest loosely against the wall of

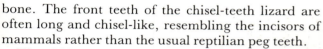

bone. The front teeth of the chisel-teeth lizard are often long and chisel-like, resembling the incisors of mammals rather than the usual reptilian peg teeth.

The 300 species of chisel-teeth lizards range throughout Africa, southern Asia and Australasia, and can be regarded as the Old World equivalents of the New World iguanas. They are small to medium in size, never exceeding 3 ft. 3 in. in length. The ground-living species have flattened bodies, whereas the bodies of many of the tree dwellers are compressed from side to side like those of chameleons. They are active during the day, and their fast, agile movements and good eyesight equip them for hunting insects, small mammals and other small reptiles. Chisel-teeth lizards include the flying dragons, the agamas, the bloodsuckers and the spiny-tailed lizards.

Dragons in the air

The flying dragons of Southeast Asia have adapted extremely well to life in the trees. Famous for their ability to glide from perch to perch among the tall trees of the tropical forests, the flying dragons sail through the air on large, thin folds of skin that extend from each side of the body between their fore and hind limbs. Elongated ribs protrude from their flanks and support these folds. Brightly colored patterns adorn the wings, and the flying dragons will flash a recognition signal to a potential mate by opening and closing the wings.

Territorial agamas

Agamas colonize habitats from deserts to tropical forests, and are particularly numerous in woodland

TOP LEFT Some basilisks can cross short stretches of water by running on their long hind legs; their hind feet are fringed with lobes of skin to increase their surface area.
TOP A flying dragon partially distends its wing flaps in preparation for flight. The brightly colored flaps of skin are supported by extensions of the ribs.
ABOVE The dark skin of the common agama absorbs heat quickly as the animal basks in the warmth of the African sun.

and savannah. Common agamas live in groups of 2 to 25 individuals that hunt together. Each group contains a single dominant adult male, a few adult females and some young. Often an adult female also occupies a favored position. The group territory is well defined, and raised mounds act as watchtowers for the dominant male, who is responsible for defending the area and the rest of the group. The territory also includes several small shelters that act as hiding places when danger threatens, and a relatively large shelter in which the community rests during the night.

Daily routine

At sunrise, the agamas emerge to warm themselves in the first rays of the new day. At this time of the morning, they have a dark brown coloration that absorbs the heat more quickly. Once warm, the

ABOVE Like many lizards, the hardun agama is equipped with spines and armored scales to deter predators. Its natural range runs from Arabia to western Turkey, and it has been introduced into northern Greece, Corfu and Egypt. Although they are chiefly insectivorous, harduns also eat some plant material.

dominant male becomes light blue in color, with orange tones on his head and tail. The male then takes up position on a mound and keeps watch for rivals.

If a rival dares to encroach on the territory, the resident male threatens it with a quick bobbing of the head and shoulders. If this warning has no effect, he whips around to face the intruder and rears up on his hind legs, keeping his head as low as possible to emphasize his impressive throat folds. As he becomes more aggressive, the defender changes color. His head turns to brown with a white stripe under each eye, and his body becomes pale and spotted.

LIZARDS CLASSIFICATION: 5

Chisel-teeth lizards

There are about 300 species of chisel-teeth or agamid lizards in 53 genera within the family Agamidae. They range over Africa, the Middle East, southern and Central Asia, Indonesia and Australia. Species include the flying dragon, *Draco volans*, of Southeast Asia and Indonesia; the common agama, *Agama agama*, of Central Africa; the common bloodsucker, *Calotes versicolor*, of southern Asia; the Egyptian spiny-tailed lizard, *Uromastyx aegyptius*, of North Africa and northern Arabia; the Australian frilled lizard, *Chlamydosaurus kingii*, the thorny devil or moloch, *Moloch horridus*, and the eastern water dragon, *Physignathus lesueurii*, all of which are found in Australia; and the Sri Lanka prehensile-tail lizard, *Cophotis ceylanica*, of Sri Lanka.

ABOVE Spiny-tailed lizards are specially adapted for life in arid terrain. They obtain all the water they need from the plants they eat, and store it in their fat reserves. They can also reabsorb much of the water that would otherwise be lost in their urine. Their tails are studded with large spines and, when threatened, the lizards use them as formidable weapons with which to lash out at predators.

During the fight that follows, the two agamas stand flank to flank and strike each other with their tails. Although they keep their teeth bared, they never bite—the tail lashing is a violent enough means of defense and often causes serious wounds. After some minutes of fighting, one of the animals—nearly always the intruder—admits defeat and flees the field.

Female dominance

The dominant female may remain close to the group of males during such encounters, and will fight intruding females if they come too close. Female agamas do not display ritualized signals before a fight, and as a result, their fights tend to be bloody—they sometimes bite one another with their long front teeth, causing serious damage.

The courtship ritual of the male common agama is similar to its territorial defense behavior, except that it moves more slowly and does not display its throat sac. The male approaches the female and, if accepted, bites her neck gently and pushes his tail under hers until their vents come into contact, the male protruding one of his two hemipenes (sacs of sperm).

The females usually lay four to six eggs in a hole that they dig among low vegetation. They then cover the eggs with sand, pushing it forward with their forelegs and patting it down with their bodies. The young agamas hatch after an incubation period of two to three months and quickly join a territorial group.

Bloodsuckers in the trees

The common bloodsucker of Asia is a lively and agile tree-dwelling lizard. It has a slender body with horny crests along the back. Like the agama lizards, common bloodsuckers are primarily insectivores. Despite their name, they do not actually suck blood.

Spiny-tailed lizards live in hot, dry deserts, where water is highly valued. The adults obtain most of their water from the plants they eat (young animals eat insects), but they also reabsorb part of the water contained in their urine.

The Egyptian spiny-tailed lizard is the largest of the spiny-tailed lizards, and is a heavily built reptile with a small head and stumpy, spiny tail. Active by day, it spends the night in a crevice or hole in the ground. If

ABOVE AND LEFT When the Australian frilled lizard is at rest, the broad mantle of skin around its neck lies in folds around its shoulders. If threatened by a predator, however, or if trying to intimidate a rival, it undergoes a spectacular transformation, raising its mantle into a broad disk and gaping with its mouth wide open. Its menacing appearance is enough to startle most enemies, but if a predator persists, the lizard will run away quickly on its hind legs.

A defensive frill

The Australian frilled lizard, another of the chisel-teeth lizards, occurs throughout the wooded areas of northern Australia, as well as in New Guinea. It is the sole member of its genus, and one of the most spectacular lizards in the world. It grows to a length of about 3 feet—although two-thirds of this is accounted for by its long tail. Its most remarkable feature is the broad mantle of folded skin around its neck that falls over the animal's shoulders. Both sexes have the frills, but the male's is always larger. Australian frilled lizards are pale brown with dark spots, though males have extra red, blue and black spots on their colorful mantles.

Active by day, Australian frilled lizards spend most of their time in the trees where they hunt for insects, spiders and other small animals. When at rest on a tree trunk or branch, they are superbly camouflaged

threatened, it retreats to one of these strongholds and enters headfirst, leaving only a small part of its tail exposed. It then swings its tail around vigorously as a means of defense.

Like the common agama, spiny-tailed lizards change their skin color during the day, starting off dark in the morning in order to absorb the sun's rays more effectively and to warm up more rapidly. As their internal temperature rises, they become increasingly pale. In extreme heat, they shelter under a stone or raise themselves off the ground to avoid absorbing more heat from the ground.

RIGHT AND BELOW RIGHT The thorny devil or moloch is a chisel-teeth lizard of the Australian deserts. Its tail and body are covered with large, spiny scales, and it has two particularly large, hooked spines on its head. Yet despite its appearance, this slow-moving lizard is harmless to humans and feeds only on black ants.

from predators. They are more vulnerable on the ground, and if one is disturbed, it will intimidate its attacker by opening its mouth to reveal its powerful teeth and red mouth lining. At the same time, it raises and fans the mantle to form a broad disk around its head, similar to an Elizabethan ruff, making itself appear much larger. If pursued, the lizard will run away on its hind legs, lashing its tail from side to side to keep its balance (the tail acts as a stabilizer in a similar way to that of a kangaroo).

Thorns aplenty

The thorny devil or moloch lives in the sandy deserts of central and southern Australia where the temperature frequently exceeds 122°F, and water is extremely scarce. One of the world's most bizarre-looking lizards, it is much smaller than the frilled lizard, measuring some 8 in. long with a 3.5 in. tail. It has a broad, flattened body whose head, limbs, trunk and tail are completely covered with thorn-shaped spines and small bumps (tubercles); the lizard's yellow, red, brown or grayish coloration alters according to its mood, and in response to temperature changes.

Thorny devils feed almost exclusively on black ants, but they often have to go without food during long dry spells in the desert, and they can withstand long periods of fasting and water shortage. They live in groups of two or three among plant tufts in the sand, and if disturbed, they hide in the scrub, moving with a slow, jerky motion. The thorny devil may protect itself by placing its head between its forelegs so that the spiny hump on its neck protrudes forward to confront the enemy.

Other Australian species of chisel-teeth lizards include the eastern water dragon, which lives along river and streambeds, and the bearded dragon. The eastern water dragon is an excellent swimmer; when threatened, it can remain submerged for up to half an hour without coming to the surface. The bearded dragon takes its name from the membranous pouch, covered with long, sharp spines, that hangs below the chin—when the pouch expands during a threat or

courtship display, it resembles a spiky beard. Two other members of the family include the Sri Lanka prehensile-tail lizard and the chameleon dragon, both of which have muscular, flexible tails, enabling them to climb securely through the branches.

Chameleons

The 85 species of chameleons are famed for their slow, deliberate movements, the fact that they can move their eyes independently, and that their bodies can change color. Although some chameleons live on the ground, they are the exceptions to the rule, most chameleons being highly adapted to living in trees. Their long, grasping tails provide a powerful grip on the branches, while the toes of their slender legs are fused into two opposing groups of digits that close like pincers on the branches as the animals creep along.

The bodies of chameleons are flattened from side to side, possibly to give the animals greater stability, since their weight is centered directly above the twig or branch on which they are walking. Their heads—particularly those of the males—are often large and heavy, and are adorned with horns, tubercles or ridges.

Quick-change artist

The ability of chameleons to change color rapidly—a mechanism probably controlled by the nervous system—serves to camouflage them from both their enemies and their own insect prey (though they may also escape predators by simply dropping off the branch and out of the enemy's view). The color that a chameleon adopts is governed by several factors, including the color of its surroundings, the local temperature and the light level—as well as the animal's mood. The chameleon's skin is usually more brightly colored when the animal is hot or sexually aroused, and duller in color when it is cool. It usually darkens in response to light, since dark skin absorbs the sun's rays more efficiently than light skin.

A chameleon's tongue is extremely long—5.5 in. in length in some species—and the animal shoots it out of its mouth with great speed to ensnare insect prey on the club-shaped, mucus-covered tip. The chameleon's aim depends on its superb eyesight: the eyes are very large for a reptile and completely covered by a mobile, scaly eyelid with a central hole revealing the pupil. Each eye can move independently, rotating through a wide arc to give the animal an extensive field of view. The two eyes can also point forward to give binocular vision, providing the chameleon with an accurate perception of distance.

Chameleons spend most of their day immobile on a branch, searching the surrounding area for food. If a chameleon spies potential prey with one eye, the other eye swivels around until the chameleon has its victim fully in its binocular sights, and can determine its

ABOVE In many lizards, the males and females are quite different in appearance. The male is usually bigger than the female and has larger, more elaborate crests, as seen in a pair of oriental water dragons from Southeast Asia.

TOP RIGHT The bearded dragon of Australia erects its spiny ruff to appear more fierce when threatening a rival male or when confronted by a predator. One of the chisel-teeth lizards, the bearded dragon grows to almost 24 in. long.

position precisely. Very slowly, the chameleon draws closer, inching along the branch until it is within striking range. It then flicks out its tongue, trapping the insect, and withdraws the tongue into its mouth to swallow the victim.

A patient hunter

Since insects are naturally active creatures, they often move off and settle on another branch before the chameleon has time to reach them. In such cases, the chameleon patiently changes direction, climbing through the branches until the insect is once again within range of its tongue.

During the breeding season, chameleons descend to the ground to search for mates, though they have some difficulty walking on the ground with feet that are adapted for climbing along branches. Despite this, the males become so excited if they spot a suitable mate that they often break into a clumsy run.

After the female chameleon has mated, she may retain the sperm in her body for several weeks before laying her eggs. She usually digs a hole for them at the foot of the bush where she normally stalks her prey. The task of digging the hole takes considerable effort, and the female lays her eggs over several days. Although most chameleons lay eggs, a few species of pygmy chameleons bear live young.

The young chameleons begin hunting insects immediately after they hatch, but their aim is not good and they often miss their target—they need practice before they can accurately judge the angle between their eye, the prey and their mouth.

Stylized battles

The males of a small East African species, Hohnel's chameleon, are bright blue and yellow in color. They occupy well-defined territories and will deny access to

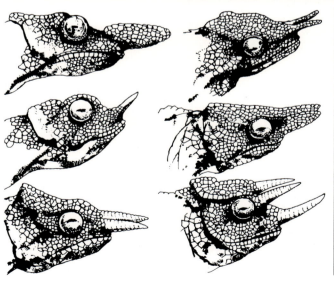

TOP RIGHT The large eyes of the common chameleon can survey the environment independently of one another, or they can both focus on one object in front of them, giving the animal sharp binocular vision.
BOTTOM RIGHT Different species of chameleons sport all kinds of horns and crests on their heads that they use in ritual combat.
PAGES 1590-1591 The chameleon can shoot out its long, sticky-ended tongue with lightning speed and accuracy to capture its insect prey. The tongue of a chameleon can reach up to 5.5 in. long. Some of the larger chameleons also feed on small birds.

LIZARDS CLASSIFICATION: 6

Chameleons

There are 85 species of chameleons in the family Chamaeleontidae, grouped in only four genera. They range throughout sub-Saharan Africa, and also occur in Madagascar, the Canary Islands, southern Europe and parts of Asia. The common or Mediterranean chameleon, *Chamaeleo chamaeleon*, occurs in North Africa, southern Spain, southeast Portugal, Crete, the eastern coastline of the Mediterranean, and parts of Arabia, while the Indian chameleon, *C. zeylanicus*, is a lizard of India and Pakistan. African species include the pygmy chameleons of the genus *Microsaura*; Meller's chameleon, *Chamaeleo melleri*; Hohnel's chameleon, *C. hoehnelii*; and Jackson's chameleon, *C. jacksonii*. The giant chameleon, *C. oustaleti*, and the stump-tailed chameleon, *Brookesia stumpfii*, both occur in Madagascar.

ABOVE The extraordinary, broad tongue of the eastern blue-tongued skink is put to dramatic use when held out in a threat display. A species of northern and eastern Australia, it is commonly kept as a pet and becomes very tame in captivity.

other males of the same species. If a stray male should wander into another's territory, a highly stylized battle results in which the males pretend to bite each other's flanks. The owner of the territory usually emerges as the victor: the defeated male signals his submission by changing from blue and yellow to light gray, and beats a slow retreat. The female Hohnel's chameleon is almost as aggressive as the male, and may even take on the male's color and behavior.

One group of chameleons, known as the stump-tailed chameleons, live on the ground in the forests of East and Central Africa and Madagascar, where they sit motionless amid the fallen leaves. Their feet are identical to those of their tree-dwelling relatives, but they lack the grasping tail. When alarmed, they sway gently on their feet, apparently in imitation of a leaf swaying in a breeze. They rarely change color, since they are already well camouflaged.

The skinks

Of the 16 families of lizards, the largest by far is that of the skinks. It comprises 1275 species distributed throughout the world's tropical and temperate regions. Skinks have evolved body shapes to suit a wide variety of habitats, though in general, they have a long, smooth, cylindrical body with a narrow head barely distinguished from the trunk, and a tapering tail.

A skink's legs are shorter than those of most lizards —so short, indeed, that they are unable to lift the animal's body clear of the ground. In some species, such as the aptly named "sandfishes," the limbs have all but vanished and the animal "swims" through the desert sand in an undulating manner similar to an eel in water. In many such species, the ears and eyes are also reduced or are protected by scales—adaptations typical of animals that live underground.

Most skink species are insectivorous, but some of the larger species prey on small mammals and other reptiles. Other species, such as the large blue-tongued skinks of Australia, feed on plants. The marine skink eats the crabs, shrimps and other crustaceans it finds on rocky, tidal shores, though it may catch some of its prey in the water. Skinks' teeth vary in shape according to the animals' diet: they are small, pointed or multipointed in carnivorous or insectivorous species; and broad and flattened, similar to the molars of mammals, in plant feeders.

A giant vegetarian

The largest of the skinks is the giant Solomon Islands skink, which can grow up to 24 in. long. Found in the forests of San Cristobal Island on the edge of the Solomon Islands archipelago (east of New Guinea), it is an aggressive animal, extremely well adapted to life in the trees, with strong limbs and claws, and a prehensile tail that can grip branches. It forages by night and feeds entirely on plant matter. Remarkably for a reptile, it bears only one offspring at a time—the young measuring just one-third the size of its mother.

The various species of blue-tongued skinks of Australia are also herbivores, although some will eat whatever they can, including worms and snails. When disturbed, a blue-tongued skink opens its mouth, hisses, and flicks out the bright blue tongue from which it takes its name. The effect of the blue tongue against the red mouth lining is startling, and may serve to scare off some of the skink's less determined

TOP The sun skink is a mainly ground-dwelling lizard of southern Asia. Though it can move fast in search of prey, it spends most of its time sunning itself in open places.

ABOVE As well as giving threat signals, the tongues of blue-tongued lizards function as insect traps, enabling the animals to snap up agile prey like this large butterfly.

enemies. Although blue-tongued skinks have sharp teeth, they rarely bite in self-defense, and if the blue-tongue fails to deter a predator, the skink will dig itself into the sand.

Blue-tongued skinks are stocky animals. The tail of the stump-tailed skink (known to Australians as the sleepy lizard, from its sluggish habits) is so short, broad and flattened that, at first glance, it resembles the animal's head. The stump-tailed skink's body is covered with large, rough scales, and its strong legs are armed with sturdy claws. Its diet consists largely of plants, but it occasionally eats insects, snails and other small animals.

Another species with a startling color scheme is the green-blood skink. Not only does it have a green tongue that may well serve the same defensive purpose as that of the blue-tongued skinks, but it has green blood—a unique occurrence among vertebrates. It spends most of its time in the trees, and even lays its green eggs high above ground level.

Designed for burrowing

The sand skinks have become adapted to life in arid, sandy or stony deserts. They spend much of their time underground, burrowing in sand or gravel, and their bodies have developed accordingly: they are

Stump-tailed skink

Chilean cave lizard

Sand lizard

Legless burrowing skink

Common tegu

Italian wall lizard
(Faraglione race)

New Guinea blind
burrowing lizard

Sand skink

Sungazer

covered in smooth scales, their necks are almost non-existent, their limbs are sturdy but very short, and their tails are short and cylindrical.

The sand skink, which ranges from Senegal to Iran, is typical of this genus. It has a pointed, streamlined head that enables it to push easily through the sand, and a mouth that opens underneath the snout, rather than at the end of it. The lower eyelid is scaly, and the front edge of the ear opening is protected by a fringe of triangular plates. The sand skink's pale coloration enables it to blend in perfectly with the sand in which it lives, and its outline is broken up by numerous black stripes running across the body. If disturbed, it digs itself quickly into the sand until it is buried.

Caring mothers

Skinks of the striped skink genus, such as the Great Plains skink, are sturdily built lizards with solid, long-toed limbs and long tails. They are distributed throughout the Americas, Asia and Africa; most live on the ground, although some species are burrowers and others are tree dwellers. These skinks brood their eggs—an unusual form of behavior among reptiles, which generally abandon their eggs after laying them.

Females of the striped skink genus lay their eggs in hollows, and then wrap their bodies around them. By doing so, they can both regulate the temperature (reptiles can raise their body temperature, if necessary, by muscular activity), and also defend the eggs. Any egg-eating animal on the prowl would have to deal with the adult skink before it could reach the eggs. The female does not stay with her eggs all the time, but when she returns to the nest after a short absence, she checks them carefully, rearranges them, and turns them with her snout.

The female Great Plains skink carries this parental care even further: when the young are ready to hatch, she helps them to break out by using her head and feet to remove pieces of shell. She then licks them clean and defends them until they are stronger. She recognizes her eggs and young by smell, using her tongue to transmit the scent to the Jacobson's organ in the roof of her mouth.

European skinks

The cylindrical skinks are found in Africa, Asia and Europe. The best-known European species are the three-toed skink and the ocellated skink. The former has a long, snake-like body with extremely short, slender limbs. It walks normally when moving slowly, but when moving fast, it slithers along on its belly,

BELOW The geographical distribution of two genera (the sand and striped skinks) and two families (the girdle-tailed and the wall and sand lizards).

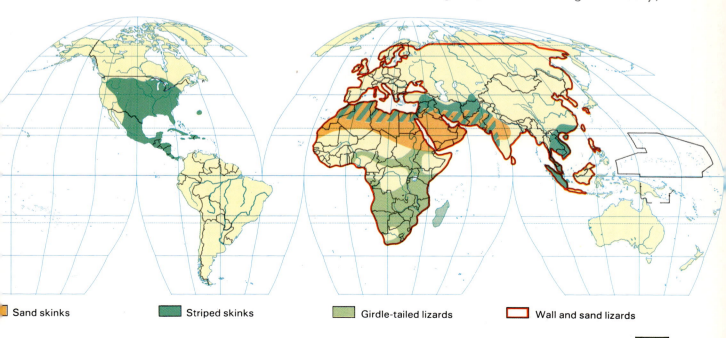

▮ Sand skinks	▮ Striped skinks	▮ Girdle-tailed lizards	▭ Wall and sand lizards

holding its limbs against the sides of its body where they fit into small depressions.

In Europe, the three-toed skink hibernates underground during the winter, not emerging until April to feed on small invertebrates. It may lay eggs or produce live young that have hatched inside its body, depending on where it lives—in warmer climates it lays its eggs. Over 20 offspring are born at a time, and they can look after themselves the moment they emerge.

The ocellated skink bears more resemblance to a typical lizard, having strong, if rather short, limbs. It is an agile animal, able to burrow swiftly into loose sand or dense vegetation. It forages mainly by day, being most active in the early morning and evening, when it hunts small insects and worms. Like its relative, the three-toed skink, the ocellated skink hibernates in winter, spending the cold months in individual or collective burrows. It may mate up to three times a year, producing from three to nine live young in each brood.

Limbless skinks

Several species of African skinks have lost their limbs altogether, and have come to resemble snakes. Those native to tropical Africa spend much of their life underground. Their small eyes are covered with transparent, protective scales, and they have no visible ear openings. They feed on termites, coming to the surface only at night or on dull, cloudy days.

The Brazilian skink is one of a group of ground-dwelling, agile skinks with long legs and brightly colored or iridescent skins. They are widely distributed across the islands of the Pacific and Indian Oceans. The group as a whole is hardy, and healthy individuals have been found on floating logs far out to sea—one reason why they may have become so widespread.

New Guinea and the Solomon Islands are the home of the casque heads. These skinks have large, keeled, bony scales, and some species have glands on their bellies and legs that secrete a substance probably used to mark their territorial boundaries.

Girdle-tailed lizards

The girdle-tailed lizards are a family of ground-dwelling reptiles that are active during the day. They are found only in Africa and Madagascar, and are adapted to life in arid, rocky areas and dry grassland. There are three main types of girdle-tailed lizards, their differing body forms relating to the areas in

TOP **The sand skink is one of a group of skinks adapted for life in hot, sandy deserts. It is active throughout the day, but spends much of its time buried in the sand, "swimming" through the loose grains by undulating its smooth body.**

ABOVE **The three-toed skink has four tiny limbs, each with only three toes. These are rarely used when the skink moves about; instead, it tucks the limbs into its body and undulates rapidly over the surface of grassy vegetation.**

which they live. The sungazer, for example, is a spiny lizard with large, pointed scales supported by bony plates. Others, such as the Cape red-tailed flat lizard, are not so spiny, but have flattened bodies that enable them to creep into narrow crevices. The third type, known as the sweepslangs, are so different that they appear unrelated. They have cylindrical bodies and very long tails, and their legs have almost entirely disappeared, giving them a snake-like appearance.

Many species, such as the sungazer and the armadillo girdle-tailed lizard, are found in rocky areas. If these spiny lizards are threatened, they wedge themselves into crevices, where, secured by their sharp-pointed scales, they are well protected and difficult to remove. If caught in the open, the armadillo girdle-tailed lizard rolls itself into an armored ball—hence the name—and grips its tail tip between its teeth, protecting its soft, vulnerable belly.

The sungazer also defends itself by lying flat on the ground and holding its limbs tightly against its body, presenting the predator with its prickly surface. If the attacker persists, it risks being injured by a blow from the animal's spiny tail. Other girdle-tailed lizards feign death in an attempt to avoid being attacked by predators.

Sun worshiping

The sungazer's name reflects the way it stares into the sun in the early morning. As with other reptiles, the sungazer needs to absorb heat at the beginning of the day, to reach its optimum body temperature. Each morning, it emerges from its burrow and moves to a suitable basking position in the full glare of the sun. It then rises up on its forelegs and faces the sun, following it around until its body is warm enough for the muscles and internal organs to work efficiently.

ABOVE LEFT If attacked in the open, the armadillo girdle-tailed lizard curls up and grips its tail in its jaws, presenting its enemy with a forbidding, almost impenetrable armor of spiny scales.

ABOVE The sungazer of southern Africa is one of the spiny girdle-tailed lizards, and has earned its name because of its habit of basking with its head raised, apparently staring into the sun.

The sungazer preys mainly on insects and other invertebrates, although it will occasionally take a young mammal or bird. Its movements are quite clumsy, but it can run fast when it needs to. Sungazers seek rocky crevices or abandoned burrows for nests, but if these cannot be found, they will dig their own burrows underneath a bush. During the breeding season, a male sungazer will fight a rival male to win a female. The females give birth to two live offspring in late summer or early autumn.

Flat lizards, as their name suggests, have extremely flattened bodies. They do not have spines, and the scales on their bodies are smooth, enabling them to slip easily between rocks. Unlike the sungazer and its relatives that have good camouflage, the male flat lizard is usually colored yellow, red and black, while the females are all black.

Flat lizards bask in high, well-exposed positions that provide a good view over their territories. They have a distinctive threat display when confronting rival males, in which they rear up on their hind legs to show off their bright throat and chest coloration. If attacked, they quickly slip away into cracks between the rocks and inflate their bodies, bracing their legs against the rock walls so that they cannot be pulled out.

Losing their limbs

The four species of sweepslangs have pointed heads and greatly elongated bodies covered with ridged bony plates, giving them the appearance of stretched pine cones. Their limbs are greatly reduced, and in some species are virtually nonexistent. Sweepslangs' tails are extremely long and can measure up to three times the length of their bodies. Despite their appearance, they do not live underground, but hunt for spiders, insects, earthworms and other small invertebrates on the surface of the African grasslands, in the highlands, or in sandy areas south of the Equator.

The size of the sweepslangs' limbs varies from species to species. The Transvaal sweepslang, for example, has retained all four recognizable limbs, complete with five toes, but the other three species have, at most, only two digits per limb. The large-scale sweepslang has no front limbs at all and only has one very small toe in place of the hind legs.

Wall and sand lizards

Most of the lizards that occur in Europe belong to the wall and sand lizards family. The family contains about 200 species ranging over most parts of the Old World. Active during the day, they mainly inhabit open, sandy terrain, but some occur in dense forests and others live in mountainous areas.

The viviparous or common lizard is widespread throughout Europe (although it is not found in the Mediterranean region). It also inhabits much of northern Asia, ranging as far east as the Pacific coast. One of the main reasons for its wide range is that it is unusually tolerant of cold weather, and can survive in near-Arctic conditions, provided there is food available. In northern Scandinavia, where the climate is moderated by the Gulf Stream (a warm ocean current that flows across the Atlantic and up the European coast), viviparous lizards are found north of the Arctic Circle and on the coast of the Arctic Ocean. In the south of its range, it often lives on mountains (up to 10,000 feet high in the Alps).

Transparent capsules

One of the secrets of the viviparous lizard's success is that the females can give birth to live young. In parts of southern Europe, the viviparous lizard lays eggs, but over most of its range, including the cold north, the female retains the eggs (usually between 5 and 8, although there may be as many as 10) inside her body until the young are fully formed. The young emerge in transparent capsules that break at birth, and the infant lizards immediately take advantage of the wealth of insect life hatching all around in the brief, but very rich, northern summer.

Viviparous lizards have slender, elongated, cylindrical bodies with narrow heads, long legs and long tails that they can shed if attacked. The discarded portion of the

---

—— LIZARDS CLASSIFICATION: 7 ——

Skinks

The family Scincidae is the largest among the lizards, with 1275 species of skinks grouped into 85 genera. They are distributed throughout the world in tropical regions, and also occur in many temperate areas such as the USA, the Mediterranean, Central Asia, Japan and New Zealand. The giant Solomon Islands skink, *Cornucia zebrata*, is confined to the Solomon Islands in the South Pacific. The blue-tongued skinks of the genus *Tiliqua* occur in Australia and New Guinea, and include the stump-tailed skink, *T. rugosa*, of southern and western Australia. The sand skink, *Scincus scincus*, occurs in North Africa, the Great Plains skink, *Eumeces obsoletus*, in North America, and the Brazilian skink, *Mabuya heathi*, in South America. The three-toed skink, *Chalcides chalcides*, inhabits the western Mediterranean region, while the ocellated skink, *C. ocellatus*, ranges from North Africa and southern Europe to Pakistan and India. The casque heads of the genus *Tribolonotus* are inhabitants of New Guinea and the Solomon Islands.

Girdle-tailed lizards

There are some 50 species of girdle-tailed lizards in the family Cordylidae, grouped into 10 genera. They are restricted to Madagascar and sub-Saharan Africa. Species include the armadillo girdle-tailed lizard, *Cordylus cataphractus*, which is confined to South Africa; the sungazer, *C. giganteus*, and the leathery crag lizard, *Pseudocordylus microlepidotus*, of southern Africa; and the sweepslangs of the genus *Chamaesaura* from parts of East, Central and southern Africa.

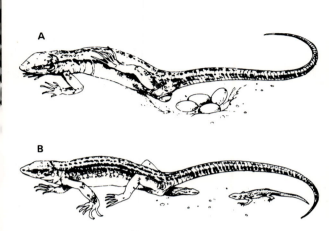

ABOVE In the south of its range, the viviparous lizard lays eggs (A), but in the north of its range, where there is insufficient sunshine to incubate the eggs, it bears live young (B). RIGHT When mating, the male Italian wall lizard entwines his body around that of the female to bring their vents together, then introduces one of his two hemipenes to fertilize the eggs. Each hemipenis is actually a membranous pouch containing sperm. When one is empty, the male switches to the other.

tail thrashes on the ground for some time after being shed, and this usually diverts the attention of the predator, allowing the lizard to escape.

The male viviparous lizards are territorial and fight with other males who invade their territory. The threatened male faces up to the intruder in an aggressive posture, with his head tilted downward and his throat region inflated, but if this fails to deter, he will bite his rival on the head or neck. A furious fight ensues, and the two contenders often finish up locked together, rolling on the ground. Eventually the intruder admits defeat by raising his head and beating his feet on the ground, before he takes flight.

Single-sex reproduction

Some populations of the closely related rock lizard, that are found in the Caucasus and the southwestern USSR, have abandoned mating altogether. The females produce young without their eggs being fertilized (parthenogenesis). Males are therefore unnecessary, and in the populations concerned, male rock lizards are extremely rare. Sexless reproduction is very common among insects, but is rare among vertebrates. The economy of the system is offset by the fact that each infant is a carbon copy of its mother. All the mother's features, both good and bad, are perpetuated through the generations. By contrast, the mixing of genes that takes place when a male and female mate, ensures that each infant is different from its parents, enabling the species to evolve.

The wall lizard is distributed over an extensive area, and unlike the viviparous lizard, it has evolved into a large number of geographical subspecies that differ from one another in color and back pattern. Wall lizards live in dry, rocky country and lay their eggs in holes in the ground.

The giant of the family is the ocellated green lizard of southern Europe and North Africa, a well-built reptile that may occasionally grow to over 31 in. long, although its usual size is approximately 8 in. It is a colorful animal, basically green with blackish speckles, but bearing intense blue eye-like spots ringed with black on its flanks. Ocellated lizards have large heads (larger in the male, as in the rest of the family) and strong legs that enable it to leap high in the air and run at great speed. It is a shy animal and hides at the first sign of danger, but it will not hesitate to bite if cornered.

The green lizard is smaller than the ocellated green lizard but is similar in appearance. It has an emerald green back with several tiny black spots. During the mating season, mature males (and some females) develop a bright blue throat.

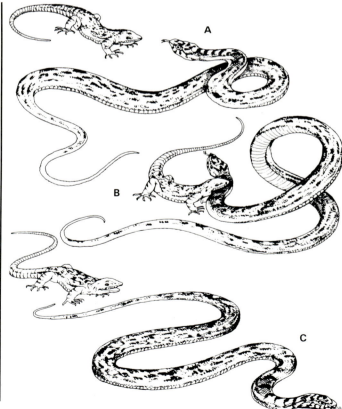

ABOVE The male green lizard usually has a more intense and uniformly green coloration than the female, which may be green or brown (as seen here) with black and white spots and stripes.

LEFT An adult green lizard confronts a snake that is about to attack it (A). Before the snake can strike, the lizard bites it on the neck (B), holding it fast until it moves off in retreat (C).

The sand lizard, which is widespread in Europe, is another species that adopts bright mating colors. It lives mainly on sandy or arid ground, such as sand dunes, dry field borders and dry heaths in Britain, including parts of southwest England and a small area of coastal dunes near Liverpool. In spring, the males shed their dull winter skins and emerge with vivid emerald-green or yellowish flanks that serve both to intimidate other males and impress females. After mating, the females lay their eggs in holes in the ground dug deep into sand or soil.

Whiptails and race runners

The whiptails and race runners are restricted to the Americas. Many species are similar to the sand and wall lizards in appearance, behavior and habitat, although they have evolved separately.

The North American whiptails and race runners include the marbled whiptail. It lives in deserts

RIGHT In the cultivated areas of Central and northern South America, farmers call the common tegu "chicken wolf," since it steals their chickens' eggs and chicks. A strong animal that lashes out with its tail and bites when cornered, it lives in holes under roots or in a burrow in the ground. Local people sometimes use its yellow body fat and flesh as a cure for various ailments.

scattered with clumps of thorny vegetation, and is active during the day. Marbled whiptails have white throats and bellies, and their tails are gray with dark undersides. They hunt their insect food in the loose litter under shrubs, and flee to the nearest cavity when they are frightened. Marbled whiptails are able to survive shade temperatures of 100.4°F or more, which few other lizards can do.

The tegus are sturdy lizards measuring up to 4 ft. long, and are found in tropical South America. Infamous thieves of eggs and chicks, they sometimes raid chicken coops. The common tegu also eats invertebrates, lizards, frogs and some leaves and fruit. The female usually lays about 30 eggs in soft soil or termite nests that she digs open with her sturdy claws. The termites then repair the damage, walling the eggs inside, where they remain until they hatch.

The semiaquatic caiman lizard is extremely well adapted for swimming. It has an oar-like, flattened tail that it uses to propel itself through the water. Its diet consists of snails, the shells of which it can break easily with its large, crushing, flat, back teeth. Its rigid skull increases the pressure with which it can crush the egg.

Alligator lizards and slowworms

Alligator lizards and slowworms both belong to the same family, the anguids, although they are quite different in appearance. Alligator lizards usually have streamlined bodies with short legs, while slowworms have no legs at all and are snake-like in appearance. Both groups have long, forked tongues that can be fully retracted, and their ears are usually an external opening (covered with scales in some species). Both groups can close their eyelids. Most alligator lizards and slowworms lay eggs, but some mountain species bear live young.

The common Eurasian slowworm is found throughout Europe (except for Ireland), northern Scandinavia and northwest Africa, while in the east, its range reaches the borders of Iran and the Urals. It has a long, cylindrical body, a short head, a practically nonexistent neck, and tough, scaly skin. When in danger, it voluntarily snaps off its tail, which initially makes up about half of its total body length of 20 in.

Slowworms have small, sharp teeth that are adapted for their diet of insects, spiders, earthworms and slugs. They inhabit overgrown places such as common land, woodland edges, gardens, hedgerows, lush meadows and especially railway embankments. They also occur in mountain pastures, and can survive at up to 6,500 feet above sea level.

The northern alligator lizard has bluish or olive colored skin with marked flexible skin folds that aid its breathing. It measures from 12 to 14 in. Living under dead wood, loose rocks or loose bark in cool, moist woodlands, it can survive at altitudes of up to 10,500 ft. As a mountain species, it is one of the live-bearing members of the family—at higher altitudes there is seldom enough warmth from the sun to ensure successful incubation of the eggs. The young develop inside the female, but they are separated from her by the egg membranes.

The southern alligator lizard, in contrast to its northern relative, lays eggs. It is a lively lizard of bushy, sunny places, including grasslands and woodland edges, especially open oak woods. The southern

ABOVE The seven-striped whiptail lives in the south-western USA and Mexico. It is most common in arid and semiarid hill country that is covered with rocks or with dry grassland broken by low bushes. Active by day, it eats beetles, grasshoppers and spiders, and if frightened, will scurry under a bush or retreat to a burrow if the danger persists.

alligator lizard's diet includes insects and other small invertebrates (including the poisonous black widow spiders and scorpions). Versatile climbers, they will steal and eat birds' eggs from nests in trees, using their semi-prehensile tail to help in grasping and balancing.

Fragile tails

Glass lizards, which are also anguids, have a broad distribution, ranging from the USA to Europe and Southeast Asia. They derive their name from their long and particularly fragile tails. The European glass lizard is the largest of all the glass lizards. It can reach a length of approximately 5 ft. from tip of nose to tip of tail (the tail when unbroken is about half as long again as the body). Resembling a giant slowworm in shape, its body may be as thick as a man's wrist, with an obvious and characteristic groove along each side. Most individuals have two small stumps on either side of the cloacal vent, all that remains of their hind legs.

The Californian legless lizard grows to about 6-10 in. long. A burrowing reptile, it has no limbs, an elongated body and a shiny, snake-like appearance. Its back is silvery or tan in color, and it has a yellow belly. As with most other members of its family, its eyes are small, but unlike snakes they are protected by movable eyelids. The Californian legless lizard prefers loose, soft, sandy soil and lives on stony stream banks, on beaches, in sand dunes and, occasionally, among leaf litter. It can dig rapidly into the ground, pushing the soil aside with its muzzle, aided by its smooth scales and blunt, rounded tail.

Xenosaurs

The xenosaurs or crocodile lizards make up a small and little-known family divided into three New World and one Chinese species. They have distinctive stout bodies and rather flattened heads, and several species have enlarged scales—scutes—along the back. All prefer damp habitats and can often be found either in or near water, generally in rain or mountain forests. They also occupy damp habitats such as hollow logs and holes in trees. Although they are largely terrestrial, they will climb trees to catch insects and other invertebrates. When near water, xenosaurs catch and eat small fish and the tadpoles of amphibians. They

LIZARDS CLASSIFICATION: 8

Wall and sand lizards

The family Lacertidae consists of about 200 species of wall and sand lizards grouped in 25 genera. They are all Old World species, occurring in Europe, Africa and Asia. The common or viviparous lizard, *Lacerta vivipara*, is widespread across Eurasia. The sand lizard, *L. agilis*, ranges over much of Europe, the green lizard, *L. viridis*, occurs in southern and western Europe, and the wall lizard, *Podarcis muralis*, is a species in southern and central Europe. The Hierro giant lizard, *Gallotia simonyi*, and the ocellated green lizard, *Lacerta lepida*, occur in southern Europe and North Africa.

Whiptails and race runners

The family Teiidae contains the 227 species and 39 genera of whiptails and race runners. They are restricted to the New World and are especially abundant in South America. They include the common tegu, *Tupinambis teguixin*, of Central and northern South America; the seven-striped whiptail, *Cnemidiphorus inornatus*, which occurs in the southern USA and northern Mexico; the six-lined race runner, *C. sexlineatus*, of the USA; the caiman lizard, *Dracaena guianensis*, of northern South America; and the giant jungle runner, *Amieva amieva*, which lives in Central and South America and has been introduced into Florida.

Anguids

The family Anguidae comprises the 75 species and eight genera of anguids—a group that includes the slowworms, glass lizards, legless lizards and alligator lizards. Most species occur in the New World, but others occur in Eurasia and northwest Africa. The common Eurasian slowworm, *Anguis fragilis*, ranges from Europe east to Central Asia and also occurs in northwest Africa. The European glass lizard, *Ophisaurus apodes*, occurs in southeast Europe, southwest Asia and Central Asia. The southern alligator lizard, *Elgaria multicarinatus*, occurs in the western USA, and the California legless lizard, *Aniella pulchra*, lives in California and Mexico.

TOP The European glass lizard is one of the many legless species of anguids. It frequently occurs around rural buildings, and is popular with farmers since it eats plenty of snails and slugs, and even catches mice.

ABOVE The California legless lizard seldom appears above ground. Its smooth body allows it to move easily through sand and soft soil, and it feeds by forcing its snout to the surface and snapping up spiders and insects.

THE SLOWWORM
— A LIZARD WITHOUT LEGS —

The slowworm is a snake-like lizard that reaches a length of 20 in. when mature. Male slowworms are brown-gray to bronze in color, and their bellies have a dark mottling of blackish or dark gray; smooth scales decorate their skin. Females often have a thin, dark line down the center of their backs and another runs along the upper part of each flank. Their young are silver to golden in color, and a black line marks their backs. The slowworm ranges throughout temperate Europe, southwest Asia and North Africa. Today, it is increasingly under threat from man, who often mistakes the reptile for a snake.

Internally, the slowworm has traces of bony arches to which limbs were once attached, evidence that its ancestors once ran on four legs. Its head is small and barely distinguishable from its neck, and its tail is more than half the length of the cylindrical body. However, the tail of a slowworm is fragile and often breaks.

Shedding its tail

Although a slowworm readily sloughs or sheds its tail, the regenerated tail never regains the elegance and length of the original. The detachment, or "autotomy," of the tail can occur at any point between the vertebrae of the tail. If a mature slowworm attempts to regrow its tail after losing it, it has to expend an enormous amount of energy in the process.

The slowworm is able to partially regenerate its broken tail on numerous occasions. Breakages to the tail rarely occur near the vent, however, and there is usually a ragged end to the old part. From this, the narrower new tail appears. The slowworm usually suffers a breakage of the tail when a predator attacks. The broken section of the tail twitches independently and distracts the attacker while the slowworm escapes. The smooth snake of the heaths of southern England and Europe is one of the slowworm's main predators. Other enemies include adders, rats, hedgehogs and kestrels.

Open woodlands, commons and heath are the favored habitat of the reptile. It prefers well-vegetated locations that offer extensive ground cover, especially well-watered meadows, woodland edges, hedgerows and banks. The slowworm seldom ventures out during daytime (except in spring and late summer). It spends the daylight hours under flat stones and logs. Burrows are also a common shelter and provide a fairly constant living temperature. The slowworm lies buried in the burrow, with only its head emerging. Occasionally, it basks openly in the sun, but it prefers to absorb heat by lying beneath sun-warmed objects such as flat stones.

During winter, the slowworm hibernates in underground burrows or in hollows below stones. As many as 20 huddle together, the largest positioning themselves on top of the group and the smallest underneath. They enter the resting place during October and do not reemerge until the spring.

Slippery prey

A slowworm is a secretive creature and moves relatively slowly. Occasionally, it will remain motionless if a predator approaches, rather than escape. Its actions are slow and deliberate, but it can move with startling speed if in danger. The slowworm does not have particularly strong eyesight and detects its prey principally by movement. Feeding on insects, slugs and earthworms, it usually seizes its prey in the middle and chews from end to end. The teeth of the slowworm are

A
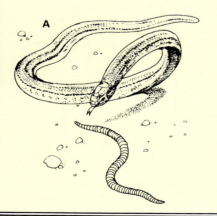

B
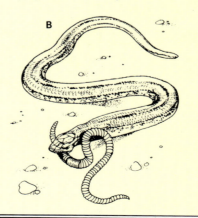

C

small and sharp, and curve slightly backward to give a better grip on slippery prey such as worms or snails. After eating, the reptile rubs its mouth against a rough surface to cleanse itself of mucus. A slowworm avoids the hairy caterpillars of butterflies and moths, but will prey on smooth larvae.

Female slowworms are egg-laying reptiles, and the eggs hatch within the body. The birth of the litter of 6-12 young occurs in late August, but cold weather often delays it until October or later. Young slowworms are active from the moment of birth.

ABOVE RIGHT When common Eurasian slowworms mate, the male grasps the female by the head, locking jaws with her. They may stay entwined all night, and by the next morning the male may have the female's entire head in his mouth.

RIGHT About three months after mating, the female slowworm gives birth to live young that are born still enclosed in very thin shells, but they soon break out and disperse. The young lizards are markedly different in color from their parents, with gold or silver on top, dark sides and bellies and thin, dark stripes running along their backs.

LEFT AND BELOW The capture of an earthworm by a slowworm: the slowworm finds and investigates the earthworm using its highly sensitive tongue (A); it bites its victim, grasping it at the rear of the body (B); and proceeds to swallow it (C and D), despite the earthworm's attempts to curl itself around the predator's head.

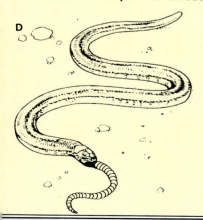

are usually active at night, although they will emerge from their retreats during the day either in shady places or after rain. Xenosaurs bear live young, which are born in early summer.

Monitors

The monitor lizards vary enormously in size, from less than 8 in. in the short-tailed pygmy monitor to more than 10 feet in the giant Komodo dragon. They have long, narrow heads with slit-like nostrils, long necks, sturdy legs armed with strong claws, powerful jaws with large pointed teeth, and a long tail that they can use as a weapon, a rudder or to grip with. Their external ear openings are exposed, and they have a long, forked tongue that they flick in and out in a snake-like way to explore the surroundings.

Monitors are distributed through the subtropical and tropical parts of the Old World, including Australia. They occupy a wide variety of habitats; some are ground-dwelling while others live in trees; some species always occur near water and others live in desert country. All monitors are active during the day and are carnivorous.

When threatened, most monitors seek refuge either in burrows or trees, or in the water. However, if they are trapped, they inflate their necks and open their mouths, hissing furiously. Monitors can also raise themselves up on their hind legs. If this display fails to deter the predator, they will lash their opponent violently with their tails and they may also bite.

Although fighting between males is ritualized, to minimize the damage to the two rivals, many mature monitors bear the scars of clashes from earlier mating seasons. When fighting a rival over a female, a male will rear up on his hind legs and grasp his opponent. Then, as in a wrestling bout, each tries to throw the other to the ground.

Having established dominance in the fight for a female, the male licks the neck and head of his mate and climbs onto her back, biting her gently. The female lays her eggs (between 7 and 56 depending on the species) in burrows, or in the canopy of trees if the species is tree-dwelling.

The smaller species of monitors feed on invertebrates while the larger ones will attack mammals and birds. The Komodo dragon, for example, can overpower wild pigs, goats and water buffalo. It is even thought to have killed humans.

BELOW The map illustrates the geographical distribution of eight species of lizards, along with the distribution of the worm-lizards that belong to a different suborder (see pages 1615-1616).

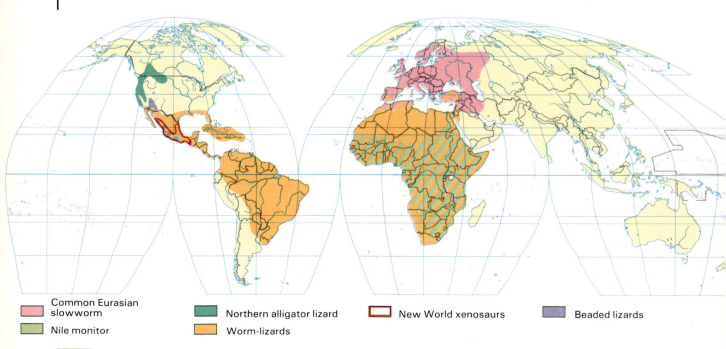

Common Eurasian slowworm | Nile monitor | Northern alligator lizard | Worm-lizards | New World xenosaurs | Beaded lizards

Tree monitor

Komodo dragon

xican beaded lizard

Galliwasp

Bornean earless lizard

Chinese xenosaur

Common Eurasian slowworm

Moroccan edge-snouted worm-lizard

California legless lizard

Somali edge-snouted worm-lizard

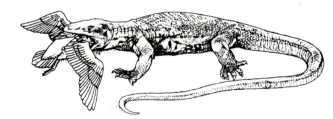

ABOVE **When threatened by an enemy or confronted by a rival, Gould's monitor rears up on its hind legs in an aggressive pose. Occupying a range of habitats, from moist coastal woodlands to sandy deserts, it is one of the most common of** Australia's monitor lizards. **It is a fast runner, and can outsprint a human over short distances.**
RIGHT **The structure of monitor lizards' skulls and throats allows them to swallow large prey whole — an ability they share with the snakes.**

Torn to pieces

The Komodo dragon, the largest of the monitor lizards, is a particularly skilled predator. It subdues its prey by holding it tightly in its jaws and beating it from side to side against the ground. If the prey puts up a fierce struggle, it will hold it down with its claws and tear it to pieces with its teeth. It can swallow surprisingly large pieces of food by expanding and dilating its throat, and it has a highly flexible skull that enables it to gape more widely than if the skull were rigid. Snakes are similar in this respect, and monitors are generally considered to be the most closely related of the lizards to the snakes (even though legless lizards, such as the glass lizards, are closer in appearance).

The Komodo dragon lives on only two small islands and two islets in Indonesia. Known to local people as the "ora," it can reach up to 10 ft. in length. As well as hunting live prey, it is a scavenger, and can detect carrion by scent from a distance of nearly one mile. Each Komodo has a large home range, and will travel up to two miles in search of food. Komodos do not defend their home ranges, which may overlap with several others. If two komodos find food where their ranges overlap, they will confront each other, and the dominant animal has first pick at the food. Komodo dragons shelter in burrows that they dig in the ground. They also rest in holes among rocks, in caves or between the buttressed roots of trees.

LIZARDS CLASSIFICATION: 9

Xenosaurs

There are only four species in the family Xenosauridae, the xenosaurs or crocodile lizards. The three New World species belong to the genus *Xenosaurus*, and live only in the rain forests of Mexico and Guatemala. The fourth species, the Chinese xenosaur, *Shinisaurus crocodilurus*, occurs in southern China.

Monitor lizards

The family Varanidae comprises the 31 species of monitor lizards, all of which belong to the same genus, *Varanus*. Most species occur in Australia and Southeast Asia, but they also range over southern and Central Asia, the Middle East and Africa. They include the Komodo dragon, *V. komodensis*, which lives only on Komodo, Flores and two small islets in Indonesia; the perentie, *V. giganteus*, and Gould's or sand monitor, *V. gouldii*, both of Australia; the tree monitor, *V. tristris*, of Australia and Southeast Asia; the water or common monitor, *V. salvador*, of Southeast Asia; and the Nile monitor, *V. niloticus*, which ranges over much of Africa.

Sturdy claws

The desert monitors of North Africa and the Middle East live in burrows abandoned by mammals that they adapt by digging with their sturdy claws. Desert monitors look similar to giant wall lizards, and they can reach over 4 ft. in length. They have long, low heads with slender muzzles. The Nile monitor, widespread across much of Africa, grows to about 6 ft. 6 in. long and lives on sandy islets, bare beaches, and river or lakeside habitats. It often lies on tree branches overhanging the water. Nile monitors are excellent swimmers and can remain submerged for some time. They eat small water animals and will also raid crocodiles' nests for the eggs. The females usually lay their eggs in termite mounds.

About half of the species of monitor lizards live in Australia. The group includes the smallest species, the short-tailed pygmy monitor lizard, which measures only

ABOVE As well as chasing its prey in the water, through which it swims with powerful sideways strokes of its tail, the water monitor climbs trees in search of food. It eats a variety of mammals and birds, and, in turn, is hunted by snakes.

PAGES 1610-1611 Komodo dragons are the largest and most powerful of all the world's lizards. They can tackle animals as large as deer, pigs and goats, often catching deer while they are asleep, and have been known to overpower and kill water buffalo.

THE NILE MONITOR
— AFRICA'S LARGEST LIZARD —

The Nile monitor ranges throughout Africa, from the upper reaches of the Nile to the Cape Province in the south of the continent. An aquatic reptile growing to 20 feet long, it inhabits riverbanks, lake shores and swamps. It is greenish-gray to brown in color with yellow "eyespots" or bands decorating its skin; the underside is yellow with grayish bars, and the tail is gray with yellow bars. Young ones have a black coloration with yellow spots and stripes. The Nile monitor's head appears small in proportion to the rest of the body. The neck is long and slender, and the animal has a long muzzle, small eyes and sturdy legs. The long body ends in a strong, crested tail that is flattened from side to side.

The Nile monitor spends much of its time basking on branches or rocks among the riverbank vegetation. When in danger, it drops into the water, and uses its flattened tail to swim to safety. If a predator threatens it and the monitor cannot reach water, it will run rapidly, outpacing even a human, especially over thick terrain. During flight, the Nile monitor holds its tail aloft in a characteristic curve, with the tip held slightly off the ground. If cornered, the monitor becomes very aggressive, rearing up on its hind legs and hissing. It attacks its enemy by grabbing it with its powerful jaws and lashing out with its tail. Pythons and crocodiles are among the Nile monitor's main enemies. As a further defense, it may also feign death.

Fierce fighters

During courtship, the Nile monitor is quick tempered and violent. If a rival male confronts it, the male opens his mouth wide, inflates his throat, hisses and lashes the air with his tail. The two rivals then stand upright and, clutching each other, begin to wrestle. Occasionally, they inflict wounds by sinking their strong claws into each other's sides. The victorious male wins by throwing his weaker rival off balance or making him submit and retreat. During the brief courtship of the Nile monitor, the male approaches the female, investigates her with his tongue, and climbs onto her back, gripping tightly with his claws. He bites her neck, sometimes violently enough to wound her.

The female Nile monitor lays her eggs in a termite nest, tearing a hole in the wall of the nest, and laying 16-34 eggs in the enlarged chamber in the center. She leaves the termites to repair the walls, sealing the eggs inside.

Termite meal

The eggs incubate in the heat and safety of the nest for five months. When the young hatch, they are strong enough to dig their way upward, eating some of the termites as their first meal. The young are mainly insectivorous and have sharp teeth. But, as the monitors grow, their sharp teeth are replaced by blunt ones perfect for crushing prey. Nile monitors eat insects, snails, crabs and other invertebrates, but will also feed on small birds and mammals.

FAR LEFT The adult Nile monitor is an excellent swimmer. It uses its tail to propel itself through the water with strong side-to-side movements. **ABOVE** Young Nile monitors rarely enter deep water. Instead, they catch frogs and insects in the shallow water of reedbeds and the margins of rivers. **BELOW** A Nile monitor's burrow seen from above. Female monitors often dig their holes in termite nests — after the lizards have laid their eggs, the termites repair the damage to the nest, covering the eggs in the process.

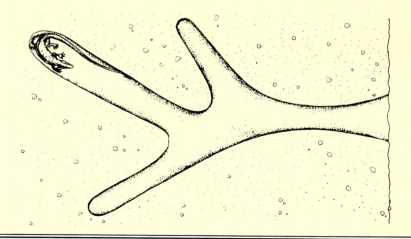

LIZARDS CLASSIFICATION: 10

Beaded lizards and the Bornean earless lizard

The family Helodermatidae comprises the two species of beaded lizards from the deserts and semideserts of the New World: the Gila monster, *Heloderma suspectum*, of the southwestern USA and Mexico, and the Mexican beaded lizard, *H. horridum*, of Mexico and Guatemala. The sole member of the family Lanthanotidae is the Bornean earless lizard, *Lanthanotus borneensis*, from the lowland forests of Borneo.

8 in. from nose to tail. It also includes Australia's largest lizard, the perentie, which can reach more than 6 ft. 6 in. in length. The short-tailed pygmy monitor is a burrowing lizard. Its back is reddish or yellowish brown, with white and dark spots, and it has a lighter belly. The perentie, or Queensland monitor, lives in arid parts of central Australia. Another burrowing lizard, it dwells in deep crevices or burrows. Its throat is ivory-colored with a coarse, black network pattern. Perenties feed on a variety of animal prey, including medium-sized birds and mammals, as well as snakes, other lizards, and bird and reptile eggs.

The tree monitors are forest dwellers of Southeast Asia. They are extremely agile in the trees, where they catch their prey. Tree monitors grow to about 31 in. and are bright green in color, giving them good camouflage in their wooded environment.

Beaded lizards

There are only two species of beaded lizard—the Gila monster and the Mexican beaded lizard. They are the only venomous lizards in the world. Their poison glands—modified salivary glands—are located on the outer sides of their lower jaws. The teeth are sharp, inwardly curved and grooved on the snout-facing surface. Unlike snakes, they do not inject their venom—instead, they let it flow into the wound by capillary action, along the grooves in their teeth. The venom works fairly quickly on small mammals and birds, but seems to be much less effective on frogs. It acts on the nervous system of the prey, causing pain

TOP Gila monsters kill prey with venom transmitted through their grooved teeth, but they do not inject the venom like some snakes. Instead, they chew into the victim and allow the venom to diffuse into the wound.

ABOVE The mangrove monitor is a colorful, semiaquatic lizard that inhabits rain forest streams and coastal mangroves in parts of Indonesia, New Guinea, Australia and some Pacific islands.

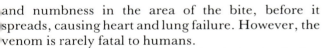

ABOVE The European worm-lizard, which looks at first glance like a fat earthworm, has its scales arranged in rings around the body. Other than after heavy rain, it is rarely seen above ground during the daytime. ABOVE RIGHT AND RIGHT Unlike most worm-lizards, which are entirely limbless, the two-legged worm-lizard from arid parts of Mexico has short, but powerful forelimbs. It uses them for digging holes in the earth and to help it clamber about on the surface. It can even climb a short distance off the ground.

and numbness in the area of the bite, before it spreads, causing heart and lung failure. However, the venom is rarely fatal to humans.

The beaded lizards are heavy-bodied animals that grow to about 24 in. in length. They have short, stout legs and short, thick tails. Both species are similar in appearance, but where the Gila monster's patterning tends to be yellowish or white on a dark background, the Mexican beaded lizard's is pinkish. Beaded lizards do not have particularly good vision as their eyes are small and they depend on scent rather than sight when catching their prey. They store fat in their large tails for periods when they are inactive, such as during the colder winter months. Their tails can lose up to 20 percent of their bulk in particularly hard times. Beaded lizards are rather sluggish, terrestrial lizards of semiarid and arid habitats. They are active mainly during twilight or at night.

The Bornean earless lizard

The rare Bornean earless lizard lives beside streams and damp ditches, especially near rice paddies. It resembles the beaded lizards in appearance, but has no venom. Its nostrils are on top of its snout, instead of at the side, and it lacks external ear openings or folds of skin on its throat. Bornean earless lizards have

small eyes with round pupils and their eyelids are movable. They are semiaquatic animals (they swim well with sideways undulations of their body) and they also burrow, digging into the soil snout first. Active at night, they probably feed on invertebrates and turtle and birds' eggs.

The worm-lizards

The worm-lizards, or amphisbaenans, form a separate suborder from the lizards. They occur in both the Old and New Worlds, and are the only reptiles to live exclusively underground. A variety of adaptations of head shape and muscle action enable worm-lizards to burrow. Rings of scales around their bodies fold up against one another or stretch out as the worm-lizards push their way through the soil, and their skulls are small and modified. In some species, tough, horny keratin shields the skull. In others, slippery scales cover the head to streamline its movement underground.

All species of worm-lizards dig their tunnels by thrusting their head into the dead end. Some species then compress the soil into the walls of the tunnel, making it unnecessary for them to deposit the soil at the surface—thus they can spend their entire lives underground. Worm-lizards have no external ear openings, their eyes lie deep beneath translucent

1615

ABOVE Like all the worm-lizards, the Moroccan edge-snouted worm-lizard is highly adapted for an underground life style. It makes a burrow with a triangular or rectangular cross-section in loose, sandy soils by rotating its body. Its head is strong and is thrust forward into the soil as the animal tunnels.

WORM-LIZARDS CLASSIFICATION

The worm-lizards or amphisbaenans form a separate suborder from the lizards, the Amphisbaenia (the second group within the order Squamata). There are about 140 species of worm-lizards grouped in 21 genera that make up four families. Burrowing reptiles, they occur in parts of North and South America, Africa, southern Europe and the Middle East.

The family Amphisbaenidae, the true worm-lizards, contains the most widespread species, including the European worm-lizard, *Blanus cinereus*, of Spain, Portugal, Morocco and Algeria, and the white-bellied worm-lizard, *Amphisbaena alba*, of tropical South America. The family Rhineuridae contains just one species—the Florida worm-lizard, *Rhinura floridana*, of north and central Florida.

Africa and parts of Asia are home to the family Trogonophidae, one member of which is the Somali edge-snouted worm-lizard, *Agamodon anguliceps*, from the deserts of Somalia and southeast Ethiopia. The Mexican worm-lizards of the genus *Bipes* make up the family Bipedidae. The common two-legged worm-lizard, *B. biporus*, occurs in arid areas of Mexico.

layers of skin, and their nostrils point backward to prevent soil getting into them as they burrow.

Worm-lizards are carnivorous and capture their prey by detecting their scent and sound. They have modified eardrums on the sides of their jaws that enable them to pick up the trail of their potential prey. They seize their food—ants, termites, spiders, worms and even small vertebrates—in their strong jaws and drag it into the tunnel to eat.

Most of the four families of worm-lizards do not have legs, but the Mexican worm-lizards do have short front legs set well forward on their bodies. These forelimbs help the worm-lizards to move above ground, and to start digging tunnels.

Rings of scales

The European worm-lizard usually grows to approximately 8 in. (although some have been recorded measuring 12 in.). Its head is small and rather pointed, and it has tiny eyes. Its scales are rectangular and run in rings around the body, separated by grooves. European worm-lizards usually remain hidden under stones or in tunnels where they forage for small invertebrates, especially ants. They inhabit pine woods and cultivated areas, but are rarely seen on the surface, except during rainstorms or at night.

The white-bellied worm-lizard is the largest of the worm-lizards. It can reach as much as 24 in. in length, with a body diameter of almost one inch. Similar to a giant reddish earthworm in appearance, its head is difficult to tell from its tail. However, when threatened, it raises its head and opens its mouth.

Flattened head

The Florida worm-lizard has a flattened head that it uses to compress the soil against the top and bottom of the tunnel as it moves along. Florida worm-lizards burrow underground, chiefly in sandy soils, after their invertebrate prey (particularly earthworms, spiders and termites). They are occasionally seen on the surface after heavy rain, but, if disturbed, will quickly retreat to their burrows.

The edge-snouted worm-lizards of North Africa and the Middle East burrow through sandy soils by rotating their bodies. Their heads are flattened at the front and the edges scrape the soil from the sides of the tunnel as the lizards advance. They then push this soil to the sides as they move along.

COILED TO STRIKE

Inspiring both awe and fear, snakes are highly
effective predators, silently stalking their victims
and then suffocating or injecting them with
lethal doses of venom

ABOVE Some snakes produce live young, but most species lay eggs, depositing them in warm places that are not too dry. In a few species the females guard the eggs, but usually they are left to incubate and hatch on their own.

PAGE 1617 A green mamba, one of the world's most venomous snakes, climbs a tree in search of eggs and fledglings. Most snakes are adept at climbing, often pulling themselves up by hooking their necks over a branch and hauling the rest of the body behind.

Snakes are famous the world over for their long, flexible, scaly bodies, their predatory habits and, in some species, their poisonous bites. They are among the most successful of the vertebrate animals, living throughout the tropical and temperate regions of the world, occurring in a great variety of habitats, and numbering some 2400 species—a total exceeded only by the lizards. A few snakes, such as the pythons and boas, retain tiny remnants of their hind legs, but all other species are entirely limbless. Though they lack legs, they are far from immobile—most species can move over land, climb trees and swim across rivers, with ease.

Large and small

Snakes vary enormously in size, from the tiny burrowing thread snakes that are only about 6 in. long to the largest specimens of reticulated pythons and anacondas that may reach over 33 ft. in length. Extra vertebral bones in the spinal column give the snakes their great length in relation to body width. Some snakes have as many as 400 vertebrae in their spines, and most species have more than 200. Human beings, by contrast, have 34 vertebrae. The bones are structured in such a way as to allow maximum movement in all directions.

Though the sinuous bodies of snakes may look similar in shape to those of the legless lizards and worm-lizards, they are, in fact, easy to tell apart. Snakes do not have the ringed scales of worm-lizards, nor the closable eyelids of most legless lizards.

The internal organs of snakes have become adapted to fit the limits of their body shapes. In many snakes the left lung has been lost and the remaining right lung carries out all the respiration. There is not enough room, either, for the kidneys to lie side by side, and they are positioned one behind the other.

Some snakes are brightly colored, with vivid markings running along the length of their bodies, but many appear rather dull in color, with various shades of grays, browns and blacks. In such species, it is the patterning of the scales on the head that provide the chief clue to identification. However, even a dull species can look attractive when it has just sloughed off its old skin, the new scales shimmering beneath. The finely sculptured surface of the new skin split light into the different colors of the spectrum.

Sliding and winding

Snakes have different methods of moving about. They can move large scales or scutes on their bellies backward or forward, and some snakes—particularly the larger and heavier species—use them to move forward while their bodies remain in a straight line. They press some groups of scutes against the ground while sliding the others freely forward. However, such a method makes for slow progress. Snakes can also move by curving their bodies into S-shapes and pressing the back part of each curve against the ground to push the body forward. The curve constantly changes as the ripple of movement runs along the length of the snake.

When climbing, a tree snake uses a concertina-like motion, pulling up and contracting its body behind it after hooking its neck over a branch. It then grips another branch with its tail and stretches the head upward again to find a new hold so that it can repeat the action. The most impressive movement among snakes is probably "sidewinding," a method used by desert species to keep only part of the body on the hot sand at any one time. By throwing themselves sideways, starting with the head and curving the body behind, they move along at right angles to the direction in which they are facing.

Flexible jaws

All snakes are carnivores, catching a variety of prey that includes mammals, birds, birds' eggs, reptiles, amphibians, fish, insects and snails. Snakes are unusual in that they can swallow large prey whole. The bones of the mouth are connected to the skull only by a soft tissue of muscles and ligaments. The arrangement is so flexible that the mouth can open wide enough for the snake to swallow prey that is much broader than its own body. A snake swallows its prey head first, working the food down its throat using its teeth. Then it sharply curves its neck and forces the food down toward its stomach. The skin is flexible enough for the food to pass along without rupturing the snake's body. Once the food reaches the stomach, digestion begins, and most snakes will not need to find another meal for at least a week.

Snakes cannot tear their prey apart because they have no limbs, but they have evolved several other methods of capturing and killing prey. Some crush their prey by wrapping their coils around them, killing them by constriction, while venomous snakes strike and kill animals with their poison fangs. The poison is produced in glands either in the upper jaw, the region of the temple or from deeper in the body, from which it is channeled to the teeth.

Snake venom has various effects on the prey, often paralyzing the animal or causing internal bleeding that quickly leads to death. The likelihood that venom originally evolved from snakes' digestive juices is emphasized by the fact that it often starts to break down body tissues. In a number of species, the snakes deliver their bites and then retreat to wait for the victim to die before they return to feed.

Eyes ever open

Snakes cannot close their eyes—for which they have gained a reputation for having cold, lifeless stares. Instead of eyelids, they have a transparent layer—the brille—that permanently covers the eye. Nocturnal species often have vertical pupils that open very wide in dim light.

Snakes are rarely able to hear a wide range of sounds—they have no external ears, and although they can hear low-pitched sounds reasonably well, they are not sensitive to high-pitched tones. They make up for these limitations by having other highly tuned senses. They constantly flick out their forked tongues, which

ABOVE Despite the small size of their heads, snakes, such as these grass snakes, can easily swallow large prey. The jaw bones can move freely, allowing the mouth to open extremely wide. **BELOW** Snakes show a variety of teeth patterns and fang shapes. Non-venomous snakes have a series of small, sharp backward-pointing teeth (A). Venomous species have pairs of small, grooved fangs (B) or enlarged, hollow fangs (C) through which venom is injected into the victim, and which leave distinctive bite marks.

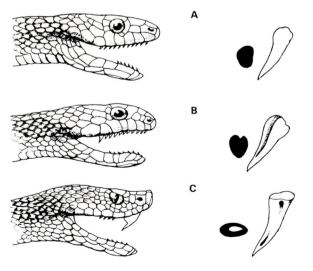

function in association with the Jacobson's organ (located in the roof of the mouth) to provide a very accurate chemical receptor. The tongue is drawn back into the mouth along with minuscule amounts of scent from the animal's environment. The snake then inserts its tongue into the hollows of the Jacobson's organ. The organ detects the chemicals allowing the snake to tell which animals are nearby—either potential prey or enemies—and gather plenty of other information about its surroundings

Some snakes also have sensory pits, either on the side of their heads or on their lips, that are sensitive to heat. They enable the snakes to detect the presence and movements of warm objects, such as their prey. The sensitivity of these heat-seeking organs is extraordinary—a snake can notice a change in temperature of two thousandths of a degree—and, using the sense, it can accurately strike in the dark to catch, kill and eat its prey.

Rituals of breeding

Male snakes possess a pair of reproductive organs, each of which is known as a hemipenis, and only one of which is used each time the animal mates. Mating generally follows a courtship ritual that involves the male and female moving closely together, and courtship itself is often preceded by fights between rival males.

Snakes use the same three systems of reproduction as lizards and worm-lizards (see page 1564). Some are oviparous, the female laying eggs and leaving them in a warm, damp place to incubate and hatch. Others are ovoviviparous, the female giving birth to live young after the eggs have developed within her body. A few species are viviparous. In these, the embryos develop inside the mother with no surrounding egg membranes, but with close contact with the body tissues of the mother (a system similar to that of placental mammals).

ABOVE LEFT The reticulated python of Southeast Asia is (together with the South American anaconda) the world's longest snake, growing up to 33 ft. Pythons do not have venom to poison their prey, but rely on the great strength of their muscular bodies to crush their victims—mammals as large as deer or pigs, and even the occasional child or small adult.
LEFT Like all snakes, the African burrowing snake sheds or sloughs its old skin—the white, papery object on the right—several times a year so that its body can continue to grow.

COILED TO STRIKE

Burrowing snakes

The blind, thread and dawn-blind families of snakes are primitive, worm-like reptiles that burrow in the ground. Because of their burrowing life-style, they have round bodies, blunt heads and stubby tails. Thick, glossy scales cover their bodies, enabling them to slither through leaf litter and loose topsoil. The bones of their skulls fuse together to form a hard, burrowing instrument useful for digging into crevices and holes in the ground. Snakes that burrow underground have poor vision, and mainly use their eyes to distinguish light and dark. Almost all burrowing snakes retain traces of the hind legs of their lizard-like ancestors.

When moving overground, certain burrowing snakes use a short, sharp spine on the end-scale of their tails to give them leverage. By anchoring the tip of the spine in the ground, they push their bodies forward or pull them backward. As the snakes travel overground, the tail spines produce a fine, wavy trail in the soil. Burrowing snakes have distinctive jaws and mouths, often no larger than tiny slits. Naturally, these narrow apertures restrict their feeding to small and slender-bodied prey.

The blind snakes

Blind snakes form the largest and most widespread family of burrowing snakes. There are as many as 180 species of blind snakes, ranging throughout Africa, Madagascar, Southeast Asia, tropical areas of the Americas and many oceanic islands. Despite their name, the blind snakes retain their tiny eyes, which lie under a layer of translucent scales.

Blind snakes differ from the other burrowing snakes in that they have backward-pointing teeth on their upper jaw. Blind snakes mostly inhabit moist, tropical regions where damp soil allows them to dig shallow burrows among the roots of plants and under rotting logs. They have a shield-like cover over their snouts. When tunneling or hunting prey, the snouts take the full impact of burrowing through the soil. Some species also live in trees, among the root masses of plants such as ferns, orchids and bromeliads that sprout on trunks and branches. Blind snakes frequently feed on the nests of ants and termites that they find in the root systems of these plants.

ABOVE Blind snakes, such as this West African species, spend most of their lives burrowing underground where they feed on ants and termites. Some species store reserves of fat in their broad tails, drawing on it for nourishment in hot, dry weather when the snakes are inactive. The eyes of blind snakes are small and covered with translucent scales, but the animals can use them to distinguish between light and dark.

SNAKES CLASSIFICATION: 1

The snakes form the suborder Serpentes (or Ophidia)—part of the reptile order Squamata. There are about 2400 species worldwide, and they are divided into 11 families. These are the Leptotyphlopidae, the thread snakes; the Typhlopidae, the typical blind snakes; the Anomalepidae, the dawn blind snakes; the Acrochordidae, the Asian wart snakes; the Aniliidae, the pipesnakes; the Uropeltidae, the shieldtail snakes; the Xenopeltidae, the sole member of which is the sunbeam snake; the Boidae, the pythons and boas; the Colubridae, the colubrid or harmless snakes; the Elapidae, the front-fanged snakes; and the Viperidae, the vipers.

TOP The western blind snake lives in the deserts and rocky canyons of the southwestern USA and Mexico. It burrows into the sandy or gravelly soil, occasionally emerging at dusk or on overcast days. CENTER The Texas blind snake usually appears above ground after spring and summer rains. To defend itself against the insects on which it preys, it smears its body with feces and a sticky fluid excreted from its anus. BOTTOM The thread snake's tiny eyes show as two dark dots (visible on the head of this animal on the upper left of the picture). Some thread snakes, such as this one from the Old World, look pink because they lack body pigment. RIGHT With their round bodies and blunt heads, blind snakes resemble large worms.

The Braminy blind snake, which is black or pearly-gray in color with a creamy-white tail tip, grows to only 5 in. in length. Distributed over much of tropical Asia, it derives its common name, the flowerpot snake, from its habit of climbing into flowerpots that stand outdoors. Once inside the pot, the snake survives for long periods by feeding on insect larvae. As a result of their curious habit, Braminy blind snakes eventually appeared in Mexico and Hawaii after ships carried them in pots containing ornamental plants. The Braminy blind snake is the only snake to produce young without mating (by a system of reproduction called parthenogenesis).

Narrow burrows

Europe has only one species of blind snake—the Eurasian worm snake or vermiform blind snake. Inhabiting the dry, sparsely overgrown earth beneath rocks and gravel, it ranges from the Balkans to the Greek islands. It also appears throughout southwest Asia, the Caucasus region of the USSR and northeast Egypt. The Eurasian worm snake grows up to 14 in. in length. Its body thickens slightly toward the tail. The tail itself is round and has a tough, spiny scale. The snake is brown in color, often with a yellow, pink or purple hue. When danger threatens, it retreats into narrow burrows similar to those of earthworms. During the hot months of summer, the Eurasian worm snake abandons the stony fields that form its normal habitat for more damp conditions further underground.

During the mating ritual, the male Eurasian worm snake, which is slightly smaller than the female, winds himself in several tight coils around the lower half of her body. He also turns his head away from the

female. The female lays four to eight long, oval-shaped eggs in June or July and conceals them underneath a flat stone. Normally, most species of blind snake lay between 5 and 12 eggs, although certain African species can lay as many as 50 eggs. Daird's blind snake of Southeast Asia lays eggs that hatch soon after being laid. It also gives birth to live young from eggs that hatch inside the female.

Thread snakes

Thread snakes are the smallest snakes in the world. They have long, slender bodies, ranging from just 3 to 16 in. in length. There are 78 species of thread snakes, living mainly in arid areas of Africa and Arabia, and in parts of the Americas from the southern states of the USA to Argentina.

The western blind snake and the Texas blind snake are both members of the thread snake family. Ranging throughout the American southwest, they inhabit arid localities, such as the bottom of canyons, where the subsoil is slightly damp. The western blind snake is purplish brown or pink in color, with a silvery sheen; its underparts are paler pink or purple. It normally hunts for invertebrates, especially termites and ant

Boa constrictor

Green tree boa

Western blind snake

Eurasian worm snake

Javan wart snake

Indian python

Anaconda

False coral snake

Sunbeam snake

larvae and pupae, in loose soil beneath rocks or inside fallen trees. As early evening falls, the western blind snake lurks above ground, but disappears again when it becomes fully dark. The Texas blind snake is more reddish brown in color, and has pinkish or whitish underparts. It inhabits the roots of trees and shrubs and also appears above ground on warm summer nights after spring and summer rains.

Hunting termites

Thread snakes only have teeth in their lower jaws, but they are able to chew their prey, usually termites. After seizing the termite at the rear of the insect's soft abdomen, the stout lower teeth of the thread snake hold and press it against the flat, grinding surface of the upper jaw. It then works its jaws in a rapid forward motion, sucking out the body contents of the insect. When it reaches the hard head of the prey, the snake writhes about and brushes it from its mouth. Thread snakes can track down termites by following the scent trails that the insects leave behind. The snakes secrete a chemical substance with a scent similar to that of termites' own scent, allowing them to enter the termite nests without risking attack.

Female thread snakes often use termite nests as a place to lay their four, oval-shaped eggs. The female Texas blind snake lays her eggs in an underground burrow. She incubates them by coiling her body around the eggs until they hatch. The eggs of some thread snakes are no larger than a grain of rice.

Dawn blind snakes

Dawn blind snakes are round-bodied reptiles that range from 5 to 6 in. in length. Tiny and thread-like in appearance, they have a dark coloration with yellow or white markings on the head and tail. There are about 20 species of dawn blind snakes, and they range throughout tropical Central and South America. Little is known of their behavior other than that they spend almost their entire lives below the leaf litter and damp soil. They have one or two teeth in their lower jaws, and there is no trace of the pelvic limb bones that are found in the other two families of burrowing snakes.

Asian wart snakes

Asian wart snakes inhabit the rivers, estuaries and seas of India, Southeast Asia, New Guinea and Australia. Unlike most snakes, the scales of the wart snakes do not overlap but lie adjacent to each other and have a sharp ridge. As a result, the skin has a rough, warty appearance, from which these aquatic snakes take their name. The heads of the wart snakes are broad and flat, and their thick, stumpy bodies end in short, slender tails, flattened at the sides to act as a rudder when they are swimming. The tails can grasp objects firmly, and wart snakes use this prehensile or gripping ability to anchor themselves when on the sea or river bed. Remarkably, these slow-swimming creatures can open their mouths below water to swallow fish, without interfering with their breathing system. One species even eats crabs.

SNAKES CLASSIFICATION: 2

Thread snakes

The thread snakes make up the family Leptotyphlopidae, with 78 species in only two genera. They occur in Africa, southwest Asia and in warmer regions of the New World. Though they belong to the thread snake family, some species are called blind snakes. Two species from the southwestern USA are the western blind snake *Leptotyphlops humilis*, and the Texas blind snake *L. dulcis*.

Typical blind snakes and dawn blind snakes

The family Typhlopidae, the typical blind snakes, contains from 160 to 180 species (depending on the system of classification) in three genera. They are widespread in the tropics, and some species also occur in temperate parts of Africa, Australia, southeast Europe and southwest Asia. The Eurasian worm snake, *Typhlops vermicularis*, occurs in southeast Europe, the Middle East, the Caucasus and Egypt. The Braminy blind snake or flowerpot snake, *Rhamphotyphlops braminus*, ranges over much of tropical Asia and Madagascar (it has also been introduced to Hawaii and Mexico). The 20 species of dawn blind snakes make up the family Anomalepidae. They belong to four genera, including *Anomalepsis* and *Typhlophis*, and all are found in Central and South America.

ABOVE The sunbeam snake takes its name from the iridescence of its brown scales. It hunts both underground, in the soft soil of the forest floor, and on the surface for small mammals, amphibians, snakes and birds.

ABOVE RIGHT As a pipesnake pulls itself down into its burrow to escape from a bird of prey, it continues to wave its tail about in the open, hoping to distract or startle the bird with the bright red coloring beneath the tail.

The Indian wart snake or Asiatic file snake adapts well to life in the water and is found far out to sea. A keel-like ridge of skin that runs along its underside improves its swimming efficiency. The larger Javan wart snake or elephant's-trunk snake grows up to 6 ft. 6 in. in length. Its flattened, broad-snouted head, powerful body and short tail give the snake a boa-like appearance. It lives mainly along coasts fringed by dense stands of mangrove forests.

The nostrils of the wart snakes are on the upper part of their heads, enabling them to surface for air without unduly alerting predators. Their eyes are also set on the upper part of the head. When underwater, a flap of skin on the roof of the mouth effectively seals off the nasal passages, and a pad of skin on the snake's chin closes a notch in the upper lip through which the tongue normally protrudes.

Pipesnakes

Pipesnakes inhabit South America and Southeast Asia. They derive their name from their cylindrical bodies that are the same thickness from head to tail. Pipesnakes are usually black in color, and they burrow in damp soils. In Asia, where the red-tailed pipesnake often constructs its underground tunnels in rice paddies, it is called a two-headed snake because of its unusual defense posture. If in danger, the red-

SNAKES CLASSIFICATION: 3

Asian wart snakes and pipesnakes

The family Acrochordidae, the Asian wart snakes, contains just two species. The Javan wart snake or elephant's-trunk snake, *Acrochordis javanicus*, ranges from India through China and Southeast Asia to northern Australia, while the Indian wart snake or Asiatic file snake, *Chersydrus granulatus*, ranges from southern Asia through Indonesia to the Solomon Islands. Of the 10 species (from three genera) of pipesnakes in the family Aniliidae, nine species occur in Southeast Asia and Indonesia. The odd one out is the false coral snake or coral pipesnake, *Anilius scytale*, of northern South America.

Shieldtail snakes and the sunbeam snake

The family of shieldtail snakes, the Uropeltidae, contains 44 species in eight genera, and includes the red-blotched shieldtail, *Uropeltis biomaculatus*. All the species are concentrated in the mountains and foothills of southern India and Sri Lanka. The family Xenopeltidae has only one species, the sunbeam snake or sunbeam python, *Xenopeltis unicolor*, which is common over much of Southeast Asia. Some zoologists include the species in the pythons and boas family.

tailed pipesnake raises its tail in the air and moves it in a manner similar to the motion of its head. The deception distracts the enemy and allows the pipesnake to strike. At the same time, the snake exposes the bright red underside of its tail to scare off a would-be predator, such as a bird of prey.

The red-tailed pipesnake is the largest species in the pipesnake family. Growing to over 3 ft. in length, it ranges throughout Southeast Asia. Although pipesnakes have large, backward-pointing teeth, their mouths cannot open very wide. As a result, they attack slim-bodied prey such as eels or other snakes—quite often, their prey are as long as the snakes themselves.

Deception plays an important part in the body camouflage of the false coral snake of the Amazon Basin. Brilliant red and black rings cover its back, providing a warning coloration that strikingly resembles the highly venomous coral snakes that live in the same region. The body markings deceive and deter many predators. The false coral snake hides underground during the day and emerges to feed at night on thin-bodied prey such as earthworms and lizards.

Shieldtail snakes

The slender, burrowing shieldtail snakes make their homes in the hilly areas of southern India and Sri

ABOVE **The Indian wart snake rarely ventures onto land, spending most of its life in water—in rivers, estuaries, and in the sea—where it feeds on fish. The middle part of its underside forms a keel-shaped fold of skin, enabling the snake to swim more efficiently.**

BELOW **Shieldtails are burrowing snakes found only in southern India and Sri Lanka. Their tails have enlarged tips made up of thickened, spiny scales on the upper surface that may serve to plug the burrow as the snake makes its way through the soil.**

Lanka. They have a scaly plate at the end of their short tails. When digging, spines on the plate collect a coating of soil particles. The purpose of the scaly plate is not known, but it may serve to anchor the snakes to the ground as they move over the surface. If the shieldtails confront a predator, they wave the plate in an intimidating display, drawing attention away from their more vulnerable head.

Shieldtails burrow in the rich soil of hill forests to a depth of 12 in. The heads of the shieldtails are narrow and pointed and their necks are extremely flexible. As they stick their sharp snouts into the ground, their necks adopt an S-shape and make sideways, sweeping movements that enlarge the width of their burrows. The scales of the shieldtails are especially glossy, allowing the snakes minimum friction as they make their way through the earth in search of their main prey of earthworms.

The largest species of shieldtail measures 12 in. in length but is only one inch wide. Most species are much smaller. Shieldtails generally have colorful skin, with red, orange, or yellow markings that mimic the warning coloration of poisonous snakes called kraits. The less colorful species have black skin with an iridescent sheen. Shieldtails give birth to about eight live young.

The sunbeam snake

The sunbeam snake of Southeast Asia is a semi-burrowing reptile that is active at night. Unusual for a burrowing snake, it spends a great deal of time above ground. It is also unusual among the group of burrowing snakes in that it has a flexible lower jaw. As a result, it can tackle bulkier prey including frogs and small mammals. A trace of the hind legs of their ancestors still remain. The sunbeam snake grows to about 3 ft. in length. It has a round body and rich brown, smooth scales that shimmer with iridescence in the sunlight. When excited, it twitches its tail in a manner similar to rattlesnakes.

Pythons and boas

Pythons and boas are heavily built snakes. They have broad, flat heads and well-defined necks. Their distinguishing feature is a pair of small, claw-like spurs that lie on either side of the cloacal opening. These are the remnants of the hind limbs of their lizard ancestors. Small, glossy scales cover the upperparts of their heads, and they have a broad row of larger plates on the underside of their tails. Their body colors tend to be relatively subdued, but bolder markings break up the body outline and camouflage the snakes against rocks, soil or background vegetation.

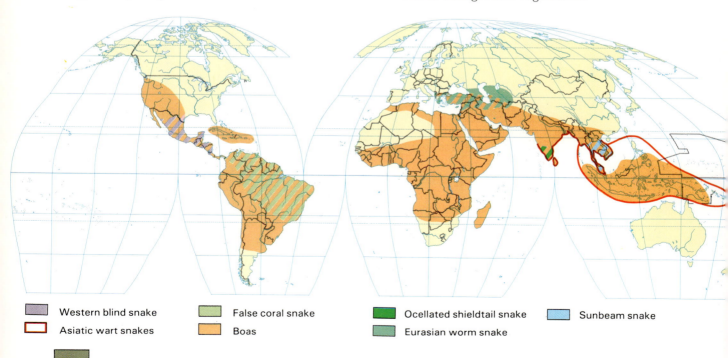

Western blind snake
Asiatic wart snakes
False coral snake
Boas
Ocellated shieldtail snake
Eurasian worm snake
Sunbeam snake

BELOW LEFT The map shows the geographical distribution of five species and two groups of snakes. **ABOVE** The royal python grows up to 6 ft. 6 in. long, and lives mainly in trees in dry, bushy areas of West Africa. It is also called the ball python, because when it is disturbed it coils up into a tight ball with its head tucked inside.
ABOVE RIGHT The intricate body markings of Indian pythons break up their outlines, making them hard to detect in the dappled light of the forest.

The 88 species of boas and pythons range throughout tropical and subtropical climates, and are famous for being the giants of the snake world. The reticulated python, one of the world's largest species of snake, reaches lengths of over 32 ft. The heaviest species is probably the anaconda, a semiaquatic snake from South America. A 29 ft. anaconda weighs over 440 lbs., almost twice the weight of a reticulated python of the same length.

Powerful predators

Despite having a layer of skin over their eyes, pythons and boas have fairly good vision. During the day, their eyes constrict to form vertical slits. At night, they widen, but are only useful for seeing prey at close range. Pythons and boas are deaf, but they have sensory pits on the scales on their lower and upper lips to detect movements on the ground. These pit linings are extremely sensitive to infrared radiation and act as efficient heat receptors. Each pit provides a wide field of detection. The heat sensing apparatus of the pythons and boas is the most sensitive of any animal, enabling them to detect the direction and distance of prey by the heat they emit. Even at night, the heat receptors detect changes of less than $0.0002°F$.

The powerful bodies of pythons and boas enable them to gain a strong hold on their prey. They catch their victims by lunging out with the front part of their bodies, securing the prey in a vice of sharp, backward-pointing teeth. Once secured, the snakes quickly immobilize their prey by wrapping coils around their bodies. At the same time, the pythons and boas contract their powerful body muscles, squeezing the victim to death.

The teeth of boas and pythons play an important role in securing their victims. The reticulated python has about a hundred very sharp teeth arranged in six rows, four above and two below. Unlike the previous families of burrowing snakes, elastic ligaments connect the two halves of their jaws, allowing pythons and boas to swallow prey up to the size of wild pigs and antelopes. Very occasionally, the largest species will kill and eat young or adult humans.

Once they have secured their prey in their jaws, pythons and boas secrete large amounts of saliva to help the food slide down their throats. If startled, they will regurgitate their prey. Although they consume large amounts at a single time, they in fact only eat their own body weight of food in a year. After swallowing a large victim, a boa or python may not need to eat again for several months.

Pythons and boas are generally able to travel skillfully and quickly across varied terrain. Large, thick-bodied individuals often move over the ground by first stretching out the front part of their bodies. The belly muscles then send waves of contraction down the body from head to tail. As the waves pass, the snake raises the underside of its body and carries it forward. Another method of locomotion involves the front third of the body thrusting forward and the rear part being drawn up behind. Boas can also move in a smooth, looping action, typical of the more advanced snakes, and they are able to climb trees.

Vibrating spurs

During the courtship of pythons and boas, males use their cloacal spurs to stimulate the female prior to mating. The male boa constrictor vibrates his spurs rapidly against the underside of the female, whereas the male python taps with slow, rhythmic movements that continue for several hours at a time.

All pythons lay eggs (although boas give birth to live young) and the number that they lay depends on the size of the female. A fully grown reticulated python lays up to 100 eggs, but a small female python lays as few as 15. After laying her eggs, the female arranges them in a heap and encircles them with her coils, bringing her head to rest on the top of the pile. The eggs stick together, helping to reduce loss of moisture from the egg surface.

Female pythons incubate their eggs for varying lengths of time. In the larger species, the female

RIGHT The reticulated python sometimes lies in wait for its prey in a tree, lunging at an animal when it passes within reach, and clamping it in its long, sharp teeth. It then coils itself around the animal, and by tightening its hold, slowly suffocates the victim or causes its blood vessels to burst. The python has an awesome capacity for swallowing large meals—one captive specimen swallowed a 77-lb. goat in the space of an hour. After feeding, a python may not eat again for weeks, or even months.

incubates them for two months until they hatch, raising her body temperature to keep them warm. There is often a difference of 12.6°F between the body temperature of the incubating mother and that of the external atmosphere. In cooler weather, the body coils of the female Indian python contract every few seconds, a habit that generates heat and maintains the heat of the egg at the 96.8°F necessary for incubation. Young pythons hatch from their eggs with the aid of an egg tooth, a sharp projection on the snout. They are usually more brightly colored than their parents.

Creatures of myth and legend

Pythons have played an important part in the traditional beliefs of some races of people who revere them for their great size and power. In former times, large villages in Liberia, West Africa, kept a living snake that represented a python god and was cared for by a priestess. Pythons were also thought to symbolize the souls of dead kings and noblemen. During the slave trade, West Africans, who were taken across to the Americas, established snake cults there, and these still exist on certain Caribbean islands and in northern Brazil. On Haiti, the snake is one of the thousands of gods or spirits that play a role in the religious cult known as voodoo.

ABOVE The African rock python is Africa's largest snake with individuals up to 25 ft. long having been recorded; most of the largest specimens have been exterminated, and the majority that are now seen are only 13 to 17 feet in length. Larger specimens prey on wart hogs, monkeys, small antelopes, and even crocodiles.

Australian Aborigines believe that before "the Dreaming"—a mythological period of time in which their tribal myths and religious rites evolved—all creation lay within the belly of Eingana (or Ungud), the Rainbow Snake. In addition, many Aboriginal myths tell of snakes swallowing people and animals.

Pythons

There are 24 species of true pythons, distributed over much of Africa, India, Southeast Asia and Australia. Most Asian forms have thick bodies and live mainly on the ground. Indo-Australian species tend to be more slender and live in trees.

The African rock python, growing up to 25 ft. in length, is the largest of the three species of pythons found in Africa. It ranges over much of sub-Saharan Africa. Adult African rock pythons frequent areas near water, but younger individuals prefer dry scrub and rocky areas. The most conspicuous feature of the

African rock python is a dark, arrowhead-shaped blotch on the top of its head. A pale stripe borders either side of the blotch.

Despite their infamous reputation for attacks on people, African rock pythons usually only attack small mammals. On one occasion, a 13-ft. snake consumed a 130-lb. impala antelope. However, in 1979, in a well-documented attack, a large African rock python seized a teenage boy in South Africa while he was herding cattle through an area of grassy plains. The boy was suffocated by the python before help arrived.

The royal python of West Africa is a small species, 6 ft. 6 in. in length, with a small head and short tail. Its markings form rosettes and contrast with its rich brown body color. It prefers dry bushland and cleared forest areas, and preys mainly on rodents. As a defense, the West African python coils up into a tight ball.

The reticulated python of Southeast Asia grows up to 33 ft. in length and takes its name from the network of dark, diamond-shaped markings on its background body color of light brown. Widespread in forested areas, it is common around villages where it feeds on rodents and domestic animals such as chickens and even dogs. It is also a powerful swimmer and has colonized islands far out to sea.

The Indian python is more strongly built, with a light gray body color and a bold pattern of rectangular markings. A darker subspecies of the Indian python occurs in Southeast Asia. Both forested and rocky areas are its favored habitats where it hunts mainly for small mammals.

Australasian species

The largest species of python to occur in Australia is the scrub or amethystine python. It also ranges through Southeast Asia, mainly in coastal mangroves. Growing up to 26 ft. in length, it can be identified by the numerous dark zigzag body markings. It lives in forested areas in the tropical north where it hunts birds and mammals, but will also take quite large prey, such as wallabies, on the ground.

The carpet python has a small head covered in small, irregular-shaped scales. Its coloration varies, but it generally has light spotted scales arranged in diamond-shaped patterns along its body. It tends to be most common in densely forested coastal regions of Australia and New Guinea. The centralian carpet python is marked with reddish or dark brown

ABOVE The carpet python of Australia and New Guinea is a slender, agile species that hunts both in the trees and on the ground. About 13 feet long, it catches small mammals and birds with its sharp teeth and squeezes them to death.

blotches. It was only described as a separate species in 1981 and appears to be confined to the rocky ranges of the interior of Australia.

Two species of Australian python, the woma and black-headed python, feed largely on other reptiles, including highly venomous types such as the tiger snake. They have rather indistinct heads and large head scales, and they lack the heat sensory pits typical of the python group. The woma is olive-green or reddish and lives mainly on the ground, in semi-desert areas of southern Australia. The black-headed python occurs over much of northern Australia and lives in a wide variety of habitats. The head, neck and throat are a glossy black. When disturbed, the black-headed python defends itself by raising the front part of its body and hissing loudly.

Tropical tree-dwellers

The 6 ft. 6 in.-long green tree python is a tree-dwelling member of the python group that ranges throughout northeast Australia, New Guinea and

LEFT The Children's python is a common Australian species that rarely grows to over 3 feet long. It lives in dry, bush country, and seeks refuge from the heat of the day by resting in the shade of tall termite mounds.

ABOVE Even carnivorous mammals, such as leopards, are not safe from attack by the larger python species—one Indian python killed and ate a full-grown leopard, an animal that weighs up to 100 lbs.

the Solomons. It has a bright green body flecked with blue, white and yellow. Often, a broken yellow stripe runs along the region of the backbone. The coloration of the green tree python merges well with the green, sun-dappled foliage, offering effective camouflage. Curiously, the head of the green tree python appears overly large in relation to its slender, flattened body and prehensile tail.

Razor-sharp teeth

During the night, the green tree python hunts for prey, especially birds that are vulnerable to attack as they settle down to roost. It has extremely sharp teeth that it uses to seize its victim. When resting during the day on a horizontal branch, the green tree python arranges its body into a series of folded loops, with its head at the center. Another python that adopts a

similar resting pose is the green or emerald tree boa of South America. Indeed, the green tree boa leads a very similar life-style to that of the green tree python, although they are entirely separate species living in different continents.

Despite the fact that it lives in trees, the green tree python lays its eggs on the forest floor. A short time after hatching, the bright yellow or brick-red young instinctively scale up trees. The young snakes then use their tails as a lure, wriggling them around to attract prey. Boelen's python is a less well-known arboreal species from New Guinea that lives only in mountain forests. It has a striking body pattern of black with conspicuous yellow bands.

Burrowing for rodents

Two species of pythons, the Calabar python and the Mexican burrowing python, belong to their own subfamilies. Although they come from different parts of the world, both species are burrowing. The Calabar python of West Africa has a small head and a round body and is less than 3 feet in length. All of these features are adaptations to aid burrowing. When threatened, it presses its head against the ground and moves its black-and-white tail in the air, mimicking the normal movements of its head so that the predator cannot distinguish the head from the tail. In addition to this form of defense mimicry, the Calabar python rolls its body coils into a tight ball if in danger.

The Calabar python hunts in the leaf litter of forested regions, mainly for rodents. It first seizes the animals and then smothers them by pressing them against the walls of its burrow. The Calabar python also climbs trees in search of prey, and is more active during the day than most species of pythons.

The Mexican burrowing python, the only New World python species, shares certain features with the sunbeam snake. Growing to 3 feet in length, it has a dark purple-brown color with paler markings and yellowish underparts. The Mexican burrowing python has a wedge-shaped head that it uses to dig into the surface of the ground. Although it burrows shallow tunnels in the ground, it does not lead an exclusively underground existence. Unusual for a burrowing snake, its eyes have keen vision. When in danger, it rolls up into a ball with the head tucked well into its body folds.

The boas

The 39 species of boa include the tree boas and the Old World sand boas, and they range throughout the tropics. Two-thirds of them inhabit the New World. One species, the rubber boa, ranges as far north as Washington State, on the border with Canada. The most famous member of the boa family is the boa constrictor of Central and South America, often believed to be a man-eating giant. In fact, most adults are about 10 ft. long and weigh around 132 lbs.

The boa constrictor has a wide geographic range, inhabiting areas as diverse as northern Mexico, the West Indies, Central America, and the southern continent of the Americas. Throughout its range, it occupies a variety of habitats from rain forest and cultivated land, to scrub and desert. The boa constrictor is especially common around crop plantations where it plays a useful role, feeding on rodent pests. Cream to brown in color, it has dark, saddle-shaped bands that widen and become more intense in color toward the tail.

The mighty anaconda

The anaconda, which can reach 32 ft. in length, is the heaviest of all the snakes. It inhabits the river

ABOVE The brown sand boa (a species also known as John's earth boa) measures less than 3 feet long, and is one of 10 species of boas that live in dry regions of southern Asia, from Iran to India. It can burrow quickly into the ground, using a ridge on its snout as a digging tool, but it moves slowly and clumsily on the surface. It kills rats, mice and other rodents by slowly crushing them, and avoids the extreme heat of the day by hiding beneath large rocks or resting in rodent burrows.

ABOVE The Calabar python of West Africa uses the similarity between its head (right) and tail to good effect when defending itself from a predator. It forms itself into a dense ball of coils in which it safely buries its head, then raises its tail and sways it about, as it would its head, in an aggressive display.

basins of the Amazon and Orinoco rivers in South America. The smaller, lighter-colored yellow anaconda lives only in wetland regions of Paraguay.

The patterning on the back of the anaconda is much less striking than that of other boas. Its background color is generally grayish brown, with large black patches that effectively camouflage the snake in the wet, thick vegetation of its habitat. It hunts both in the trees and in water, and its nostrils are placed on the top of its snout, rather like those of a crocodile (and for the same reason) to allow it to breathe easily when swimming. Anacondas are excellent swimmers, and are far more agile in the water than on land, where they spend much of their time coiled up on riverbanks or on branches overhanging the water. On occasions, they allow themselves to float downstream on mats of uprooted vegetation or fallen trees.

Attacking caimans

Despite the sensational tales about the anaconda's danger to humans, it never attacks people—on the contrary, it prefers to glide quietly away if it senses them nearby. It preys mainly on warm-blooded animals, usually birds and mammals up to the size of a capybara (a large, semiaquatic rodent), but it will also eat reptiles, such as turtles and the South American alligators known as caimans. There are reports of anacondas killing caimans over 6 ft. 6 in.

long. They seize their prey at the water's edge and quickly drag it into the water.

During the anacondas' courtship ritual, the male entwines his body round the female, and tickles her in the cloacal region with his vibrating spurs (vestiges of his hind limbs), stimulating her to mate. The female then raises her tail and opens her cloaca; the male inserts his hemipenis into the cloaca and mating takes place. Some months later, the female gives birth to up to 40 live young measuring about 24 in. long.

Coiled in the branches

Tree-dwelling species of boas from South America have large heads. In contrast to the pythons, the heat-sensitive organs of the tree boas lie between the scales of the lips rather than on the lips themselves.

The green or emerald tree boa of northern South America and Brazil grows to 6 ft. 6 in. in length and has bright green skin with a yellow underside. It has long, powerful foreteeth, and feeds mainly on birds. The powerful, prehensile tail of the green tree boa allows it to move effortlessly through trees with a concertina-like movement. First, it extends its body fully to reach a branch. Then it coils the front part of its body around the branch and hauls up the rear end. The powerful grip of the emerald tree boa also enables it to strangle its prey while hanging from a branch. The garden tree boa occurs in Central America, South America and the Antilles. It has a basic gray coloration with brown blotches edged with yellow. It feeds on birds, small mammals, especially bats, and lizards. Another species of tree boa, the Madagascar tree boa, closely resembles the boa constrictor.

North American scrub dwellers

The rubber boa of North America is a nocturnal snake that lives in diverse habitats from grassland and scrub to altitudes of up to 10,000 ft. in the mountain forests of the Rocky Mountains. Dark, shiny scales resembling rubber cover its stout body. The rubber boa grows to less than 6 feet in length. During the day, it rests under rocks and logs.

Leaf litter and topsoil are the principal hunting areas of the rubber boa, which burrows to shallow depths in search of small rodents. It also feeds on lizards and birds. When defending itself, the rubber boa lashes its tail from side to side to ward off rodents that prey on its young. It is a good climber, using its prehensile tail to investigate bushes and small trees for nestling birds. The other North American species is the rosy boa. It inhabits areas of scrub and rocky hillsides, often near oases or streams in the arid southwest of the USA. The body color of the rosy boa varies from a grayish pink to brown. It has three gray stripes running down the length of its body. The rosy boa is active mainly during the night, hunting for small mammals and birds.

Ambush in the sand

Sand boas form a group that have been separated from the other boas for over 50 million years of evolution. They are sometimes put in a separate family from the other boas. Sand boas inhabit hot, sandy desert regions of northern and eastern Africa and the Middle East, and they extend into Central Asia. One species lives in southeast Europe.

Sand boas have stout bodies, usually less than 36 in. long, and broad, spade-shaped heads that they use to unearth topsoil. Their bodies are often sandy in color, broken up by darker bars and blotches. They mostly live underground, hunting rodents in their burrows, but they appear above ground at night. They also catch prey by lying just below the surface of the soil. From this vantage point, they seize passing prey with a rapid, sidelong strike. Similarly, the rough-scaled sand boa of India and Pakistan lies half-buried beneath trees waiting for palm squirrels to descend. It also hunts ground-feeding birds such as hoopoes, babblers and quails. The rough-scaled sand boa is easy to identify because of the viper-like zigzag markings running down its back.

One of the smallest species, the 12-in. Mueller's sand boa of Africa, is a pale orange-brown with darker blotches. It lives at the edges of deserts where it hunts small rodents such as jerboas, as well as lizards.

Wood snakes

Wood snakes are often considered to belong to a separate subfamily from the other boas. Their center of distribution is the Caribbean islands. They have a more slender shape than other boas, and enlarged head-scales typical of more advanced snakes. Female wood snakes no longer have any traces of the small cloacal spurs that typify other boas and pythons. Their color and body patterns vary considerably, but they generally have a combination of fine markings,

SNAKES CLASSIFICATION: 4

Pythons and boas

The pythons and boas form the family Boidae, with 88 species grouped into 27 genera. They are distributed over most of Africa, southwest, Central and southern Asia, Indonesia, Australasia and South America, and also occur in a few parts of North America and southeast Europe. They are often divided into six subfamilies. (However, the number of subfamilies and the species within them differs from one system of classification to another, and some authorities prefer to consider them as separate families altogether.)

Most of the pythons are grouped in the subfamily Pythoninae, including the reticulated python, *Python reticulatus*, of Southeast Asia and the Philippines; the African rock python, *P. sebae*, which occurs over much of sub-Saharan Africa; the royal python, *P. regius*, of West Africa; the Indian python, *P. molurus*, which occurs in India, Sri Lanka and Southeast Asia; the Children's python, *Lialis childreni*, of Australia; the green tree python, *Chondropython viridis*, which ocurs in New Guinea and northern Australia; and the black-headed python, *Aspidites melanocephalus*, of Australia.

The subfamily Calabariinae contains only the Calabar python, *Calabaria reinhardti*, of West Africa, while the Mexican burrowing python, *Loxocemus bicolor*, from the Pacific coasts of Mexico and Central America is the sole member of the subfamily Loxoceminae.

Most of the boas belong to the subfamily Boinae, including the boa constrictor, *Boa constrictor*, of Mexico, the West Indies, Central America and much of South America; the green or emerald tree boa, *Corallus caninus*, and the anaconda, *Eunectes murinus*, both of northern South America; the rubber boa, *Charina bottae*, of western North America; the rosy boa, *Lichanura trivirgata*, of the southwestern USA and Mexico.

Members of the subfamily Tropidophiinae include the wood snakes of the genus *Tropidophis* and the rainbow boas of the genus *Epicrates*. These genera are both confined to the West Indies. The Round Island boa, *Bolyeria multicarinata*, is one of only two species in the subfamily Bolyeriinae, both of which are confined to Round Island in the Indian Ocean.

1637

LEFT The green tree boa lives in the tropical forests of northern South America, where it hunts birds and lizards at night, seizing them in its large jaws that are armed with forward-pointing teeth. When resting, the green tree boa folds its coils evenly over a horizontal branch with its head positioned at the center.

RIGHT The boa constrictor lives in Central and South America in a range of habitats, from deserts to rain forests, though it avoids water. A ground dweller, it is one of the largest of American snakes, growing to over 18 ft. long. On some Brazilian plantations, boa constrictors are valued, since they keep down the rodent populations.

speckles, spots and stripes. Most species live in rocky, wooded localities near caves. They hunt mainly lizards and sometimes seize bats as they fly to and from their roosting sites within caves.

Defense ritual

Wood snakes have a strange defense ritual. After coiling into a tight ball, the eyes and roof of the mouth exude blood, and, at the same time, the snake emits a foul smell from glands at the base of the tail.

There are many other species of boas, spread throughout the West Indies and Central and northern South America. Spiny boas live on the forest floor. They have ridged scales on their backs and upturned, spiny scales on their heads. The Oaxacan boa lives only in the mountain cloud forests of southern Mexico, where it hunts amphibians in the earth, under rocks and in fallen timber. It is completely black in color, with highly iridescent, polished scales.

The rainbow boa

Rainbow boas from the West Indies occur throughout the Caribbean. One of these, the Cuban boa (the largest boa on the island of Cuba), sometimes grows up to 10 feet long. As with all snakes, it is at risk from those who kill it out of fear and from those who wish to make a profit from its skin. As a result, few specimens of Cuban boas live long enough to grow to their full size. Cuban boas have become increasingly rare in recent years, but their decline began when sugarcane cultivation was introduced to the island, and the snakes lost their natural forest habitat. They might well have adapted to living in the sugarcane fields, but for the sugarcane harvesters who kill them with their machetes when they find them among the crops.

A particularly handsome species is the rainbow boa, with its orange back marked with large, irregular hoops, set off by a pearly, iridescent sheen. A docile snake that lives throughout the forests of Brazil and in Central America, it is one of the most long-lived of the boas, surviving for up to 27 years in captivity and reaching a length of 8 feet.

Madagascar boas

Little is known of the two species of boas that live on the island of Madagascar. They strongly resemble the typical boas and were once classified in the same genus as the boa constrictor. Nowadays, they are known as the Madagascar boa and the Madagascar tree boa. The latter has a shorter tail than a typical boa. It measures only one-tenth the length of the head and body combined (which amounts to 4 ft. 3 in.). The Madagascar tree boa lives in the rain forests of the eastern coast, where it preys almost entirely on birds.

Last of the Round Island boas

Round Island, a tiny island lying some 15 mi. northeast of Mauritius in the Indian Ocean, is home to two rare species of boa—both slender snakes that burrow. One of these, the Round Island boa, may already be extinct. It was last seen in 1974 and that was the only

ABOVE The anaconda is a massively built reptile that may weigh 485 lbs. or more, making it the heaviest snake in the world. One specimen, which was 27 ft. in length, measured more than 3 feet around the thickest part of its body.

BELOW An anaconda can kill animals as large as a 6-ft.-6 in. caiman (a type of alligator) by strangling it in its coils. Every time the prey breathes out, the snake tightens its grip still further, until eventually the victim dies of suffocation.

sighting in 40 years. The other species is the keel-scaled boa. Thought to number around 75 individuals in the wild, the species is being bred in a zoo in Jersey. The snakes have become rare due to the destruction of their palm forest habitat on the island, together with the introduction of domestic animals such as pigs and rats that prey on the young snakes.

The advanced snakes

The last three families of snakes are known as the advanced snakes, a category that includes most of the species alive today. These are the colubrid or so-called "harmless snakes"; the front-fanged snakes, or elapids, such as the cobras, taipan, kraits, mambas and sea snakes; and the vipers. All have venom glands, a specialization that varies with their degree of evolutionary development. In the harmless snakes, these glands are fairly simple (although most harmless snakes are no danger to humans, a few from tropical Asia and Africa are capable of killing people, and some have mild venom for subduing small prey). The venom glands of the front-fanged snakes are much more developed, while those of the vipers are the most highly refined.

Venomous colubrids have long, tusk-like back teeth, often with grooves running down their length,

connected to the venom-producing glands in the upper jaw. When the snake grasps its prey in its mouth, the venom pours down the grooves, entering the skin of the snake's victim through the wounds. Among these snakes, the venom is used mainly for hunting.

The evolution of the poison apparatus evolved further with the appearance of the front-fanged snakes. As their name indicates, the poison fangs of these snakes are located in the front part of the mouth. They are longer than those of the harmless snakes, and the grooves are partly closed at the surface, so that most of the venom travels down an inner channel. In this way, the poison can be injected into the victim more directly. The fangs are fixed in the upper jaw, and when the snake closes its mouth, they fit into pockets in the lower lip.

Storing the poison

As the fangs of front-fanged snakes developed, so the poison glands grew larger, with several lobes acting as storage chambers for the poison. When the snake bites its victim, special muscles squeeze the storage chambers, forcing the venom down through the grooved fangs and into the wound.

Some cobras have modified, forward-facing fang grooves, enabling the spitting cobras—such as the black-necked cobra, for example—to spit their venom over a distance of up to 10 feet. If it enters the eyes of a threatening animal or human, the venom can cause temporary or even permanent blindness, allowing the snake to make its getaway in safety. By spitting venom, the snake is able to keep its predator at a distance. Spitting is usually used only for defense, rather than for capturing prey, when the snake generally uses an ordinary bite to overcome its victim.

The poison apparatus has developed to an even greater degree among the vipers and pit vipers. In these reptiles, the fangs are also located in the front of the mouth, but they are even longer than those of cobras. When the snake is at rest, the fangs fold back against the upper jawbone. When the mouth opens, a simple mechanism constructed from several bones swivels the fangs forward, ready for action.

Death by injection

The grooves in the fangs of vipers and pit vipers are fused at the surface to form open-ended tubes. These act as hypodermic needles when the snake sinks them

ABOVE The rainbow boa occurs in Central America, the Caribbean and northern South America. It lives in rocky crevices, among loose stones and on farmland, where it feeds on birds and rodents that it captures at night among the trees. Like many boas, it can become quite tame—boas are kept in some villages to keep down the numbers of rats.

into its victim, injecting venom pumped out by the poison glands. In many species of vipers, such as the Gaboon viper, these glands occur at each side of the head. Because the glands are so large, their heads are much broader than those of non-venomous snakes.

The effectiveness of a snake's bite depends partly on the potency of the venom and partly on the length of the fangs—the longer the fangs, the deeper the poison is injected. Among the deadliest venoms are those of two Australian snakes, the taipan and the eastern brown snake, and several of the sea snakes.

One group of snakes that do not fit into the general pattern of fang development are the burrowing asps. They are classified among the harmless snakes, but despite this, have folding fangs similar to those of vipers instead of the short, rear fangs typical of their family.

Colubrid snakes

The family known as the colubrid or "harmless snakes" is by far the largest of the snake families, with 1562 species found throughout the tropical and temperate world (with the exception of southern Australia). They include snail-eating snakes, hognosed snakes, egg-eating and rear-fanged snakes, as well as water snakes and king snakes. These snakes have diversified to occupy the widest range of habitats: some tree-dwelling species, such as the vine snakes, have long, extremely slender bodies that allow them to

Boomslang

Tentacled snake

Corn snake

Mangrove snake

Red-striped ribbon snake

Egg-eating snake

Horseshoe snake

King snake

Cat snake

lurk unseen among creepers; aquatic types, such as the spotted water snake of northern Australia, have nostrils on top of their snouts, enabling them to breathe while almost totally submerged. Burrowing snakes, such as the southern mole viper of South Africa, have reinforced heads that they use to drill underground tunnels.

The diet of colubrids varies considerably among the different groups, and some species have become specialists at preying on particular animals. Many have developed poison glands connected to short, rear fangs, but few are capable of poisoning large animals. One exception is the boomslang (the Afrikaans word for "tree snake"), a tree-dwelling snake that readily uses its venom for defense, and is quite capable of killing an adult human.

Alternating scales

The fossil records suggest that one group of colubrid snakes, the xenodermin snakes, were once far more numerous and widespread than they are today. Now confined to southern and Southeast Asia, they have unusual vertebral bones that have flattened and broadened to form plates. Most xenodermin

ABOVE When threatened, the eastern hognosed snake of eastern North America flattens out its head and neck, inflates its body with air, opens its mouth with its curious upturned snout, and hisses loudly. Though they are completely harmless to humans, the startling defensive displays of hognosed snakes have earned them a fearsome reputation and their popular names "hissing adders" and "blow vipers" (in fact, they belong to a separate family from the adders and vipers).

snakes are heavily built, but one species from Indonesia and Malaysia has a slender body. Unique for a snake, the scales on its flanks are of different sizes and run alternately—one large, one small. It spends most of its time underground, digging its way into sand, soft cultivated soil or swampy ground. It preys on amphibians such as frogs and toads, and, like other xenodermin snakes, it lays two to four eggs.

Snail eaters

The Asiatic snail-eating snakes or bluntheads are dietary specialists, for they prey almost exclusively on snails and slugs. Mostly nocturnal in their habits, they have slender bodies, large eyes and short, broad heads with strong jaws. The jaws are reinforced with fused scales that give the mouth greater rigidity than the mouths of other snakes.

The chins of Asiatic snail-eating snakes lack the distinctive fold (called the mental groove), that in most species enables the mouth to stretch out and engulf large items of prey.

Asiatic snail-eating snakes are unable to break snail shells with their jaws. Instead, when a species has a snail in its grasp, it pushes its blunt snout against the shell and inserts its lower jaw into the opening (the lower jaw can be extended independently of the upper jaw). It then sinks its two sharp, curved teeth into the snail's soft body and retracts its jaw to hook the victim out of the shell.

The American snail-eating snakes include several species, such as the common snail-eating snake, that range over Central and South America from Mexico to Brazil. They are very similar to their Asiatic relatives, and use the same technique to extract snails from their shells.

The dwarf snakes and reed snakes of southern Asia comprise some 80 species of colubrids that are all similar in appearance. Their small, blunt heads blend smoothly into their bodies, with no obvious neck, their eyes are small, and their cylindrical bodies are encased in extra-smooth scales. In many ways they resemble worms, and they spend much of their life concealed in soft earth. Worms make up a large part of their diet, but they also feed on the larvae of ants and termites. The many-toothed snake and its relatives form another group of southern Asian colubrids, with thick-set heads and no obvious necks. Their teeth are broadened into blades which give them a secure grip on the tough-skinned lizards that form their main prey.

Upturned snouts

The hognosed snakes of North America and the toad eaters of Central and South America share a curious facial feature—they have upturned snouts, formed from pointed, curved scales on the upper jaw. All are excellent burrowers, though they spend most of their lives above ground.

Although they sometimes feed on turtles' eggs, small snakes, lizards, frogs and salamanders, hognosed snakes and toad eaters mainly prey on toads. Toads might seem easy prey, but many of them secrete

BELOW The map shows the geographical distribution of three species of colubrids—the grass snake, rhombic egg-eating snake, and mussurana; two species of front-fanged snakes—the Egyptian cobra and common sea snake; and two vipers—the cascavel and southern fer-de-lance.

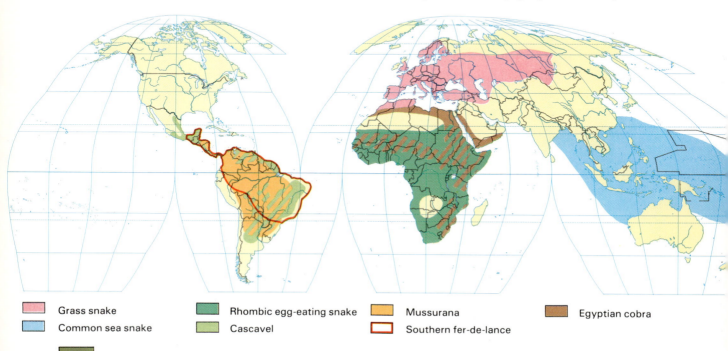

- Grass snake
- Common sea snake
- Rhombic egg-eating snake
- Cascavel
- Mussurana
- Southern fer-de-lance
- Egyptian cobra

poisonous substances from their skin that, in some species, are powerful enough to kill predators. Hognosed snakes combat this defense mechanism with their own venomous saliva. The saliva seems to neutralize the poison from the toads' skin and render it harmless. It is not powerful enough to kill prey immediately, and a toad bitten by one of these snakes will take about 24 hours to die.

Playing dead

The western hognosed snake of the USA has smooth scales and large eyes with round pupils. It reaches up to 32 in. in length. In appearance and behavior it resembles a viper, but it is unable to defend itself with poison fangs in the way that a viper can. When disturbed near cover, it immediately retreats to safety, but if it is caught out in the open, far from shelter, it resorts to a dramatic sequence of defensive tactics. When first attacked it reacts with rage, flattening its head and neck, spitting and hissing loudly and striking out furiously at its enemy. It performs the angry scene several times, but if it is unsuccessful, the snake will try a different tactic. Leaving a short pause after its final strike, it suddenly freezes, opens its mouth wide, stretches out its trembling body and gives a few spasmodic twitches of its tail. A few convulsive jerks of the body follow, before the snake rolls over on its back and lies on the ground as if dead. If lightly pushed, it rocks to and fro like a rigid corpse.

The snake continues to feign death for some time. It then lifts its head—still keeping its body rigid—and glances around to assess the danger. If the enemy is still close by, it resumes its corpse-like position, but otherwise it slowly straightens up and slides away.

Egg swallowers

The egg-eating snakes of Africa and India are famous for their ability to swallow hard-shelled birds' eggs that are much larger than their own heads. Most snakes are adapted to swallow large objects. They have loosely attached jawbones that give them an extremely broad gape, and their skin is elastic enough to stretch well beyond the limits of most other animals' skin.

In the case of the egg-eating snakes, the ability to swallow large objects has been refined. The skin at the sides of the snake's mouth can stretch to an extraordinary extent, and the two halves of the lower

SNAKES CLASSIFICATION: 5

Colubrid snakes

The colubrid or harmless snakes of the family Colubridae form by far the largest family of snakes, with 1562 species grouped in 292 genera. They occur on all the continents except Antarctica, reaching as far north as Arctic Scandinavia, and as far south as the tip of South America. Zoologists have classified the family in a variety of different ways, some suggesting as many as 20 subfamilies.

Some members of the family are the common snail-eating snake, *Dipsas indica*, of tropical South America; the dwarf snakes of the genus *Calamaria* from Southeast Asia and Indonesia; the western hognosed snake, *Heterodon nasicus*, of the western USA; the rhombic or common egg-eating snake, *Dasypeltis scabra*, of Africa; and the Cape centipede-eater, *Aparallactus capensis*, of southern Africa.

The rear-fanged snakes form a large group within the colubrid family. Members of this group include the tentacled snake, *Erpeton tentaculatum*, the mangrove snake, *Boiga dendrophila*, and the Asian vine snake, *Dryophis nasuta*, all of Southeast Asia; the flying snake or golden tree snake, *Chrysopelea ornata*, of Southeast Asia, Sri Lanka and parts of India; the boomslang, *Dispholidus typus*, of tropical and southern Africa; the cat snake, *Telescopus fallax*, of southeast Europe, Malta and southwest Asia; the Montpellier or lizard snake, *Malpolon monspessulanus*, of southern Europe; and the mussurana, *Clelia clelia*, of tropical South America.

Another group of colubrids is the water snakes and garter snakes, two members of which are the European grass snake, *Natrix natrix*, of Europe, northwest Africa and Asia, and the common garter snake, *Thamnophis sirtalis*, of southern Canada and the USA. The rat snakes, racers and king snakes make up a further group of colubrids that includes the common king snake, *Lampropeltis getulus*, of North America; the western whip snake, *Coluber viridiflavus*, of southern and central Europe; the Aesculapian snake, *Elaphe longissima*, which ranges from France through eastern Europe to northern Iran; and the smooth snake, *Coronella austriaca*, which is widespread in Europe and also occurs in the western USSR, Turkey and Iran.

jaw are highly flexible, allowing the mouth to expand around the largest eggs. Extensions of the neck vertebrae protrude through the wall of the gullet and are enameled like real teeth. These "vertebral teeth" act like a saw blade to slit the shell of the egg as it passes down the gullet on its way to the snake's stomach.

Once it finds an egg, an egg-eating snake grasps it in its mouth and, angling its head down to stop the egg from slipping away, it pushes the bulky object through its jaws. The skin at the sides of the mouth and throat stretch so much that the scales become widely separated. When the egg reaches its neck, the snake closes its mouth and rests its snout on the ground. It then contracts its muscles to push the egg still further backward. As the egg passes the vertebral teeth, the shell splits open lengthways and the contents are squeezed into the snake's stomach. As soon as the food reaches its stomach, the egg-eating snake opens its mouth and, with a series of convulsive movements, regurgitates the unwanted shell.

The most common African species is the rhombic egg-eating snake, which lives in a wide variety of habitats south of the Sahara. It reaches about 30 in. in length, and is active both during the day and night. It feeds ravenously in the spring and summer when birds are nesting, laying down a store of fat for the winter. The coloration of individuals varies to match the local soil color, and some species mimic the colors and patterns of venomous snakes, such as night adders, to gain protection from predators.

Battles with centipedes

The burrowing asps and centipede eaters of Africa and the Middle East have all the features typical of an

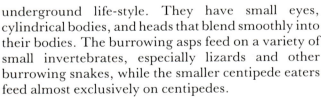

LEFT AND ABOVE An egg-eating snake has a head that is less than half the diameter of a hen's egg, yet it has little difficulty in swallowing an egg whole. In the top row of pictures (from left to right) the snake opens its lower jaw, which is only loosely attached to the rest of its skull, and begins to engulf the egg. It leans down on the egg to keep it still, and gradually works it inside its mouth cavity. In the lower row of photographs the snake starts to push the egg down its body by strong movements of its muscles (far left). When the egg reaches the part of the gullet where sharp extensions of the vertebral bones slit the shell open, it collapses and the contents are sucked out (center left). Finally, the empty shell is cast out of its mouth and the snake settles back to digest its meal (left). Egg-eating snakes only swallow fresh eggs, and can judge whether eggs are still good to eat by testing the shells with their sensitive tongues. They occur in both Africa and India.

underground life-style. They have small eyes, cylindrical bodies, and heads that blend smoothly into their bodies. The burrowing asps feed on a variety of small invertebrates, especially lizards and other burrowing snakes, while the smaller centipede eaters feed almost exclusively on centipedes.

The Cape centipede eater is a small snake, generally measuring 10-12 in. in length, though some specimens reach 16 in. It inhabits the open savannahs of southern Africa, where it lurks among grass roots or on top of low bushes, clumps of earth and termite mounds. Though it is attracted to termite mounds by the large amount of eggs and larvae there, centipedes remain its favorite prey. These creatures can present a major problem for a small snake, since a tropical centipede may measure over 6 in. in length and is armed with its own poison fangs. Fierce battles are quite common, both animals giving powerful bites. The snake usually wins, however, and celebrates its victory by swallowing the centipede headfirst.

Rear-fanged colubrids

The rear-fanged group of colubrids have venom glands that secrete poison through grooved fangs at the rear of their upper jaws. These venom glands are separate from their salivary glands. In many cases, they produce an extremely potent poison, but the fact that rear-fanged snakes have no venom storage sacs limits the amount of toxic substance available for a single bite. The snakes also lack the specialized venom-pumping muscles of more advanced snakes. Instead of pumping its poison directly into the wound, the venom is secreted into the snake's mouth to find its own way into the bite wound—although channels in

ABOVE The mangrove snake is a nocturnal hunter from the rain forests and mangrove swamps of Southeast Asia. It is mainly a tree dweller that hunts for birds and their eggs in the branches, but it also descends to ground level to prey on rodents.

the fangs direct it into the bite holes. Few of these snakes have venom strong enough to be of danger to humans.

Species of rear-fanged snakes range throughout Southeast Asia, New Guinea and northern Australia. Inhabiting fresh and brackish water, and marine tidal zones, aquatic rear-fanged snakes have adapted well to their habitat. Their nasal openings are on the upperpart of their snout, enabling them to breathe while swimming half-submerged. In addition, they have valves in their nostrils which they can close, enabling them to swim underwater. As with many types of water snakes, they give birth to live young. Aquatic rear-fanged snakes have reduced ventral scales across their underparts, since they do not need them for movement over land.

Tree-dwelling species of rear-fanged snakes are extremely long and slender. Instead of the usual flat scales, they have keeled scales on their underparts. Ground-dwelling species of rear-fanged snakes, which have shorter, tapering bodies and well-defined heads, resemble other typical colubrid snakes.

Nocturnal hunter

A common species of long-tailed water snake inhabits areas of Southeast Asia. Although it can move over ground, this 3ft.-long species never strays far from water. It has small eyes with vertical pupils—an indication of its nocturnal habits. It stalks frogs, toads and fish by moonlight in the swamps and paddy fields of its watery habitat. Occasionally, it emerges from the water to pursue amphibians, but it rapidly returns at the first hint of danger.

Unique plant eater

The tentacled snake, or fishing snake, is another aquatic species. Reaching a length of 28 in., it ranges throughout southern China, Thailand and northern Malaysia. As with other water snakes, the tentacled snake prefers brackish waters that are rich in vegetation, although it occasionally strays from river estuaries to the seashore. The tentacled snake usually preys on fish and other small animals, but it also feeds on plant matter, a unique feature among snakes.

Another distinctive feature of this strange-looking snake is its head. Slightly flattened in shape and broad at the rear, it has two sealed, movable appendages at the front of the snout. These are tentacle-like in appearance, extending forward like antennae. Their

purpose is unknown, but they probably have some sensory function. The tentacled snake's body is round and covered with small, keeled scales. Its eyes are small with vertical pupils. As with all water snakes, it has nostrils on the upperpart of its snout.

The mangrove snake, an arboreal creature that descends to the ground to hunt, has narrow, oval pupils that dilate in darkness. As a nocturnal reptile, it preys chiefly on birds, but also takes mammals, amphibians and even other snakes—both harmless and venomous—hunting them by night through the long, external roots of mangrove trees near swamps and groves in Malaysia. It also ranges throughout Southeast Asia, Indonesia and the Philippines. In color, the 6 ft.-6 in.-long body of the mangrove snake is blue-black and usually has lateral yellow crossbands, a yellow top lip and yellow underparts with black spots. It is a highly venomous species.

Airborne species

Several tree-dwelling colubrids, including the flying snake and the various species of whip snakes, are spectacular fliers, able to take off from branches and glide to a landing site. The twig snake, originating in tropical Africa, is a typically arboreal snake and has a very slender body that measures up to 5 ft. in length.

ABOVE Elegant even when at rest, the paradise flying snake becomes a spectacular sight when it flattens out its body and launches itself into the air to glide from branch to branch in the forest canopy, or from the top of a tall tree to the ground.

It also has an equally slender, slightly pointed head and large eyes with horizontally elongated pupils. Normally, the twig snake populates treetops, bushes or luxuriant vegetation that harbor the small birds and lizards that form much of its diet.

Two ridges of scales run along either side of its body, enabling the twig snake to climb trees, and it can make its way up the smoothest trunks with ease. Once among the branches, it glides through the foliage, clinging to branches with its tail. When descending, the snake holds itself rigid, spreading its body flat to lower air resistance.

The most dramatic of all the tree-dwelling snakes are the two species of flying snakes—long, slender-bodied reptiles with large, round pupils and grooved fangs. Their elongated bodies end in a very slender tail, giving the snakes excellent grip and allowing them to climb smooth tree trunks without difficulty. In addition, both species of flying snakes can move extremely quickly through the branches to catch fast-moving geckos and other tree-dwelling lizards.

1649

LEFT The grass-green vine snake curls its sinuous body around creepers and vines in the tropical forests of southern Asia. It hunts for small prey, especially young birds.
ABOVE The boomslang is one of the few colubrid snakes that are venomous enough to kill a human being. It delivers highly toxic venom to its victims through three large, grooved fangs.
RIGHT The cat snake feeds almost entirely on lizards, and takes its name from the stealth with which it stalks them.

The most startling characteristic of the flying snakes is their ability to fall through the air and land without injuring themselves. They cannot actually fly, but they drop from one branch to a lower one so quickly that they appear to be gliding. During flight, the snake flattens its whole body to lower air resistance. It can glide down to ground level from the treetops, resuming its normal rounded shape when it lands.

Slender coils

The vine snakes of southern India and Burma are similar, having extremely slender, laterally compressed bodies and long, fine, whip-like tails. They have stream-lined pointed heads and their large eyes have horizontal pupils. The Asian vine snake is brilliant green in color, with two yellow stripes running the length of its underparts. Its green body-color provides excellent camouflage among the vines and creepers of its natural wooded habitat. It grows to 5 ft. in length and hunts by day among the bushes and treetops, preying on lizards, small birds and snakes that it kills by crushing in its slender coils.

A distinctive facial feature of the Asian vine snake is the set of grooves that decorate the upper part of its snout. Together with the elongated shape of the pupils, these grooves give the Asian vine snake some measure of binocular vision. By swiveling both eyes forward, it can peer down the grooves to focus on a target with both eyes at once, an ability that allows it to assess distance with considerable accuracy. When threatened, the Asian vine snake raises itself partly off the ground and widens part of its body and neck scales to reveal the black, underlying skin. At the same time, it opens its mouth to display its black lining threateningly. Although venomous, it is not harmful to humans.

Docile but dangerous

In contrast to most colubrids, the venom of the tree-dwelling boomslang of tropical and southern Africa is capable of killing a man. But the boomslang rarely bites humans and is fairly docile. It has a slender body and grows up to 6 feet long. The boomslang has a short, stumpy, slightly curved snout with round eyes and round pupils. Its slender body is green-brown in color with compressions from side to side and a covering of narrow, ridged scales.

Because of its body camouflage and slender shape, the boomslang is ideally suited to tree dwelling. It moves swiftly through the tree canopy in search of lizards, birds and eggs, killing its prey with large, grooved poison fangs mounted at the back of its jaws.

TOP AND ABOVE The coloration of the mussurana from tropical South America changes dramatically from the juvenile (top) to the adult (above).
BELOW The mussurana preys on other snakes, including highly venomous lance-heads. Immune to its victim's venom, a mussurana (A) subdues a fer-de-lance (B) by crushing it in its coils. The mussurana also kills small mammals using its poison fangs.

A

B

The position of these fangs, coupled with the fact that the snake lacks the venom-pumping muscles characteristic of more highly evolved snakes, means that relatively little venom enters the prey.

Deadly venom

Even though the boomslang injects no more than one milligram of venom into its prey, the power of the venom is sufficient to kill a monkey or dog in under an hour. It will also kill an adult human. The venom of the boomslang is more powerful than that of cobras and vipers. However, these more advanced snakes inject more venom in a single bite. The boomslang prefers small prey that it can immobilize with a deep bite. Venom enters the wounds caused by the fangs, killing the small victim almost immediately. If annoyed, the boomslang will puff up its neck and the front part of its body, staring straight at its enemy. In the process, it doubles in girth and the scales covering the distended skin move far apart. If this threat posture has no effect, it will strike.

Vertical pupils

The ground-dwelling cat snake of Africa has highly toxic venom, but its fangs are positioned even further back in the jaw than those of the boomslang, making it incapable of injecting a lethal dose into a human. It has a well-defined head, large eyes with vertical pupils and a slender body. The cat snake grows to 31 in. in length and is active at dawn, dusk and during the night. Occasionally, it appears during the day. The cat snake prefers stony ground, as it provides an ideal purchase for the reptile's body, giving it a good turn of speed. Usually, it preys on small birds and mammals, as well as the occasional lizard. It lays 5 to 7 eggs, each measuring about one inch.

Metallic highlights

The largest of the European colubrid snakes is the Montpellier or lizard snake, found throughout the coastal regions of the Mediterranean. The females are bigger than the males (as in most species of snakes), and can reach over six feet in length. Their coloration varies greatly, although most typically they are olive with metallic highlights. The Montpellier snake has a slender body with a long, thin tail and a long head, equipped with large eyes with round pupils. In the forepart of the upper jaw, the

Montpellier snake has several small teeth, followed by a short gap and a pair of grooved fangs at the rear of the upper jaw. Its venom is highly potent and probably dangerous to man if a large specimen delivers the bite. The venom causes numbing, stiffness and fever for several hours in humans.

Montpellier snakes are extremely agile—they are fast-moving, excellent climbers and fearsome hunters. They hunt by day, preying on mammals, birds and their young, lizards, and other large snakes. They are aggressive creatures and, if disturbed, often turn on their attackers, hissing and biting at the same time. Montpellier snakes mate in spring, and in early summer the females lay from four to 20 eggs, each about two inches long, amid vegetation on the ground. The adults spend the cold European winters hibernating in deep holes.

Snake killer

The richly vegetated area between Guatemala and Brazil is the home of the mussurana, a large, harmless snake that preys on other snakes. It also preys on small mammals, crushing them between its coils and then poisoning them by delivering a fatal bite with the large fangs positioned far back in its mouth. The mussurana preys particularly on rattlesnakes and the venomous lance-head snakes.

After spotting a rattlesnake, the mussurana attacks quickly with its head raised high off the ground. Once within range, the snake lunges forward, bites the rattlesnake and wraps four or five coils around its body. The victim defends itself by repeatedly delivering deep bites into the mussurana, injecting doses of venom that would prove fatal to any other animal, but to no effect. Similarly, the venom of the mussurana has no effect on the rattlesnake, and the two enemies wrestle fiercely. Deprived of its main weapon, the rattlesnake stands little chance, and invariably succumbs from suffocation following prolonged constriction. The mussurana then swallows it whole. In South America, farmers are generally careful to leave the mussurana unmolested, since its taste for rattlesnakes helps rid the farm of a dangerous pest.

The water and garter snakes

Water snakes and garter snakes are a large group of aquatic and land-dwelling colubrids that are found throughout the temperate and tropical world. Despite

ABOVE A Montpellier or lizard snake of southern Europe is a fast, agile predator that mainly catches lizards and small birds. Adults also eat other snakes and small mammals, and the young eat invertebrates. Montpellier snakes usually live in warm, dry habitats, but they sometimes occur in damp woods and on riverbanks, occasionally entering the water to swim. It is the largest of all the colubrid snakes that occur in Europe, with a maximum length of over six feet.

ABOVE A group of newly hatched European grass snakes bask in the sun, their distinctive yellow collars standing out against the olive and gray coloration of their bodies. Up to 40 white eggs are laid in each batch, and they are placed in warm locations that include manure or compost heaps.

their adaptability in colonizing wide varieties of habitat, they are strikingly similar in appearance.

Ranging in size from 24 in. to 6 ft. 6 in. long, many water and garter snakes have powerful bodies and well-defined heads. Their teeth increase in size toward the rear of the upper jaw, while teeth on the lower jaw are regular. As aquatic and semiaquatic snakes, they are excellent swimmers, preying largely on fish and amphibians. Other species are mainly land-dwelling reptiles.

The range of the water snakes is vast, spreading from North America to Africa and into Indonesia. A particularly familiar species of water snake is the European grass snake, ranging throughout Europe, North Africa and Central Asia. Because of the isolation of numerous local populations of European grass snakes, several subspecies have evolved. Generally, these differ in color, size and shape. An identifiable feature of all the subspecies is a yellow-white collar on the nape of the neck. Sometimes the collar divides into two sections at the nape. The body color of the European grass snake varies according to its habitat, but it is normally olive-green or gray, with dark speckles on its back. In shape, its head also varies according to subspecies. An adult grass snake usually measures from 35 to 47 in. in length. On rare occasions, there are sightings of female European grass snakes that measure 6 ft. 6 in. in length.

Swimming for prey

The European grass snake inhabits dry and wet terrain. It mainly hunts in moist places and swamps. The snake often appears swimming half-submerged in marshes and ditches or crossing slow-running rivers. Although the European grass snake swims with its head above water, it can remain submerged for long periods of time if a predator is nearby. Occasionally, the grass snake swims out to sea, reaching a distance of several miles from the shore. It also appears far from its watery habitat—on chalk hills, sandy heaths, in open woodland and under hedges.

When hunting in water, the European grass snake preys on fish, frogs, toads and newts. It also takes mice, lizards, eggs and even small birds. When the snake captures its prey in water, it carries the victim onto dry land and then swallows it alive. European grass snakes are venomous, but the venom largely helps in digestion, speeding up the breakdown of the prey's skin. It is not potent enough to overcome the prey, and the snake relies largely on its sharp, backward-pointing teeth to grip its prey and prevent its escape. Once the victim is inside the jaws of the European grass snake, a gland in the snake's mouth secretes a lubricating mucus that coats the prey and allows it to slip into the digestive tract more easily.

Foul-smelling liquid

When disturbed by a predator, the European grass snake usually slips away as quickly and quietly as possible. If escape is impossible, it emits loud, intimidating hisses, similar to those of an adder. In addition, the European grass snake produces a foul-smelling liquid from its cloacal gland. Another feature of the defense ritual is mimicry. After enacting convulsions, the European grass snake feigns death and remains motionless on the ground, upturning its

underparts. Its mouth lies open and its tongue hangs out. It even produces a few drops of blood from its mouth by the voluntary rupture of certain minor blood vessels in its palate. If the danger subsides, the snake then escapes.

Compost heaps

Mating takes place in spring, soon after the snakes emerge from their winter hibernation. In mid-summer, the female lays a cluster of 10-45 elongated eggs. These adhere to each other by a jelly-like substance. Sometimes, several females lay their eggs in the same nest. Compost heaps provide particularly suitable sites for a nest since they generate heat and thereby incubate the eggs—up to 1500 eggs have been found in a single common nest. Incubation usually lasts for two months. The newly hatched snakes are 7.5 in. long and double in size in the first year of their lives. Initially, the young feed on worms, tadpoles and insect larvae, but as they grow, they graduate to larger prey such as frogs and toads.

Colorful stripes

The garter snakes live in ponds and streams ranging throughout North America, Canada and Mexico. Garter snakes are non-venomous, slender snakes marked with long stripes. The common garter snake is black, brown or red in color with yellow, orange or red stripes. In length, it rarely exceeds 24 in., although exceptional individuals of more than 3 feet in length occur occasionally. They are the commonest snakes in North America, appearing throughout southern Canada and the eastern USA.

Like grass snakes, garter snakes adapt well to water, and they often hunt aquatic prey such as fish and

ABOVE LEFT The dice snake is a close relative of the European grass snake. Both species are aquatic, but whereas the grass snake often inhabits woodlands and hedgerows, the dice snake comes onto dry land only to bask or hibernate.

ABOVE Garter snakes are common throughout North America, reaching as far north as Alaska. Most species are patterned with thin, horizontal stripes, like the fancy garters that were once fashionable for holding up men's socks.

frogs. Their land-based prey includes toads, salamanders, mice and occasionally birds' eggs. Young garter snakes survive almost exclusively on earthworms for their first year.

Remarkably for snakes, garter snakes are sociable creatures. They live in large groups made up of several hundred individuals. The groups spend the winter in communal underground nests, coiled together for warmth. Because garter snakes have the most northerly distribution of any reptile in the Western Hemisphere, reaching the sub-Arctic areas of the Yukon, their communal nests are important for their survival. Garter snakes have a high level of cold tolerance and enter hibernation later than any other reptile. Conversely, they are the first to emerge from their winter quarters in early March.

After hibernation, garter snakes begin to mate, often at a place near to their winter quarters. If climatic temperatures are unsuitable, garter snakes will not mate. In Canada it has been observed that the right temperature for one subspecies of the common garter snake is about 59°F.

The mating ritual itself can be spectacular. When a female garter snake emerges from her winter nest, rival males compete to mate with her by wrapping themselves around her. As a result, the female

THE SMOOTH SNAKE
— AN ELUSIVE LIZARD EATER —

The smooth snake ranges throughout Europe, from Norway to southern Italy and into Iran and Turkey. It also inhabits scattered lowland heaths in southern Britain. With a population of only 2000, it is Britain's rarest snake. Sometimes mistaken for an adder, the male smooth snake has a brown back, while the female's is gray-brown. Two to four rows of dark brown spots run down their backs.

The 29.5 in.-long smooth snake has several distinguishing features. Its head is small, oval and flat, and a dark streak runs from the nostrils through each eye to the corners of the mouth. It has small eyes with round pupils, quite unlike the vertical slit pupils of the adder. It is also slimmer than the adder, and its body scales have no keels or ridges, giving it a smooth body surface—as its name suggests.

If cornered, the smooth snake coils its body into an S-shape, hisses and then strikes with the intention of biting. However, its small teeth can only cause minor injuries. It is an elusive snake, and normally avoids confrontations by slipping away into the undergrowth. In Britain, the smooth snake was not discovered by scientists until 1853.

Semiaquatic reptile

Smooth snakes inhabit sunny, stony or sandy areas in scrub or scattered woodland, particularly clearings, paths and forest edges. Difficult to spot, they prefer to lie under hot stones rather than in the open. The smooth snake is a burrowing reptile, and spends much of its time underground. It is also at home in the water, and when alarmed, it will slide into a pool or stream and hide in the mud on the streambed.

Lizards are the favorite prey of the smooth snake, but it also hunts slow-worms and young snakes—including adders—mice, voles and small birds. It attacks its victim by grasping its neck and coiling its body around the struggling prey. If the victim is small, the smooth snake will suffocate it with three convolutions of its body before swallowing it head-first.

Some prey, particularly green lizards and slowworms, will defend themselves from attack by inflicting vicious bites on the smooth snake as they struggle. On occasions, the defensive action of the prey will actually force the smooth snake to release its grip, allowing its victim to escape. In the struggle, it is common for a lizard or slowworm to discard its tail, which remains twitching in the dust to distract the snake as its owner makes off.

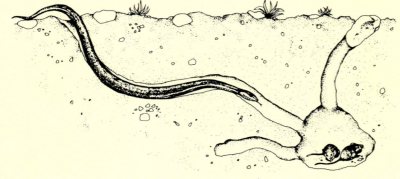

Venom gland

Although the smooth snake has a venom gland, it never uses it to capture prey or to defend itself. Although the venom is strong enough to kill a small animal, the snake does not have the specialized venom-pumping musculature needed to inject it. Instead, the venom acts as a strong solution to break down the prey's skin during digestion.

Males reach sexual maturity in their second year, whereas females must wait until they are 4 or 5 years old before they are ready to breed. The female bears 13-18 live young in summer. Bearing live young is a characteristic adaptation of reptiles that inhabit cold latitudes. At birth, a fine membrane often envelopes them, but the convulsive movements of the newborn young soon rupture the film. The steel-blue colored young molt shortly after birth, and usually they do not eat until the following spring.

A close relative of the smooth snake, the southern smooth snake is almost identical in appearance and habits, but has a more southerly distribution and it lays eggs instead of bearing live young.

TOP LEFT Lizards often provide more than two-thirds of a smooth snake's diet. The snake swallows its prey alive, making sure it is engulfed head first.

BOTTOM LEFT Smooth snakes spend much time burrowing underground, and are adept at finding their way into the runs and nests of mice and other small mammals.

ABOVE RIGHT Two adult smooth snakes bask in the sunshine to raise their body temperatures. More common in warmer, southerly parts of Europe, the smooth snake is the rarest species of snake in Britain.

RIGHT The southern smooth snake is a close relative of the smooth snake and lives only around the Mediterranean. Unlike its relative, it is rarely active during the day but comes out to hunt in the evening for lizards, small snakes and insects.

ABOVE The bright, banded color scheme of scarlet king snakes is similar to that of coral snakes (see page 1667). The similarity between them may have evolved as mimicry. The bright colors of the venomous coral snakes warn predators to keep clear, for their poison can be deadly. It is thought that the non-venomous king snakes adopted the same coloration as the coral snakes as a means of fooling predators into leaving them alone.

becomes submerged under a squirming knot of up to one hundred smaller males, each intent on mating. Occasionally the males inadvertently form a knot around each other. Sometimes they will even attempt to mate with a dead female.

Only one male succeeds in mating with the female. The male has tiny barbs that he passes along her back as he prepares to mate. Once mating occurs, the writhing mass of males separates—usually about ten minutes after it has formed. The fertilized female then leaves for her summer range, giving birth in the summer to 12-78 live young. The young garter snakes measure 8 in. long at birth, and reach full maturity after two years.

Garter snakes do not eat during the mating season, a common practice among reptiles. If the males fail to mate during the spring, they will try again in the autumn. If they succeed, the females store the sperm in their bodies during the winter months, and use it for fertilization the following spring, after they have emerged from hibernation.

Whips and kings

Western whip snakes, racers and king snakes belong to a group of colubrids that range throughout the Northern Hemisphere. Occasionally, they also appear in South America and Africa and throughout Southwest Asia to northern Australia.

The king snakes of North America are the most celebrated of these snakes. Despite their name, they only grow to a length of 6 ft. 6 in. In fact, they derive their common name of king snake from their habit of attacking and eating other snakes. They are distinctive in appearance. Bright, transverse bands of color decorate their sides. These vary in color and size according to the species. Some king snakes have red, yellow and black rings on their body and closely resemble the highly venomous coral snake—a relative of the cobras. Their body markings are almost certainly adaptations designed to exploit the fearsome reputation of the coral snake and scare predators. In fact, the body patterns of the king snakes are not identical to those of the coral snake, the bands of color occurring in a different order.

Preying on snakes

The medium-sized king snakes are ground dwellers that range across North America, from sea level up to altitudes of 6500 ft. They inhabit a wide range of habitats, including conifer forests, prairies, desert regions and along riverbanks. King snakes hunt small mammals, usually rodents, as well as lizards, frogs, fish and earthworms, and they will attack any snake that they encounter. During the attack, the powerful king snake grips the neck of its victim with its teeth and coils its body around the snake to suffocate the victim.

Hunting rattlesnakes

King snakes are immune to the venom of other snakes, including that of rattlesnakes. When confronted by a king snake, a rattlesnake displays alarm, a unique reaction since it does not respond with fear to the sight of any other snake. Instead of coiling its body to strike, the rattlesnake attempts to flee. If the rattlesnake is cornered, it flattens its head and neck against the ground and attempts to beat off the attacker with a loop of its heavy body. The defenses of the rattlesnake rarely succeed, however, and the king snake will crush the victim in its coils and consume it head-first.

Another curious feature of king snakes is their defense ritual. If it perceives danger, the snake imitates a rattlesnake, coiling itself up. It rears its head into the air and vibrates its tail rapidly—which in dry grass makes a similar sound to that of a rattlesnake's rattle. Another defensive reaction is to produce a foul-smelling substance from the cloaca.

Communication

The defense ritual of king snakes may act as a form of communication to other members of the same species. Evidence for this theory comes from experiments in America, which involved a captive female king snake. Despite being handled frequently, the female never emitted the cloacal discharge until it was brought into contact with a second king snake. The female promptly discharged onto the laboratory bench. This suggests that the odor acts as a recognition signal between king snakes, and possibly plays an important role during the mating season. Mating occurs in spring, and the female lays her 10-30 leathery eggs in summer. Usually, the female lays her eggs underneath leaves and plant litter.

TOP The bull snake of the western USA has excellent camouflage that allows it to lie unnoticed among rocks or vegetation while it basks in the sun.

ABOVE The western whip snake is a fast, agile hunter that tracks its prey by sight. BELOW Rat snakes can climb well, and snatch eggs and young from birds' nests.

1659

Agile and adaptable

The racers include the western whip snake or dark green racer, and the European whip snake. The western whip snake is the most widespread species in Europe, ranging from France to northwest Yugoslavia, Italy, and the Mediterranean islands of Sicily, Corsica and Sardinia. There are several subspecies of western whip snake, each with differing body coloration. The most common of these grows to 6 ft. 6 in. in length and has a green-brown body color with yellow markings. Western whip snakes are agile, adaptable creatures that flourish in markedly different habitats, from ground level to altitudes of 6500 ft.

Unlike the ground-dwelling smooth snakes, western whip snakes are extremely irritable in behavior. If disturbed, they race about frantically and will bite anything that threatens them. However, their needle-sharp teeth cannot inject venom. Their prey consists largely of small mammals, lizards, frogs, toads and birds. The slender racers feed on beetles, crickets and lizards, but western whip snakes have been known to attack the venomous horned viper. In addition to their speed of 4 mi. per hour, they can dodge and turn with great speed, making them difficult to catch. Western whip snakes hibernate in winter in large groups, secure from the cold in a deep hole. When they awaken in the spring, western whip snakes shed their skin and almost immediately search for a mate.

Entwining tails

Although the males court females singly or in groups, the frenzied communal courtship of the garter snakes does not occur. Once the female accepts a mate, the male wraps himself around her and bites her gently on the neck to hold her down. The two snakes then entwine their tails until their cloacae come into contact, enabling the male to insert his hemipenis and fertilize the developing eggs. The female lays her eggs during the summer in natural shelters, such as rocky crevices, or in the ground under bushes. Incubation takes about two months, and the offspring measure some 8 in. long when they hatch.

A symbol of healing

The Aesculapian snake takes its name from the legendary Greek figure Aesculapius, a son of the god Apollo, who in mythology became the first physician and possessed such skill that he could restore the dead

TOP The Aesculapian snake thrives in hot climates and probably colonized central Europe in the distant past when the climate was warmer than it is now.
ABOVE Despite their name, racers such as the green racer are not exceptionally fast movers. Their top speed is about the same as most people's brisk walking pace.
BELOW Courting snakes twist their bodies together before mating, and they may stay entwined for an hour or more.

to life. In ancient Greek and Roman art, Aesculapius was generally shown holding a staff with a snake entwined around it, and this symbol is still used by the medical profession today.

Occurring in the open, broad-leaved woodlands of southern and central Europe, the Aesculapian snake is an agile climber and spends much of its time slipping through the branches in search of mice and small birds. It hunts by day in order to take advantage of the warm daytime temperatures, since the climate of the temperate north is generally too cool for reptiles to be active at night.

Another member of the colubrid family is the dhaman or Indian rat snake, a fast, aggressive snake occurring from Afghanistan across to China and on the islands of Sri Lanka and Java. It has the unusual habit of defending itself by mimicking a cobra: it rears up and flattens out the ribs of its neck to form a hood similar to that of the cobra. (In India, some snake charmers use this snake instead of the potentially deadly cobra.)

Front-fanged snakes

The true cobras belong to the family of front-fanged snakes, a group that is divided into two subfamilies: the cobras, mambas and their relatives; and the sea snakes. Although their fangs are not as highly developed as those of the vipers, the front-fanged snakes are more deadly owing to their powerful, quick-acting venom. The poison acts on the nervous system, causing a paralysis that often leads to heart failure and death.

Modified salivary glands lying behind the snake's eyes secrete the venom; when the snake bites its victim, strong muscles compress the glands, forcing the venom through the fixed, grooved fangs in the front of the upper jaw, and deep into the wound. Spitting cobras expel their venom with such force that they can spray their enemies with poison from up to 10 feet away.

Most of the snakes in the subfamily containing cobras and mambas are of moderate size, although there are a few impressively large species. The black mamba of Africa may grow to as much as 11 ft. 6 in. long, while the king cobra of India is the world's longest venomous snake, growing to almost 20 ft. in length. The coloration of the snakes in this subfamily is varied: they may be completely green (the green

ABOVE **The king cobra of Asia is the longest venomous snake in the world, growing to well over 16 feet. When it rears up with its hood spread, ready to strike, it presents a terrifying** spectacle. **The female king cobra lays her eggs in a nest of leaves and rotting vegetation; she then covers them and, unusually for snakes, curls up on top to protect them from predators.**

mamba), patterned with colored hoops (the coral snakes and many cobras), or have special markings (the Indian cobra). In many cases, these eye-catching colors and markings, together with physical modifications—such as the "hood" of the cobra—act as signals to potential predators, warning them to keep away. Most of these snakes lay eggs, but some of the Australian species bear live young.

Most cobras, mambas and their relatives live in forests, but some occur in grassland or even desert. Only one species, the water cobra of southern equatorial Africa, is aquatic. It lives on riverbanks and lakeshores, and enters the water to prey on fish. It is active by day and rests hidden in the vegetation by night. Similar to a true cobra in appearance, its body is covered with large, smooth scales and is colored brown with broad, black bands and fine, white stripes; it can even broaden its neck into the cobra-style hood

ABOVE Snake venom evolved as a means of killing or immobilizing prey, but in many species it has become an effective defense. The black-necked spitting cobra can force venom out through slots in the front of its fangs, and shoot it into the eyes of its enemy from up to 10 ft. away. Then, with its attacker temporarily or permanently blinded, the cobra can escape.

(though it is not as broad), and uses this as a threat display before striking at an aggressor with its fangs.

A deadly giant

Of all the many venomous snakes, the largest by far is the king cobra of India and Southeast Asia. Most individuals measure between 10 and 13 ft. long, and an old specimen may grow up to nearly 20 ft. long. Being a slender animal, however, it never achieves a great weight (one specimen measuring 15 ft. 7 in. long weighed only 26 lbs. 5 oz.). Its head can grow as large as a man's hand, and with its fangs and poison glands, it is an extremely dangerous animal. It is also irritable, particularly during the breeding season, and it may attack without cause. In India, its reputation for aggressiveness is such that, if one is discovered in a town, police will evacuate the area.

Humans rarely interfere with the king cobra, partly because it is so frightening, and partly because many regard it as a sacred animal. In parts of Burma, the Burmese capture these snakes alive for religious festivals, using them for a form of snake charming, then releasing them back into the wild. To capture a king cobra, the hunter takes advantage of the snake's threat display: as the king cobra lifts up the front part of its body by 3 ft. or more and flattens its neck into a hood, the hunter keeps it in this position by distracting its attention with one hand, while grabbing it behind the neck with the other.

The king cobra feeds mainly on snakes that it hunts in the undergrowth of the lush tropical forest, though it also occasionally eats rodents and monitor lizards.

Before mating, the male and female king cobras dance in front of one another with their heads raised off the ground. The performance may continue for an hour before the male entwines his body around the female's to mate. The female builds a nest of vegetable material, pushing it into a heap with her head. She lays her eggs on top of this bed and covers it with more plant material, coiling up on top and staying there to protect her brood until the young hatch—an unusual display of mother care among snakes. The female king cobra regards any animal that approaches the nest with great suspicion, and may attack it without warning. The young measure about 20 in. long when they hatch.

True cobras

The true cobras are much smaller than the king cobra, rarely growing to more than 5 ft. long, or 6 ft. 6 in. at maximum. Cobras are probably the most notorious of all snakes, partly due to the number of people they kill with their venom (many thousands each year in rural Asia) and partly because of their dramatic threat display, which involves the broadening and flattening of the neck into the distinctive hood. They feed mainly on rodents, frogs, and even birds, climbing into trees to steal nestlings. Some species eat snakes, including other cobras.

The most common species of cobra is the widespread Asian or Indian cobra. Many of the local cobra populations have become sufficiently distinct to be classified as separate subspecies. Cobras also occur in Africa; one of these, the Egyptian cobra, is known as Cleopatra's asp, since it is believed that this was the species of snake used by the Queen of Egypt to commit suicide following the Roman invasion of her country in 30 BC. With its quick-acting venom, it would certainly have been a better choice than the true asp—a viper whose equally deadly poison is slower to take effect and produces greater pain.

A spitting image

Another dangerous African cobra is the black-necked spitting cobra. It closely resembles the Egyptian cobra, sharing its habitat and displaying similar behavior, but it does not occur north of the Sahara. When disturbed, it expands its neck to form a hood, stares at its enemy, opens its mouth slightly and squirts its venom through the air for a distance of up to 10 ft. The snake always appears to aim for the eyes, which, if hit, swell up and become inflamed, causing temporary or even permanent blindness. The snake only uses this method of poisoning in defense, and never to capture prey.

Deceptive mambas

The mambas are another group of African snakes notorious for their venom. In contrast to the cobras, the mambas look quite harmless: the green mamba, for example, resembles an ordinary colubrid snake. It has a narrow, elongated head that is quite distinct from the neck, a slender body with smooth scales, a long, narrow tail and round pupils—all characteristics of the colubrid snake family. In reality, however, it is a dangerous animal: not only does it have well-developed fangs supplied with highly toxic venom that can kill a cow within a few hours, but it can move very fast and attack before its victim has a chance to escape.

The black mamba is extremely large for a venomous snake: although it normally grows to 8 ft. in length, specimens up to 13 ft. long are not uncommon, making it the second largest venomous snake after the king cobra. It spends much of its time in the trees, climbing through the branches with great speed and agility to capture birds, reptiles and small mammals.

Fastest snake on earth

The green mamba is a relatively shy animal, but its relative, the black mamba, is highly aggressive and will not hesitate to bite if it is disturbed. Unlike many poisonous snakes that normally disappear into the undergrowth rather than risk injury through confrontation, a black mamba will attack any animal that disturbs it. It will actually give chase, writhing through the dust at high speed while keeping the front

ABOVE The Cape cobra of southern Africa measures 47-59 in. in length. It is an agile climber, gliding swiftly through the foliage of low trees in search of small reptiles and mammals. It often raids the nests of social weavers for nestlings, and sometimes enters domestic gardens—and even houses—to hunt for rats and mice. The Cape cobra is a highly venomous species, and is responsible for most of the snakebites that kill people in South Africa's Cape Province.

THE ASIAN COBRA
— A CHARMING SNAKE —

The Asian cobra is one of the world's most dangerous venomous snakes. Its venom is extremely powerful and can kill a person within 15 minutes of being injected. In India alone, the Asian cobra is responsible for up to 10,000 deaths per year.

The Asian cobra is an adaptable snake. It ranges across a huge area from Central Asia through India, China and the Philippines, and it inhabits areas as varied as arid semidesert, scrubland, forests, rice paddies and swamps. It will even inhabit heavily populated urban areas.

The Asian cobra is light brown, olive-gray or black in color, depending on its habitat. Its throat is usually yellowish brown.

The most distinctive feature of the Asian cobra is the expandable hood behind its neck. Essentially an area of elastic skin, the hood expands outward when the reptile spreads its neck ribs, in much the same way as the ribs of an umbrella stretch the fabric. The snake spreads its hood when it is angry or excited, or in the event of danger from predation and disputes with other cobras. In the case of the Asian cobra, the scales separate to reveal eyespots on the upper surface.

Mock eyes

There are conflicting theories as to the purpose of these mock eyes. Possibly they act as a deterrent to predators. Eyespots on insects, such as caterpillars and adult moths, are effective because, when revealed, they give the predator a sudden shock. In its confusion, the predator mistakenly believes that the victim has suddenly grown, making it potentially more dangerous.

The function of the cobra's eyespot pattern is not so easily explained, since the Asian cobra is already a dangerous and intimidating foe. Possibly, the inflated hood and eyespots together make the snake instantly identifiable to its enemies.

The eyespot markings are on the back of the hood rather than the front, and the snake always faces its enemy when in danger. Therefore, although the eyespot pattern is faintly visible from the front through the translucent hood, it is more striking from the back. The markings vary according to the subspecies and are especially prominent on subspecies in western India. In the east of the Indian subcontinent, the cobras tend to have a single ring mark. In the north, the snake's hood has black transverse bars, suggesting that the eyespots are simply a variation on a pattern rather than a deterrent.

Striking out

The Asian cobra strikes at an enemy if it feels threatened. It first rears up and raises its hood. The amount of the body that the cobra raises in threat depends on its level of excitement, and it may vary from one-fifth to one-third of its total length. If the cobra rears back until its head touches its back, it is usually about to flee. Before it attacks, the Asian cobra executes a mock strike with its mouth closed.

When a cobra strikes, it lunges forward and downward (it never bites upward). Snake charmers, who always

nain just beyond striking range,
loit this behavior in their act. They
on the fact that the cobra is
ically a nocturnal animal. When the
ian cobra emerges from the dark
ket into bright sunlight, it becomes
fused and defensive. It rears up and
eads it hood in a threat display,
ing its gaze on the nearest moving
ect—the snake charmer's pipe. As
charmer waves the pipe through the
, the snake sways in unison. The
e that the charmer plays is irrelevant
ause snakes are deaf to normal
nds and react only to vibrations
sing through the ground.
The tendency of the Asian cobra to
ome easily mesmerized by moving
ects makes it vulnerable to the
ngoose, one of its main predators.
ring a confrontation, the mongoose
rsues the Asian cobra until it takes

up a defensive position with its hood
spread. It then jumps around the snake
until the cobra becomes disorientated.
Usually, the mongoose attacks from
above, biting into the back of the cobra's
neck before devouring it head-first.

FAR LEFT AND ABOVE When an Asian
cobra feels threatened or prepares to
defend itself, it spreads its hood by
pulling the neck ribs out and back,
stretching the skin of the neck into
the shape of a flattened spoon.
Though they are prepared to bite if
severely provoked, most cobras first
launch mock attacks with their
mouths closed. The distinctive
"eyespot" markings on the neck of
the Asian cobra are visible only from
the back, when the snake expands its
hood (left).
RIGHT The cobra will often share the
same sleeping quarters with other
animals, including potential prey,
such as rodents.

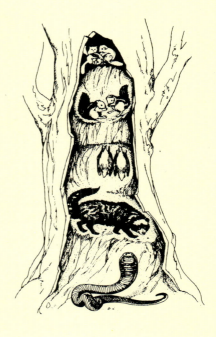

of its body completely clear of the ground. The black mamba holds the record for being the fastest snake on earth—one individual reached a speed of 7 miles an hour (it was chasing a man at the time, but was shot before it reached him).

Before mambas mate, they have a drawn-out courtship ceremony in which the male and female "dance" in front of each other before entwining their bodies together. The female lays about 15 eggs among the tree roots, and these hatch after four months.

The coral snakes

In the Americas, coral snakes are the only representatives of the front-fanged snakes. These highly poisonous, brightly colored reptiles occur throughout much of the New World, from the United States to Argentina. Coral snakes take their name from the broad, coral-red bands encircling the bodies of most species. The red bands alternate with black bands, and the two colors are divided by yellow rings. The sequence of the colors provides an important means of identification, since the similar-looking, but harmless, king snakes have the same colored bands but arranged differently—the red and yellow bands are divided by black rings. Coral snakes usually have black heads, with a yellow band.

ABOVE A shy snake that is rarely seen, the green mamba lives in the forests and coastal bushes of East and southern Africa, where it feeds on small mammals and birds. It is less aggressive and less poisonous than its relative, the black mamba, although its bite does cause some paralysis in humans, and in a few cases, the venom can be fatal.

Coral snakes are the same shape as burrowing snakes. Their small heads are the same width as their bodies (and therefore lack distinct necks), and they have small eyes and short, thickish tails. However, despite all these features, coral snakes rarely burrow into the ground, preferring to rest under stones or vegetation during the day. They usually hunt at night, preying on frogs, small lizards and other snakes. Having only small heads, coral snakes cannot open their mouths very wide, and as a result, can swallow only slender prey.

Coral snakes have short fangs, and after biting they need to "chew" on their victims in order to inject increasing amounts of venom. Bites nearly always prove fatal—taking only about 24 hours in the case of a grown man. However, deaths among humans from coral snake bites are uncommon, mainly because the snakes' secretive, nocturnal habits keep them out of the way of people.

ABOVE **The vivid markings of the eastern coral snake of the southeastern USA and Mexico are a warning to predators not to attack. Coral snakes remain hidden during the day and emerge at night to hunt other snakes and lizards.**
ABOVE RIGHT **The tiger snake of Australia is one of the most venomous of all snakes, and takes its name** from its body pattern— broad, dark bands on a light background. When angered, the tiger snake spreads its neck into a hood, similar to that of the cobra, and strikes with great speed. The tiger snake is a common species in much of southern Australia and Tasmania, and even occurs in the suburbs of Sydney.

Australian front-fanged snakes

Two-thirds of all the snake species in Australia belong to the front-fanged family, and most of these are highly venomous. Australia is the only continent where poisonous species outnumber non-poisonous species. One of the deadliest of Australian snakes is the death adder, whose triangular head resembles that of the viper (vipers do not occur in Australia). Its venom is more potent than a cobra's venom.

Australians regard the taipan as the country's most poisonous snake. It is an aggressive animal that lives in northeast Australia, in coastal rain forests and dry, inland regions, and it can reach a length of 10 feet. Its venom paralyzes the nerve centers that control the heart and lungs.

Sea snakes

Most sea snakes occur in the shallow seas of the southwest Pacific Ocean, between Malaysia and Australia. Some species range further afield and one, the yellow-bellied sea snake, occurs throughout the tropical Pacific and Indian Oceans.

The majority of sea snakes spend their whole lives at sea. The exceptions are the sea kraits, which stay near the

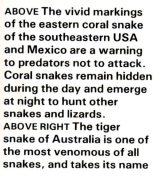

SNAKES CLASSIFICATION: 6

Front-fanged snakes

The front-fanged snakes of the family Elapidae consist of 236 species grouped in 61 genera. They inhabit mainly tropical regions of North and South America, Africa, Asia and Australasia. They are often divided into two subfamilies: the Elapinae, which includes the cobras, mambas and kraits, and the Hydrophinae, the sea snakes.

Among the cobras of the subfamily Elapinae are the king cobra, *Ophiophagus hannah*, of India and Southeast Asia; the Asian or Indian cobra, *Naja naja*, which ranges over Central Asia, India, southern China, Southeast Asia and the Philippines; the Egyptian cobra, *N. haje*, which is widespread in Africa and also occurs in Arabia; and the black-necked spitting cobra, *N. nigricollis*, of much of sub-Saharan Africa. The kraits make up the genus *Bungarus*, and occur in Southeast Asia and Indonesia. The mambas of Africa include the black mamba, *Dendroaspis polylepis*, of much of sub-Saharan Africa and the green mamba, *D. angusticeps*, of East and southern Africa. The subfamily also includes the eastern coral snake, *Micrurus fulvius*, of the southeastern USA and Mexico; and the death adder, *Acanthophis antarcticus*, and tiger snake, *Notechis scutatus*, both of Australia.

The smaller subfamily Hydrophinae includes the yellow-bellied sea snake, *Pelamis platurus*, which ranges over much of the Indian Ocean and the south Pacific, and the sea kraits of the genus *Laticauda*, which live in shallow waters of the southwest Pacific, from Malaysia to Australia.

Gaboon viper

Western diamondback rattlesnake

Red-headed krait

Sea krait

Sidewinder

Death adder

Southern fer-de-lance

Asian cobra

Eastern coral snake

shore at all times, frequently emerging onto the beach to bask in the sun and occasionally foraging for food on tropical islands. They move with great agility on the ground, almost as well as ordinary land-dwelling snakes. They also lay their eggs on land, beneath vegetation that has been washed up on the beach above the high-water mark.

Like other sea snakes, sea kraits are not aggressive toward humans, and prefer to swim away rather than risk a confrontation. However, they will fight if they are disturbed. If they do bite, the consequences are serious, since the venom of all sea snakes is extremely potent and takes effect within three to five minutes.

Apart from sea kraits, sea snakes never come ashore, even to breed. They do not lay eggs, but give birth to three to eight live young at sea. Compared with the sea kraits, the other sea snakes, such as the yellow-bellied sea snake, are much better adapted to life in the water and have lost many features that are essential to land snakes. Their belly scales are small and similar to the scales on their backs, whereas the

ABOVE The death adder of Australia is a highly poisonous snake that seldom grows more than 24 in. long. With its short, bulky body and broad head, it resembles a viper, but is, in fact, more closely related to the cobras and the kraits.

PAGES 1770-1771 The cottonmouth of the southern USA is a venomous snake that takes its name from the white color inside its mouth, visible when the snake opens it in threat. It catches frogs and fish, lying in wait for them at the water's edge.

SNAKES
CLASSIFICATION: 7

Vipers

There are 187 species of vipers in the family Viperidae, grouped into 17 genera. They range over much of North and South America, Africa and Eurasia. They are divided into two subfamilies (considered by some zoologists to be separate families)—the Viperinae, containing the 45 species of true vipers, and the Crotalinae, with the 142 species of pit vipers.

The Viperinae includes the European adder or common viper, *Vipera berus*, which ranges from Europe across Eurasia to the Pacific coast of the USSR; the asp, *V. aspis*, of western and central Europe; the common puff adder, *Bitis arietans*, of most of Africa; and the Gaboon viper, *B. gabonica*, of East, Central and southern Africa.

The pit vipers of the subfamily Crotalinae mostly occur in the New World. The southern fer-de-lance, *Bothrops atrox*, and the bushmaster, *Lachesis muta*, both range over tropical parts of South and Central America. The cottonmouth or water moccasin, *Agkistrodon piscivorus*, occurs in the southern and eastern USA, and the copperhead, *A. contortrix*, lives in the eastern USA. The Asian tree vipers of the genus *Trimeresurus* range from India east to Japan and the Philippines. The pit vipers also include the rattlesnakes, such as the sidewinder, *Crotalus cerastes*, and the western diamondback rattlesnake, *C. atrox*, both of North America, and the cascavel, *C. durissus*, of South America. The pygmy rattlesnakes of the genus *Sistrurus* include the massasagua, *S. catenatus*, which ranges over much of central North America.

TOP The black-banded sea krait occurs in the waters of the southwest Pacific Ocean. Though it is adapted for a marine life, it can move quickly overland, and has even been seen basking in the sun on coral atolls.

ABOVE Sea kraits rely on their potent venom to paralyze and kill fish within a few minutes. Quick-acting venom is essential to prevent the victims from disappearing into the lower depths, beyond the reach of the snakes.

scales of land snakes are large plates that allow the animals to grip the ground. The lengthways muscles that they use to swim are well developed, but the muscles that run crossways through the body have virtually disappeared. As a result, sea snakes are almost incapable of moving on dry land.

Sea snakes sometimes make mass migrations. One naturalist reported seeing a vast group of snakes traveling out at sea. They were grouped together in a long column at least 10 feet wide and dozens of miles long, and were so densely packed that the column was visible from several miles away. The migration probably numbered several million individuals, but where they were going, or why, remains a mystery.

Vipers

Vipers are often regarded as the most highly developed of the advanced snakes. Their sophisticated venom mechanisms ensure that they are among the most effective of all hunters—and the most feared.

Vipers' fangs are sharp, hollow tubes. As they bite, the fangs act as hypodermic needles, directing the venom deep into the victim. The venom itself is extremely painful and destroys the blood and tissues. It is produced in large quantities by glands on either side of the snake's head. The venom is squeezed out of the glands by large jaw muscles, and the whole arrangement of glands and muscles gives the viper its characteristically broad triangular-shaped head.

The fangs can be rotated by a complex arrangement of bones that swivel the teeth into position when the viper opens its mouth. When it is resting, the fangs fold back horizontally. If the fangs drop out or break, they are replaced by others further back in the jaw.

Vipers are typically thick-set, with relatively short, fat bodies, and easily distinguishable short tails. Their broad heads are distinct from their necks—mainly because of the poison glands and their associated muscles—and they have large eyes, often with upright pupils. Their scales may be ridged, giving the animals a rough, unpolished appearance.

True vipers

There are two main types of viper: the true vipers of Eurasia and Africa, and the pit vipers, most of which live in the Americas. The true vipers include snakes such as the European adder and the Gaboon viper, while the most familiar pit vipers are the rattlesnakes.

The most impressive of the true vipers are the larger African species, such as the puff adder and the Gaboon viper. True vipers are found in a variety of habitats, from open savannah to forests. Many have bold patterns, but in their natural environment these act as camouflage, breaking up their outlines and making them almost invisible among the ground vegetation.

The puff adder is a stout reptile, with a flattened body and a broad, flattened head that contains its large venom glands and two long fangs. It grows to about 5 ft. long and ranges in color from pale yellow to reddish and brown, patterned with dark brown and black markings and spots. Its name reflects its habit of inflating its body with air and hissing loudly when disturbed. After this warning, the hissing snake

rears up into an S-shape and lunges at its enemy, sinking its fangs deep in the victim's flesh and injecting a lethal dose of venom.

Puff adders live in semiarid or desert environments, at altitudes of up to 6500 ft. They are sedentary creatures who lie in wait for their prey rather than actively hunting. They remain motionless for hours, relying on their camouflaged coloring to keep them concealed, until their prey is within striking range. Puff adders are at their most active during the night, but their movements are slow and clumsy. They feed mainly on small mammals, and some will even follow their prey into houses, putting humans at risk.

The largest member of the true vipers group is the Gaboon viper. Although it is not very long, only growing to a maximum of 6 ft. 6 in., its body is stout, and can measure as much as 6 in. in diameter. Gaboon vipers have large, blunt, triangular heads with a slightly upcurved snout, and small, silvery eyes. Their fangs may be as long as 2 in., and are linked to large venom glands. Gaboon vipers have complex coloring consisting of diamond, triangular and rectangular markings in a combination of dark and pale shades, and, as with the puff adder, this acts as camouflage, concealing the snakes from their prey.

Gaboon vipers are found in the coastal forests around St. Lucia, east of Zimbabwe and Mozambique. They hide in the debris on the forest floor and strike when their prey (small mammals, the occasional monkey, and birds) comes within range. When threatened, Gaboon vipers hiss loudly in warning, before striking. Their venom is injected deep into the victim and acts on the nerves, blood and tissues. Despite this, the Gaboon viper causes fewer deaths among humans than the puff adder—possibly because there are fewer of these snakes around.

Night hunting for frogs

Night adders are found in tropical and southern Africa. Many of these vipers lack the characteristic viper features and are more similar to the harmless snakes. Their heads are narrow and not distinct from their necks, since their venom glands are not housed in the sides of the head, as in most vipers. Instead, they occur in long cavities running along the sides of the head and continuing beyond the neck almost to the heart. When the night adder bites, the gland muscles push the glands forward against the sides of

ABOVE Massive and slow-moving, the puff adder of Africa is a typical, large-bodied, lance-head viper. It uses ambush tactics to capture its prey, lying quite still until the victim comes within range, and then striking with its long poison fangs. Its venom is very potent, and although puff adders are not aggressive, their bite is usually fatal.

the head and the neck, changing the snake's appearance completely. These snakes prey mainly on amphibians such as frogs, hunting at night on damp and marshy ground. Unlike most other vipers that are usually live bearers, night adders lay eggs.

An African sidewinder

Some true vipers have adapted to life in stony or sandy deserts, and these are known as sand vipers. One of these is the horned viper, so called because of the two scales on its nape that have become elongated to form short "horns." Its head is broad with a well-defined neck, and its stumpy body ends in a short tail. The horned viper is easily recognized by its movement. It travels sideways, arching the front of its body across the sand to one side, then shifting the hind part across while repeating the procedure at the front. Sidewinding is an efficient method of crossing soft sand, the snake stepping across it instead of

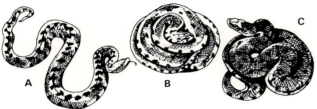

TOP **The horned viper is the African equivalent of the American sidewinder, for it uses the same unusual, but efficient, side-looping technique for making its way across hot, soft desert sand.**

ABOVE **The temperament of a snake can sometimes be deduced from the way it lies. The harmless lizard snake (A) and grass snake (B) tend to lie in relaxed coils, but a viper (C) is always ready to strike.**

pushing its way through. It thereby reduces the amount of its body in contact with the hot desert sand, preventing it from overheating.

If disturbed, the horned viper quickly digs itself into the sand, leaving a distinctive pattern on the surface. When it cannot escape in this way, it coils up and rubs the ridged scales on its body against each other to produce a sound similar to the threatening rattle of a rattlesnake. If these threats do not stop the attacker, the horned viper strikes.

Unlike most of its family, horned vipers lay eggs (from 8 to 22), but the young snakes inside the eggs are already fully formed when the eggs are laid and hatch within a few hours.

A northern viper

The most widespread of the true vipers belong to a group that includes the European adder. They probably originated in temperate areas, particularly in southern Europe. One species, Russell's viper, is found throughout Asia and is responsible for more deaths from snakebite than any other venomous snake. It is particularly common in highly populated areas.

These snakes are usually live bearers, but in some cases the female lays eggs. They are relatively small, rarely growing to more than 3 ft. long, although Russell's viper can grow to 5 ft. Usually most active at night, or at dawn and dusk, they may be seen by day during the spring, when they bask in the sun.

The European adder has a large range since it is tolerant of low temperatures. Adders have been found further north than the Arctic Circle in Norway, and they are the only venomous snake to occur in Britain (renowned for its cool, wet climate). They have slender bodies covered with broad scales, and have the typical viper head—a broad arrow with a well-defined neck. Adders are usually gray or brown in color, with a dark zigzag pattern running down their spine. The zigzags may broaden into a series of diamonds, or the snake may be completely black, with no visible markings.

Adders are adaptable reptiles, and are found in a variety of habitats ranging from arid, stony, mountainous terrain to grassy pastures, open woodland and riverbanks. They are most commonly found on dry heaths, open hillsides and moorland. European adders are more active during the day, when the temperature is slightly warmer, and they usually hunt in the morning, after they have basked in the sun to warm up. They are often seen basking in sheltered, sunny spots, although they rarely bask in the hot midday sun.

The adder feeds mainly on small mammals, but also preys on amphibians, lizards and insects. It slides up to its prey and strikes, sinking its fangs deep into its victim, injecting its venom. The adder immediately pulls its head back and waits for a few minutes for the poison to take effect, before following the victim by tracking its scent. It then moves around to the dead animal's head, and swallows it whole. If the prey is large, the adder will not kill again for several days.

Adders are shy animals and will disappear into the undergrowth rather than encounter people. If cornered, they hiss threateningly and then bite. Their venom is extremely painful but rarely fatal to humans. Most people who have died from the effects of an adder's bite have been small children or people already weakened by illness.

In winter, adders hibernate, sheltering in underground burrows until early spring. Often several

snakes hibernate together. The males emerge first, and after basking for a time in the sun, they prepare for the mating season.

During the mating season, rival males face each other and engage in ritualized duels. They approach each other, rear up and attempt to intimidate the other with loud hisses. They then entwine their bodies, swaying to and fro. The victor is the one who forces the other to the ground. The courtship is a much more gentle procedure. The male approaches the female from behind, slides up her back and eventually entwines his body around hers, gripping her neck in his jaws as they mate.

Once a year, in summer, and every two years in colder regions, the female adder gives birth to between 5 and 20 young. They emerge swathed in light membranes, but break these immediately. The young disperse shortly after birth to fend for themselves.

Pit vipers

The second group of vipers are the pit vipers. These have conspicuous pits on each side of their snouts, between the eyes and nostrils. The pits contain heat-sensitive organs that enable the snakes to sense infra-red radiation, and hunt their warm-blooded prey in total darkness. Pit vipers also have highly sophisticated venom apparatus that, together with their ability to locate prey in the dark, makes them formidable predators. Most pit vipers live in the Americas, although some species are found in Asia.

The most numerous of the pit vipers—and some of the most dangerous—are members of the group of lance-head snakes that are found throughout much of Central and South America. The most notorious of these is the southern fer-de-lance, a large snake that can grow to 6 feet long. It is extremely venomous, and often lives on sugar plantations, where it causes a large number of human deaths. Fer-de-lances eat small mammals, frogs, lizards and small snakes. The females give birth to approximately 60 live young in each litter, all of which are potentially fatal to humans.

RIGHT (top to bottom) The three subspecies of the European adder vary in color and pattern: some have a marked black zigzag line down the spine, or a series of black diamonds, while others are entirely black. Females tend to be browner and duller than the males, and their markings are less well defined; they are also longer and fatter.

THE ASP
— A EUROPEAN VIPER —

Poisonous snakes mainly populate tropical climates of the world. But two members of the viper family occur in temperate parts of Europe. The European adder and the asp are members of the same family and share common physical characteristics. Generally, the asp inhabits more southern areas of Europe, ranging through the hilly or low, mountainous regions of Italy, southern France and southern Germany. The habitat of the asp is warmer and drier than that of the adder. It lives in rocks, scrub and heaths rather than in the sandy terrain of the adder.

A distinctive feature of the asp is the tip of its snout, which turns up to form a small spike. Otherwise the asp is typical of the viper family. It has a broad, pointed head, and a slender neck that runs on to a thick-set body; its tail is short. The asp's eyes have the vertical, oval-shaped pupils typical of nocturnal snakes. Usually, the scales on its head are small, while the back scales are ridged, giving the animal a rough appearance. In color, the underparts of the asp are gray, yellowish or brown. A pattern of dark bars crosses its back. When contracted, they form a zigzag pattern similar to that of the adder.

The asp is active depending on its surrounding temperature. If it is too cold, the asp retires to its hole in the earth or between rocks. In winter, it hibernates in an underground chamber, either alone or in a group of several individuals coiled together.

When the weather improves in spring, the asp emerges from its winter nest to bask in sunlight, to hunt for food and to find a mate. The males emerge above the surface first, followed by the females about two weeks later.

The asp often climbs onto a branch or into a low bush to bask in the sunlight. Normally, each individual has its own favored basking site, and, although suitable places may be infrequent, it is unusual to see two asps basking together—except during the period immediately after hibernation.

The basking site of the asp usually enjoys full exposure to the sun and is near a covering of rock crevices or low

LEFT Completely black asps are fairly common in the mountains of France and northern Italy.
BELOW Two male asps intimidate each other during a fight over a female.
ABOVE RIGHT The asp keeps her 4-18 young inside her body until they are ready to break free of their embryonic sacs; this may occur inside the body or immediately after birth.

vegetation. It can then seek refuge if in danger, or slip into the shade when the heat becomes oppressive. Since the sun moves during the day, the snake may have two or more favored sites, moving from one to the other as the day progresses.

The asp is a slow-moving snake, but it is aggressive and more dangerous than the adder. Hunting mainly at night, it preys on small mammals and reptiles such as mice, voles, young birds and lizards. The young often eat invertebrates such as earthworms. Instead of pursuing its prey, the asp normally conceals itself among dead leaves and vegetation, waiting to ambush its victim. As a result, it rarely strays beyond a limited home territory of several square yards. When its prey comes within range, it strikes, injecting a lethal dose of venom through its hollow fangs. It then waits until its victim is dead before swallowing the prey head-first.

The asp is not truly territorial, but the small size of its home range means that each individual effectively dominates its area. Other snakes rarely hunt over the same ground. The actual size of the living space depends on several factors, such as exposure to sunlight, the amount of food available and the type of vegetation. Over the years, the local population of snakes within a given area remains almost constant. Males tend to be more mobile than females.

Mating takes place in April or May. The courting ritual includes fights between rival males. First, the males attempt to intimidate each other by rearing up in an S-shape. During the battle, the rivals lock their necks together and pull or push their opponents to the ground. They never attempt to bite each other.

During mating, the male vibrates his body, approaches the female and touches her gently on the back. He then

slides his head along her body until he is resting on top of her, and rolls his tail on top of hers. The female often frees herself and moves swiftly away.

The male pursues her and repeats his caresses. As a result, the mating ritual may last for several hours. Occasionally mating takes place in autumn, and the offspring are born in late spring. The eggs remain in the mother until they are due to hatch.

The female can reproduce annually in favorable climates, but in colder regions the snakes breed once every two to four years. During gestation, the female requires high food consumption, and a female that lives in a cold climate is frequently unable to accumulate sufficient fat reserves for her winter hibernation when she is breeding.

At the end of summer, the falling temperature encourages the snakes to return to their winter burrows. The females hibernate first, the males following after about 15 days.

The bushmaster of South and Central America is the longest viper and can grow to over 13 feet in length, but its body is relatively slender and almost triangular in section. Its head is large and lance-shaped (broader at the rear), and its fangs can be as long as 1.5 in. Bushmasters are not rattlesnakes, but shake their tails in a similar way if disturbed. They then bend the top half of their body into an S-shape, and strike.

Bushmasters live in forests where they hunt their food among the ground vegetation. They prey on small mammals, particularly rodents, following them with their heat receptors and killing them with their venom. Unlike the other pit vipers, bushmasters lay eggs that the females brood until they hatch.

Rattlesnakes

The most notorious of the pit vipers are the rattlesnakes of North and South America, whose appearances in innumerable "cowboy" films have made them familiar throughout the world. The sinister dry rattle of warning is produced by large, horny rings on the end of the tail that rub against each other as the snake vibrates its tail. These snakes gain an extra segment on their rattle each time they shed their skins. There are about 25 species, ranging in length from 20 in. to nearly 7 feet, all with the stout bodies and lance-shaped heads typical of vipers.

Rattlesnakes usually live in arid, stony or bushy terrain with plenty of cover, but some prefer woodland. Those living on open terrain are active at dawn and dusk, while woodland species tend to be more active during the day. The rattlesnakes that live in northerly latitudes hibernate during the winter in communal nests, often gathering in hundreds with snakes of other species.

Rattlesnakes hunt small mammals, the occasional ground-dwelling bird, lizards and small snakes. If a rattlesnake is disturbed, it coils its body, lifts its tail and vibrates it to produce the unmistakable rattle. If this warning is not heeded, the snake will bite, injecting an extremely potent venom that, in several species, can kill a fully grown human within an hour.

Courtship battles

In spring, rival male rattlesnakes fight ritual duels similar to those of the European adder. The two contenders raise the front of their bodies, resting on

TOP **The bushmaster is the largest of the venomous American snakes, measuring about 12 ft. in length. It lives in the tropical rain forests of Central and South America where its body patterning provides an effective camouflage when it lies** among the leaves on the forest floor. Rodents make up the bulk of its prey. ABOVE **The southern fer-de-lance is notorious for its habit of lurking on footpaths and among crops, and is much feared by farm workers in South and Central America.**

one another as they sway and push, trying to force the other to the ground. It is rare for either snake to be injured during this ritual, and the fight ends when the loser retreats.

During courtship, the two rattlesnakes entwine their tails to bring their cloacae together, allowing the male to insert one of his hemipenes. Mating may be interrupted and resumed several times, and can last all day. The young, usually between 10 and 20 but occasionally as many as 60, are born live. In northern areas, rattlesnakes usually breed every other year.

The sidewinder of the southern states of the USA is the most intriguing of the rattlesnakes, for, like the horned viper of Africa, it moves sideways across the soft sand of its desert home, leaving a curious track behind it—a series of parallel, slanting grooves. The continuous curl of its body as it moves gives it the appearance of a rolling coil spring.

The cascavel is the only true rattlesnake of South America. It is probably the most deadly of all the rattlesnakes since its venom acts on both the blood and the nervous system. It is extremely aggressive, but always sounds its rattle before attacking, giving its

TOP The rattle on the tip of the eastern diamondback rattle-snake's tail is composed of old, horny scales that are loosely attached to one another.
ABOVE The western diamondback rattlesnake is an excitable, aggressive snake, and causes more deaths in the USA than any other species. Though it lives in the semiarid regions of North America, it is an agile swimmer that is quite prepared to pursue its prey through the water.

LEFT The flattened, spade-like head of Pope's tree viper owes its shape to the large venom glands and venom-squeezing muscles on the sides of its skull. The junction between the snake's body and tail is clearly visible in the photograph.
BELOW LEFT Two rival male rattlesnakes engage in a wrestling match during the spring breeding season.

victim a chance to escape. Cascavels prey on rodents and often hunt rats near human dwellings, increasing the risk of human deaths.

Most rattlesnakes are found in arid places, but the related cottonmouth or water moccasin is semi-aquatic, and lives in flooded fields and swamps in the southeastern United States. It is an excellent swimmer, and will chase and kill fish and amphibians in the water. It also hunts reptiles, birds and mammals on the banks. The snake's bite is extremely painful but rarely fatal to humans. When disturbed, it opens its mouth to display its white lining (hence the name cottonmouth).

The cottonmouth grows to about 5 ft. long and has the broad, pointed head typical of the vipers. Young individuals are pale with dark, transverse bands that merge as the animal grows older.

Cottonmouths mate in March, and the females give birth to their young almost 12 months later. The young are born live, enclosed in a membrane that is immediately broken by their convulsive movements. Females reproduce every other year. The young are able to feed as soon as they are born, and will often prey on animals larger than themselves.

The smaller copperhead, a relative of the cottonmouth, is the commonest venomous snake in the eastern United States. It is less poisonous than the cottonmouth, and although people are frequently bitten, it is rare for the victims to die.

Coiled in the branches

Several Asiatic pit vipers have adapted to living in trees, and have prehensile tails that enable them to grip branches. One of these Asian tree vipers, the bamboo viper, has all the typical viper features in miniature. It has a broad, triangular head and a distinct neck, a short tail and a venomous bite, but is only 24 in. long. The bamboo viper lives in bushland and hunts amphibians, small mammals, small birds and large insects. Its venom is not particularly poisonous to humans, and does not cause serious injury.

WATCHFUL GIANTS

Survivors from the great Age of Dinosaurs, crocodiles and alligators are the world's largest reptiles. Despite their sun-basking habits and clumsy appearance, they are fast movers, able to capture all kinds of prey in surprise attacks

ABOVE **In India, the female gharial lays 16-61 eggs in pits that she digs in sandbanks alongside rivers. After 80-90 days, when the young are ready to hatch, they use the "egg tooth" at the end of their snouts to break out of their shells.**

PAGE 1681 **The 16-ft.-long black caiman is the largest caiman species and lives in the quiet backwaters and lagoons of the Amazon Basin.**
BELOW **The map shows the geographical distribution of the three families of crocodilians.**

Crocodilians—which include crocodiles, alligators, caimans and the gharial—are the only survivors of a group of ancient reptiles that flourished 225 to 65 million years ago during the great Age of Reptiles. Known as the archosaurs or the "ruling reptiles," the group also included the dinosaurs and the flying pterosaurs.

Fossil evidence reveals that early crocodilians were small, lizard-like reptiles that resembled the ancestors of the birds. By contrast, some of the later crocodilians were very large, with broad-snouted forms up to 39 ft long. Their size may have made it possible for them to hunt small dinosaurs.

Until recently in geological terms, the distribution of crocodilians was much wider than it is today. Fossil remains show that until 15 million years ago, they basked on the sandbanks of subtropical lakes in Switzerland. With the cooling of the climate, however, crocodilians moved south to the tropics and subtropics, where most of the 22 living species can now be found.

Modern crocodilians look little different from their relatives of 65 million years ago. They represent a small but successful group of reptiles that have declined in numbers only because they have been overhunted for their skins, their habitats have been destroyed or their breeding and feeding grounds have been disturbed.

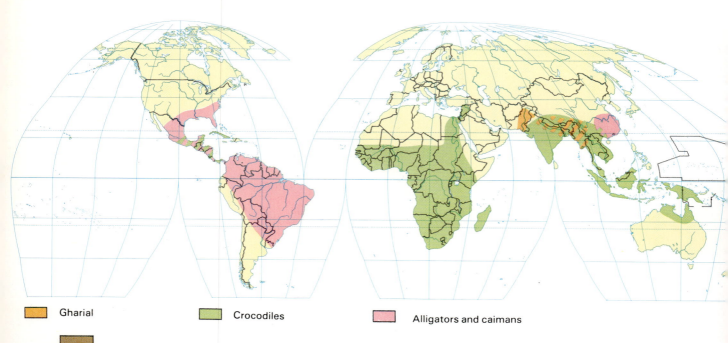

▮ Gharial ▮ Crocodiles ▮ Alligators and caimans

Floating logs

All crocodilians have a characteristic and instantly recognizable appearance. Their heads are large, and their long jaws are lined with sharp teeth. Their bodies are heavily built and rather flattened, and their tails are large, compressed and powerful. Most are dull brown, green and black—a coloration that allows them to blend in with the muddy water and aquatic vegetation in which they live.

When resting in the water, crocodilians look like floating logs. The resemblance is partly due to the roughened texture of their skin. It is made up of horny, shield-like scales, called scutes, that cover the neck, back and tail.

Bony plates underneath the scutes give added protection and strength to the already thick body covering. In some species, including many caimans, the body armor extends to the underparts. However, the flanks of most crocodilians are covered with large, rounded scales, with more oblong-shaped scales on the underside. The scales, especially on the flanks and on the underside of the head, are well supplied with nerve endings that make them sensitive to touch.

Since crocodilians are cold-blooded, they tend to spend long periods on land, sunning themselves to raise their body temperature. In addition, all species

ABOVE The African slender-snouted crocodile lives in the rain forest regions of West and Central Africa, where it feeds almost exclusively on fish. The narrow, streamlined snout offers little resistance to the water during chases after prey.

BELOW To assert its dominance within a territory, the American crocodile places its head on the water surface (A), opens its mouth so that the lower jaw remains submerged (B), and makes a large splash by closing its jaws together (C).

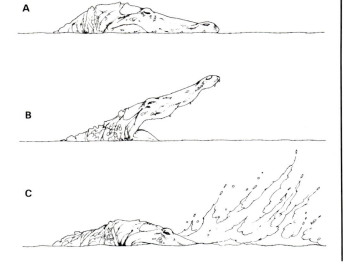

A

B

C

1683

Gharial

False gharial

Nile crocodile

African dwarf crocod

ay their eggs on land. However, most obtain their food in the water, and their bodies show many adaptations to aquatic life.

Crocodilians propel themselves through the water by slowly and rhythmically undulating their long, muscular tails—a method that is effective even when they are moving against the current. To create a streamlined shape when gliding at speed through the water, they press their small limbs against the sides of their bodies.

The hind limbs of most species are webbed and act as efficient rudders. With a sudden upward movement of the feet and with the toes fully spread, a crocodilian can move down and backward quite suddenly. It can also use its feet to paddle through the water when moving along slowly.

A crocodilian's nostrils and eyes are set on the top of its head so that it can see and breathe while most of its body is submerged. When the animal dives underwater, special muscles close the crescent-shaped nostrils on the tip of the snout. In a similar way, two flaps of skin at the back of the mouth seal off the windpipe and gullet so the animal can open its mouth freely underwater. Large species can stay submerged for up to an hour at a time.

The ears are located high up on the sides of the head, hidden by two scaly flaps of tissue. The flaps close around the ears when the animal submerges, protecting them from injury and from increases in pressure. The eye also has a "third eyelid," a blinking membrane that sweeps sideways across the eye to give added protection when diving.

CROCODILIANS CLASSIFICATION

The crocodilians belong to the order Crocodylia, a group of reptiles that contains 22 species distributed throughout the tropical and subtropical regions of the world. They are divided into three families: the Crocodilydae, the crocodiles; the Alligatoridae, the alligators and caimans; and the Gavialidae, the gharial.

Crocodiles

The 14 crocodile species in the family Crocodylidae are divided into three genera, though the majority belong to the genus *Crocodylus*. They live in freshwater, the brackish waters of estuaries and in the sea, and include some of the largest reptiles in the world. These include the saltwater or estuarine crocodile, *Crocodylus porosus*, which ranges from India to northern Australia; the Nile crocodile, *C. niloticus*, which occurs over much of sub-Saharan Africa; and the mugger, *C. palustris*, found across much of the Indian subcontinent. There are several smaller species of crocodile, such as the African dwarf crocodile, *Osteolaemus tetraspis*, of West Africa; the Cuban crocodile, *Crocodylus rhombifer*, which occurs in two swamps in the west of Cuba; and the Siamese crocodile, *C. siamensis*, which inhabits Thailand and parts of Indonesia. Other species include the American crocodile, *C. acutus*, of southern Florida, the slender-snouted crocodile, *C. cataphractus*, of western and Central Africa, and the false gharial, *Tomistoma schlegelii*, of Southeast Asia.

Alligators and caimans

Except for one species, all the members of the family Alligatoridae occur in areas of tropical freshwater in the New World. They consist of seven species of alligators and caimans placed in four genera. The two species of alligators in the genus *Alligator* are the American alligator, *Alligator mississippiensis*, of the southeastern USA, and the Chinese alligator, *A. sinensis*, which lives along the lower Yangtze River in southern China. Both of these species extend well into temperate regions. Caimans range from Central America to the central regions of South America and include the spectacled caiman, *Caiman crocodilus*; the black caiman, *Melanosuchus niger*, of central South America; and the dwarf caiman, *Paleosuchus palpebrosus*, of northern and central South America.

The gharial

The family Gavialidae contains just one species of crocodilian, the gharial *Gavialis gangeticus*. It inhabits the rivers and pools of northern India, Pakistan, Bangladesh, Nepal and Burma.

Black caiman

American alligator

Smooth-fronted dwarf caima

Spectacled caiman

Efficient hunting machines

Crocodilians are predators that feed on any animal they can overcome, and they also feed on carrion (the dead bodies of other animals). Young crocodilians—and the adults of some species—take small prey such as insects, mollusks, crustaceans and fish. They are good climbers, able to scramble up small trees and bushes in search of food.

Adults and larger species take correspondingly larger prey including other reptiles such as snakes, turtles and smaller crocodilians, as well as birds and mammals. Some species, such as the gharial, feed mainly on fish, while the slender-snouted crocodile takes freshwater crabs as well as fish.

Crocodilians are well equipped as meat eaters. They have large heads and strong jaws armed with sharp, cone-shaped teeth. The lower teeth fit into sockets in the upper jaw, and the jaws have strong muscles that enable them to snap shut and hold prey securely. Crocodilians have long, low and massive skulls—adapted to resist the great pressure created when they snap their jaws together. The teeth are replaced as they wear out, and although the process slows down in old age, a large crocodilian may replace each of its teeth at least 40 times during its life.

Surprise attack

In a zoo, crocodilians often lie motionless for long periods, but that does not mean that they are incapable of moving quickly. In the wild, they frequently unleash the full force of their powerful bodies—especially in a surprise attack on their prey or when seeing other crocodilians off their territory.

Waterholes are favorite hunting grounds for the larger species. While their prey is stooping to drink at the water's edge, the crocodilian closes in unseen. Once within striking distance, it makes its surprise attack. The crocodilian accelerates for its final lunge by digging its feet into the riverbank and levering its body upward with its legs. It can also attack by leaping out of the water suddenly, and seizing its unsuspecting prey by the head or forelegs.

The crocodilian's surprise attack usually knocks its prey off balance. If not, the crocodilian twists its body around its victim or lashes its powerful tail from side to side to bring the animal down. Then it drags its prey to the water's edge and drowns it before it can struggle free and escape.

ABOVE The Australian freshwater crocodile is a fish-eating species with a slender snout that lives only in the small rivers and streams of northern Australia. Measuring 10 feet long, it is a particularly agile species, able to gallop fast on land. Toward the end of the dry season, the female lays her eggs in a hole dug in a sandbank. Incubation lasts for about eight weeks, and the young hatch just before the arrival of the monsoon rains.

Tug-of-war

Common prey animals include antelopes and wild pigs, although animals as large as cattle are also attacked. A crocodile can maintain a tug-of-war against a large mammal because it has extremely strong neck muscles attached to long, bony extensions of the neck bones. The backbone is also very flexible, since it is made up of ball-and-socket joints.

Once a crocodilian has drowned its prey, it feeds on the carcass by tearing off large chunks. To do so, the reptile sometimes has to grip the body tightly with its jaws and twist it around vigorously until the flesh comes apart. To eat prey caught in the water, such as fish and soft-shelled turtles, the crocodilian may bring the victim up to the surface and toss it into the air to flip it into the correct position for swallowing. It comes to the surface because the air offers less resistance to jaw movements than the water.

THE NILE CROCODILE
— ON GUARD AT THE NEST —

Nile crocodiles do not reach sexual maturity until they are 12-15 years of age. At this stage they measure from 6 ft. 6 in. to 10 ft. long and weigh 154 to 220 lbs. Early in each mating season, the mature males fight for dominance, threatening each other by blowing bubbles out of their open mouths, arching their necks and lashing the water with their tails. The bubbling display is accompanied by grunts and growls and the male may partially submerge himself to blow water through his nostrils. If one reptile proves the weaker, he will quickly scurry off the territory chased by the more dominant male. If he is slow to move, the weaker of the two raises his head almost vertically to expose his throat, and the dominant crocodile may seize him in his jaws.

Sunbathing by the Nile

Nile crocodiles can most often be seen sunning themselves on riverbanks, often in the company of water birds. The Egyptian plover is believed to enter the crocodile's mouth to feed on the leeches and other parasites that are found there, but this behavior has never been confirmed. The bird does, however, pick at insects on the crocodile's head and back.

Another wader, the water dikkop (Afrikaans for "thick head"), gains protection for itself by nesting near crocodile nests that are guarded by the female crocodiles. It is thought that the cries of the dikkops warn the crocodiles of approaching danger.

Courtship and egg-laying

The courtship behavior of the Nile crocodile involves a series of displays. A male and female come together, raise their heads and rub each other's jaws. The pair also lie near each other with their jaws wide open for long periods. The female lays her eggs five months after mating, during the dry season when there is less of a risk from flooding. She chooses the nest site, usually on a sandy bank near the river, and guards it until she is ready to lay the eggs. She then digs a hole, approximately 24 in. deep, with her hind legs and lays 16-80 eggs,

BELOW LEFT By keeping its mouth wide open, a basking Nile crocodile may be able to lose some excess body heat, but its toothy gape is more likely to be a warning to possible intruders to keep their distance.

RIGHT The Nile crocodile spends many hours sunning itself on sandbanks to maintain an even body temperature. It usually feeds from the early evening into the night.

BELOW RIGHT In response to the piping calls of her unborn young, a female Nile crocodile uncovers her eggs before they hatch (A). After the young have broken out of their shells, the mother delicately picks them up in her mouth (B), and carries them down to the water (C) where she releases them.

which she then buries under about 16 in. of earth. The females use the same nesting sites for years.

The female Nile crocodile is an attentive mother and will stay by the eggs for up to 90 days until they hatch. While guarding the eggs, the female does not feed. The male also stays in the vicinity of the nest area. Despite a constant guard, nests are frequently raided by a variety of animals, including monitor lizards, baboons, hyenas, marabou storks, fish-eating eagles and even other crocodiles. Of the many predators, the most dangerous are the Nile monitor lizards. They often work in pairs, one distracting the female crocodile while the other digs up the eggs.

High-pitched signals

To help them break out of their shells, young crocodiles have an egg tooth on the top of their snouts. Before they hatch, they utter high-pitched sounds that can be heard several yards from the nest. The female is stimulated by the sound and digs up the earth using her forelimbs and jaws. Once the nest has been uncovered, she picks up the hatchlings one by one in her mouth. Safe between her jaws, the young crocodiles change their call to a gentle chirping.

The female crocodile is able to locate any of her young that wander away by tracing their distress calls. Once she has collected all the hatchlings, she enters the water and releases the young by opening her mouth and swinging her head from side to side in the shallows. Washed clean of sand from the nest, the young crocodiles swim ashore and rest on the banks.

The young Nile crocodiles are between 10 and 13 in. long when they hatch, and at first, their diet consists of snails, beetles, dragonfly larvae and other insects. As they grow older, Nile crocodiles eat frogs, toads, rodents and small birds. When mature, their diet is more varied, including fish, birds and hoofed mammals.

The young crocodiles do not disperse for up to eight weeks, and during that time they are guarded by both parents. Whenever her young are in danger, the female crocodile protects them by putting them in her mouth.

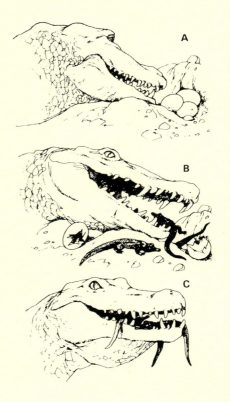

ABOVE The saltwater or estuarine crocodile of southern India, Indonesia, the Philippines and other islands of the southwest Pacific lives mostly along the coast, both in brackish estuaries and in the sea. The largest of the crocodiles, it grows to over 26 ft. in length; the world record holder measured 28 ft. 4 in. long and weighed over 2 tons.

Nile crocodiles help one another when tackling large carcasses. One crocodile may hold the dead animal underwater while the other feeds off it, or both may rotate it in different directions to tear the carcass apart more easily. Young Nile crocodiles also feed cooperatively. During the spring floods, they form a tight semicircle with their snouts pointing in the direction of the rushing water, enabling them to trap and snap up fish.

Man-eating crocodiles

There have been many gruesome stories about crocodilian attacks on humans. Most are far-fetched, but these animals are certainly capable of killing people, just as they can kill most other large mammals. However, only a few of the 22 species have a reputation for being man-eaters. These are the Nile crocodile of Africa, the mugger of India, and the saltwater crocodile of Southeast Asia and northern Australia.

Most injuries take place near the water's edge and usually involve women who are washing clothes or children who are playing in the water. There have also been many accounts of people involved in shipping accidents being killed in the water by crocodilians.

Attentive mothers

All crocodilians lay hard-shelled eggs that may number up to a hundred depending on the age and size of the female. The mothers are attentive, guarding their nests until the offspring hatch. Many species even carry their young in their mouths to nursery grounds in shallow water.

The female sometimes digs out a nest for the eggs and covers them, or she may build a mound of vegetation and lay eggs in the center of it. These trench and mound type nests are extremes, between which are many intermediate types. The American crocodile, for example, buries her eggs in high, moist ground, and during incubation she may scrape additional soil over it with her hind feet to form a low earth mound.

Crocodilians grow at a fast rate, especially when young. The mugger of India grows from about 10 in. in length at hatching to 3 ft. by the end of the first year, and the young of most species grow more than 12 in. each year.

Crocodile or alligator?

There is one easily recognizable feature that distinguishes a crocodile from an alligator. When a crocodile's jaw is closed, its pair of enlarged lower fourth teeth are visible. They fit into notches in the upper jaw rather than into bony pits, as in the alligator's mouth. The position of the two exposed teeth gives the crocodile its typical "grinning" expression.

It is commonly supposed that alligators have broad snouts and crocodiles have more pointed ones. This is not necessarily the case, however. Snout size and shape vary with individual species of crocodilian. For example, crocodiles of the Americas tend to have narrower snouts than their Old World counterparts.

Generally, crocodile species are more common in the Old World and alligators and caimans have their center of distribution in the New World. Of the 22 surviving species of crocodilians, most have suffered in numbers because of the demand for their skins.

The crocodiles

The 14 species of crocodiles range in size from the 5-foot African dwarf crocodile to the massive saltwater crocodile that attains a length of over 26 feet. They are distributed across warmer regions of both the Old World and the New World.

TOP The African dwarf crocodile is an extremely rare species that lives in swamps and slow-moving streams in the tropical forests of West and Central Africa. Reaching only 5 ft. long, it is a slow-moving animal that feeds on fish, amphibians and, unusually for crocodilians, fruit. As well as being small, it has a proportionately shorter snout than most other species of crocodiles. ABOVE In Thailand, the Siamese crocodile is rare in the wild, but it is bred in captivity on a commercial scale.

The American crocodile is an uncommon species due to overhunting for its skin and habitat loss. In southern Florida, much of its favorite natural habitat—coastal mangrove forests—has been destroyed. It manages to survive in small numbers, having colonized the cooling channels of a nuclear power station. It uses both mound and hole nests, and feeds mainly on fish.

Morelet's crocodile of Central America lives in freshwater lagoons and swamps in forested areas, while the Orinoco crocodile inhabits lakes and the deep, slow stretches of large rivers in northern South America. The Cuban crocodile is extremely rare, living only in two swampy areas on the island of Cuba in the Caribbean.

Several species of crocodile live in Asia and Australia, though most of them are now endangered

THE CROCODILIANS

Most of the world's crocodiles and alligators are under threat from hunting and loss of habitat. Many are already extremely rare: the Chinese alligator is the rarest crocodilian in the world with a total population estimated at only 700-1000 individuals. Crocodilians are mostly hunted for their valuable skins. They are used by the luxury leather trade to make items such as shoes and handbags. Although about half a million skins are legally received each year to be processed for the market, untold numbers of caimans from South America are killed yearly for the illegal leather trade.

Fortunately "crocodile farms" in some 200 places around the world are helping to reduce the pressure on the wild populations. In Australia and Zimbabwe, crocodile farming is part of a general conservation management policy; while in Papua New Guinea, there are many small farms where saltwater and freshwater crocodiles are reared. The gharial has only recently won the battle for survival: in 1974 there were no more than 60 adults left. Since then their numbers have increased to several thousand by conservation projects that involve raising the young in captivity and releasing them into protected areas. When they are about 3 ft. long, large enough to protect themselves from predators, the young are finally transferred to the wild.

TOP The broad-nosed caiman of South America grows to over 8 ft. long and eats aquatic insects, snails, crustaceans and fish. Large numbers of this species are caught for their skins, while their young—such as the individual seen here—are collected and sold as pets or stuffed for sale as curios.

ABOVE With its long, slender snout, it is unclear whether the false gharial is more closely related to the gharial or to the crocodiles. It lives in freshwater in parts of Southeast Asia, where it feeds on fish.

ABOVE Some two months after mating, the American alligator lays 30-50 leathery eggs in a mound of mud and vegetation; as the plant matter rots, it generates enough heat to incubate the eggs. During this time, the female stays near the nest, hissing and charging at intruders that stray too close.
RIGHT The American alligator splashes to advertise its ownership of a territory: it holds its snout above the water (A), opens its mouth (B), and then shuts it to create a powerful splash (C).

through hunting. The mugger lives on the Indian subcontinent in various freshwater habitats, from hill streams to man-made reservoirs. Measuring over 16 ft. long, it digs burrows in which it can take refuge during the extreme temperatures of winter and summer. Muggers may wander great distances during the dry season in search of new ponds, and they also migrate during the monsoon floods. The saltwater or estuarine crocodile is the largest known reptile, reaching more than 26 ft. long. It favors the brackish water found in estuaries along the coasts of southern India, the Philippines, the Moluccas and other islands down to northern Australia.

Nile dweller

The Nile crocodile was once found as far north as Syria and Palestine (now Israel), and there was even an Asiatic population on the Seychelles Islands in the Indian Ocean. Its range, like that of many other species, has been reduced by hunting for its skin and meat, but the animal is still a feature of the Upper Nile and the rivers, lakes and swamps of parts of tropical and southern Africa.

The two other species of crocodiles from Africa are the slender-snouted crocodile and the African dwarf crocodile, both of which live in the heavily forested regions of West and Central Africa. The African dwarf crocodile rarely grows above 3 ft. in length.

The alligators

The alligator family contains two species of alligators and five species of caimans. The alligators have the most northerly distribution of all the crocodilians: the American alligator ranges up the east coast of the USA

ABOVE The broad, rounded snout of the American alligator distinguishes it from the only other crocodilian native to the USA, the American crocodile, which has a long, tapering snout. American alligators range along the coast from North Carolina, south to Florida and across to Texas. They now number more than one million, and since legal protection of the species was lifted in September 1988, the public is once again allowed to hunt them.

as far as North Carolina, while the much rarer Chinese alligator lives along the lower Yangtze River in southern China. Both species hibernate in burrows in the colder part of their range.

Throughout its swampland habitat, the American alligator digs large holes connecting to underground passages up to 66 ft. long. The alligator hibernates in these passages, since they provide stable temperatures during the winter cold and summer heat.

The diet of the alligator changes with age. Young alligators eat smaller creatures such as insects and snails, but large alligators have a preference for certain fish such as bowfin, catfish and gar. Adults also feed on freshwater turtles and water snakes, as well as on water birds and mammals such as muskrats and raccoons.

The American alligator's nest consists of plant matter, such as leaves, mixed with mud and sand that the female scrapes together with sideways movements of her body and tail. She builds the nest at night, and may take several nights to complete the 3 ft. high mound. She then uses a hind foot to scoop out a cavity in the top of the nest in which to lay the eggs. The rotting vegetation inside the mound acts in a similar way to a compost heap, generating enough heat to incubate the eggs. Meanwhile, the female guards the nest until the young hatch.

In the USA, the conservation of the American alligator has resulted in a marked recovery of its numbers, and it is no longer on the endangered list. Unfortunately, its Old World counterpart, the Chinese alligator, is today very rare due to the loss of its habitat. It lives in fertile lowlands that are intensively farmed and have high human populations. Despite being protected by law, Chinese alligators are still killed for both their meat and their skins. They emerge from hibernation in late April, and during May are active mainly during the day while the weather is still cool; in summer, they become more nocturnal.

RIGHT The dwarf caiman of the Amazon Basin is one of the smallest of the caimans, measuring about 4 ft. 9 in. long.
CENTER The snout of the gharial of India is equipped with over a hundred sharp teeth. When hunting fish, the gharial waits until they swim by, then swings its narrow snout out into their midst, catching several fish at one time.
BOTTOM Black caimans are large enough to feed on capybaras—the largest of all the rodents. They catch their prey both on land and in the water.

Armored undersides

Several species of caimans live in the wetlands of South America. They range in size from the 3-ft.-long dwarf caiman to the black caiman that grows up to 13 ft. in length. Caimans are often boldly marked and usually have armored undersides made up of broadly overlapping bony plates. Smaller species, such as the broad-nosed caiman, feed mainly on aquatic invertebrates, especially water snails, while the larger black caiman preys on fish as well as on semiaquatic mammals such as capybaras.

Caimans are illegally caught in huge numbers for their skins, and their decline in number has seriously changed the ecology of many stretches of water in the Amazon Basin. Caimans' droppings had a fertilizing effect on the water, enabling it to support rich invertebrate life; the invertebrates, in turn, attracted large shoals of fish. But today, with a decrease in caimans, the fish stocks are smaller and fewer fish spawn in the Amazon's tributary lakes and streams.

The gharial

The gharial is a distinctive-looking crocodilian with a long and slender snout that lives in northern India, Pakistan, Nepal and Burma. It is often called a "gavial,", though this was an early misspelling of the original name ("gharial" comes from the Hindi word *ghara* meaning "pot," and refers to the pot-shaped lump on the male's snout). Gharials prefer deep, fast-flowing rivers with clear water, and deep pools with high sandbanks where they can bask and nest.

Gharials grow to about 20 feet long and have weak legs—since they stay mostly in the water they do not need strong, supportive limbs. Their teeth are long and sharp, enabling them to grasp slippery fishes and frogs. The gharial catches its fish prey with a sudden, sideways sweep of its slender jaws. It then comes to the surface and tosses its catch into the correct position for swallowing.

THE
AMPHIBIANS

BUILT FOR TWO WORLDS

The amphibians constitute the smallest group of vertebrates, with some 4000 species. They display an immense variety of forms, and while many are familiar, others have rarely been seen. Present-day amphibians belong to three orders: the frogs and toads; the salamanders and newts; and the caecilians. These are the only surviving representatives of a group of animals that, several hundred million years ago, was the most advanced and dominant form of life on earth. The amphibians reached that position because they were the first vertebrates to successfully leave the water and conquer the land. It was an important step in the evolution of animals, and later gave rise to the reptiles. The reptiles went one stage further to become completely adapted to living on dry land. In contrast, nearly all amphibians are dependent on water for at least part of their development.

The word "amphibian" comes from the Greek *amphibios* (*amphi* meaning "of both kinds" and *bios* meaning "life"). It refers to animals that can live two kinds of lives—one on land and one in the water. The life cycle of amphibians begins with the larval stage, which is the first stage of development after hatching from the egg. The larvae live in water, where they use gills to breathe (by extracting oxygen from the water) in much the same way as fish. They then undergo a radical transformation when they are ready to move onto land. The gills are reabsorbed into the body, and the animal starts to breathe air, using lungs. It is this adaptation to breathing air, along with the growth of limbs capable of supporting the animals on land, that enabled the first primitive amphibians to develop.

Amphibian ancestors

The oldest known amphibians lived on Earth some 350 million years ago, during the Devonian period. Their fossil remains were found in Greenland, and

TOP LEFT The most familiar types of amphibian larvae are the tadpoles of frogs and toads. These common toad tadpoles have begun to grow their back legs, but they will need to undergo many other physical changes before they can live on land.

LEFT The stripeless tree frog of Europe has sticky pads on its fingers and toes, enabling it to climb smooth surfaces.
PAGES 1696-1697 The muscular legs that allow the edible frog to leap away from danger are valued by humans as luxury food.

ABOVE The back legs of toads are not as muscular as those of frogs, and they tend to walk on all fours rather than hop, except when alarmed. The European common toad— the largest of the European toads—returns to the same pond each year to breed. It travels along the same route and covers as much as three miles.

show similarities to ancestral fish groups. But instead of having fish-like fins, these early amphibians were already equipped with well-developed, bony limbs, enabling them to support their lizard-shaped bodies on land. Amphibians are believed to have evolved either from lungfish or from a group of fishes called lobefins. However, it is not clear exactly how or when the change to land-living forms took place, since remains of the very earliest amphibians have yet to be discovered. But once they started to colonize the land, the number of their fossils increased dramatically. With far less competition for space and food on land than there was in the water, many amphibian species evolved to take advantage of their new environment. In time, a great diversity of types evolved, some of them growing to over 13 feet long.

These ancient amphibians dominated the land for several million years, but most became extinct before the more advanced reptiles took over late in the Permian period, about 225 million years ago. Links between the ancient and modern amphibians are still unknown, since gaps in the fossil record prevent scientists from tracing the amphibians' evolution fully.

Advances in evolution

The body structure of amphibians, both past and present, shows the advances made on their fish ancestors. The amphibians' bones, in particular, differ greatly from those of fishes. Amphibians have fewer skull bones, and they are broader and flatter. Their teeth, when present, are different from all other land vertebrates: a weak joint between the root and crown of each tooth enables it to bend inward.

Since an amphibian lives partly on land, it has evolved limbs and a backbone to support its weight. Because of this, the backbone has strengthened, and the internal leg joints have modified into supporting limb girdles. The ribcage is also well formed to prevent the internal organs from damage.

Several features present in the higher vertebrates first evolved in the amphibians, and were adaptations to living on land. Amphibians were the first vertebrates to have eyelids, preventing the surface of the eyes from drying out; and some of them were the first to develop true tongues for moistening and

ABOVE A frog's eyes, such as those of this moor frog, are placed high on the head so that the animal can keep watch while most of its body stays submerged in the water.
ABOVE RIGHT The male frog's croak announces his presence to other males, but its main purpose is to attract females. In the male pool frog, the inflated vocal sacs on each side of the head greatly amplify the animal's distinctive "purring" calls.

manipulating their food. The amphibians also evolved the first true ears, along with a sound-producing organ, the larynx.

Major modifications of the nervous system occurred in the amphibians. The spinal cord—the part of the central nervous system contained in the backbone—became enlarged in the region of the limbs, to coordinate movement. However, the most important advance among the amphibians was the increase in the area covered by the nerve cells. These invaded the outer layer of the two halves of the brain, beginning a process that ultimately resulted in the enlarged brain of the mammals.

Amphibians have thin, moist skins that serve a variety of functions vital to their survival. They breathe through their skins (as well as their gills and lungs) by absorbing oxygen from the air, in a process called osmosis. The skin also absorbs water from humid air and loses the water—and a certain amount of heat—through evaporation.

Amphibians that live in dry places have thicker skins than those living in humid areas, enabling them to conserve water. They breathe by using their lungs more than their skin. Unlike higher vertebrates, amphibians lack the muscles necessary to fill and empty their lungs of air. Instead, they use the bases of their mouths, which rise and fall rhythmically like bellows.

Skin-deep defense

The skin of present-day amphibians lacks the obvious protection evident in other vertebrate groups. Fish and reptiles, for example, have scales that, while different in structure, provide highly effective protection for their bodies. Birds have feathers, while mammals are well equipped with fur and hair.

Although amphibians have delicate skins, the animals are not as exposed and defenseless as they may seem. Their skin is covered with a large number of fluid-secreting glands that produce a slimy mucus, keeping it moist when the animal is on land and exposed to the air. The mucus provides a basic form of protection against water loss and also prevents too much fluid from entering the animal's body when it is immersed in water. In frogs, the mucus acts as a

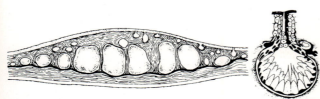

RIGHT Mucus-secreting glands in the skin of an amphibian prevent the animal's body from drying out and give the skin surface a moist, shiny appearance. Many frogs also have poison glands in their skin to deter animals from eating them, while some have glands that give off a pungent odor. **ABOVE** Two cross-section drawings show small mucous glands opening onto the surface of a frog's skin (A); and a magnified view of a single, flask-shaped mucous gland (B).

main form of defense, making the animals too slippery for predators to catch.

Some amphibians have skin glands that secrete a toxic liquid as an effective means of defense against enemies. These glands are highly specialized in their structure and function. Large numbers of them are either evenly distributed over the entire skin surface, or are located at specific points on the body. Toads, for example, have toxic glands behind and above their eyes. Called parotid glands, they are so large that they are easily visible to the human eye. The marine toad can squirt its poison over quite a distance.

Some frogs have poison glands that run in chains down the sides of their bodies. The poison-arrow frogs of Central and South America have a poison so lethal that a tiny dose will kill a human. The Indians of Colombia tip their arrows and blow darts with the skin secretions of at least three species of these frogs when they are hunting.

A sticky end

Although certain species of amphibians lack tongues, most have long tongues that may extend up to several inches. An amphibian uses its tongue to capture small prey, hitting the victim with its sticky tip which is coated with a thick, slimy mucus. The prey sticks to the tongue and is quickly carried to the back of the predator's mouth and swallowed.

An amphibian's stomach can expand to an enormous size when necessary, and is capable of holding large amounts of food compared to the size of its body. Because an amphibian does not possess teeth suitable for chewing, it crushes its prey between its jaws and swallows it almost whole.

AMPHIBIANS CLASSIFICATION

There are 4015 species of amphibians distributed through all the continents except Antarctica. They are classified in three orders: the order Gymnophiona, which contains the 163 species of caecilians; the order Urodela, containing the 358 species of salamanders and newts; and the order Anura, by far the largest of the orders, which comprises the 3494 species of frogs and toads.

Blood circulation

In amphibians, the blood circulation system is unique in that it changes dramatically during the course of the animal's development. In the larval stage, the blood circulation is similar to that of fish. Blood passes through the heart only once and is then pumped to the gills and the various parts of the body. The heart is an extremely simple structure. It has one chamber that receives the blood in need of oxygen from the body, and another, more muscular one that pumps blood to the gills. After the larva has developed into an adult, the blood circulation system becomes more complex, with the heart containing three chambers instead of two.

Development of the senses

Depending on their life-style, some amphibians use certain senses more than others. Most groups rely on sight to find their food, but since their vision is not

well developed, they generally spot their prey only if it is moving. However, amphibians living permanently in subterranean waters or underground have under-developed eyes. Newts and salamanders rely mainly on their sense of smell to locate breeding grounds.

Many types of frogs and toads have a well-developed sense of hearing, usually with quite obvious external ears. The visible part of the ear is called the tympanic membrane, or eardrum, and is located behind the eye. Frogs and toads use their hearing to detect food, such as flying insects, as well as to locate other members of the same species. Amphibians use sounds to identify prospective mates for breeding. Males also call and listen for the croaks of other males as a means of marking their individual territories.

The sense of taste plays a less important role. Amphibians swallow most items of prey without delay, but react quickly if they taste animals that have unpleasant defensive chemicals. Some insects—for example stinkbugs—and many millipedes defend themselves by emitting a foul-tasting and foul-smelling fluid. Amphibians either avoid them entirely or drop them immediately if they pick them up by mistake.

Amphibians are patchily distributed throughout all the continents. The largest number of species, mainly frogs and toads, inhabit humid equatorial regions.

ABOVE The long-tailed salamander belongs among the American brook salamanders and ranges from southern New York state to Alabama and Illinois. It measures from 4 to 6 in. long and lives in or under rotting logs, under stones, in caves and beside rivers. In the adult, the tail measures more than half the length of the body.

However, a few species of amphibians live within the Arctic Circle, some have adapted to living in hot, tropical and arid areas, and a few survive in deserts—so long as traces of water are available. A small number of amphibians live on mountains at altitudes of up to 14,800 ft. With the exception of the Argentinian and Californian toads, no amphibians tolerate saltwater.

Various species survive in the more inhospitable regions by restricting their activities to the night and to rare moments of rain. Some amphibians are well adapted to living in areas where the climate changes regularly. They escape cold, temperate winters by burying themselves in the ground or taking shelter in burrows built by other animals, such as small rodents. Amphibians can stay dormant for several months. However, unlike mammals that hibernate, they will move slowly away if disturbed while they are resting during the winter. Similarly, if there is a warm spell, they might become active and look for food.

ABOVE Most frogs and toads spawn in water, but some species lay their eggs in damp areas on land. These miss out the tadpole stage of their development and the young hatch directly from their eggs as miniature frogs. The eggs are wrapped in a slimy substance called mucilage that protects them from drying out.

Amphibians cannot survive excessive heat and dry periods. Those that live in hotter regions escape otherwise unbearable conditions by taking refuge underground. When they become inactive, they do not need to feed, and so can survive for extremely long periods in their underground shelters until conditions improve.

In very hot climates, it is essential for amphibians to conserve water. Frogs manage to survive in areas with extended periods of drought by filling their bladders with water when it rains, and then burying themselves. When they need the water, they reabsorb it through the bladder walls. In Australia, when Aborigines are in the outback and need a drink, they may seek out these water-holding frogs.

Food and enemies

Amphibians are predators—they feed on small to large invertebrates such as spiders, insects and insect larvae, land- and water-living crustaceans, worms, slugs and snails. Larger species even feed on small vertebrates such as young lizards and mice. Only the marine toad and the tadpole larvae of frogs and toads are vegetarian. They feed either by filtering particles of food from the water, or by scraping at plant material with their specially adapted mouths.

Amphibians are themselves prey to larger vertebrates. They fall victim to many animals, such as other amphibians, reptiles (particularly snakes and terrapins) and marsh and woodland birds (for example, rails, cranes, ducks, birds of prey and owls). Larvae are much more vulnerable than adults. Tadpoles are eaten not only by vertebrates, but also by dragonfly larvae, larvae and adult water beetles, some species of spiders and many types of fish. Amphibian eggs are also eaten by other amphibians, particularly newts.

Amphibians use various strategies to avoid being eaten. If they have defensive chemicals in their skins, they usually advertise the fact by exhibiting a warning color, often red or yellow. The fire salamander, for example, becomes strikingly marked in yellow and black. Some species conceal the fact that they are poisonous until they are attacked. The fire-bellied toad raises the sides of its body to show its bright red and black underside when it is provoked.

ABOVE In the breeding season, the male alpine newt can be identified by the yellowish crest that runs along its back and tail and is marked with bars or, as seen here, with black spots. Alpine newts usually occur in or near ponds, lakes and slow streams.

FAR RIGHT Found only on the Iberian Peninsula and in western France, the marbled newt is distinguished from other European newts by its bold blotches and green coloration. The newt on the left is an adult female, recognizable by the bright orange stripe on her back.

As another form of defense, some edible species pretend that they are distasteful. They mimic poisonous types by matching their colors and thereby gaining the same protection from predators. The harmless North American red salamander, for example, mimics the red eft, the land-living stage of the red-spotted newt.

Most amphibians camouflage themselves to match their backgrounds. The majority of tree-living frogs, for example, are green, to blend in with the leaves. Many are able to change their color, making them even more difficult to see. Some ground-dwelling frogs resemble dead leaves, even possessing fleshy projections on their bodies that look like the edges of the leaves.

Leaping to safety is another defense typical of frogs and toads. As soon as an intruder approaches the pond, they dive into the water, and swiftly burrow into the mud at the bottom. Several species of toads puff themselves up and stand on all fours in times of danger to make themselves appear more aggressive. Some predators retreat, but others, such as medium-sized snakes, may not be deterred. However, they cannot swallow the victim because of its bloated size.

Reproduction

As a group, amphibians exhibit the most varied forms of reproduction of any of the vertebrates. Eggs can be fertilized either inside or outside the body. In most salamanders and newts, fertilization is internal. Frogs and toads usually fertilize their eggs externally. Normally, the male holds onto the female with his front legs and deposits sperm over the eggs as the female lays them. Little is known about the caecilians' mating habits, except that in most species the eggs are fertilized internally.

The majority of amphibians produce a large number of eggs, as many will be eaten by predators. Species that look after their young lay fewer eggs. Parental care varies from simple to more complex behavior, depending on the species. Among giant salamanders, the male merely keeps a watch over the eggs until they hatch. Among the numerous advanced species, the male midwife toad wraps the string of

LEFT The bright markings of the turquoise poison-arrow frog warn predators that it is extremely poisonous. The Indians of South American forests skewer and roast this small frog over a flame, causing its poison glands to secrete their toxins. After they have left the poison to ferment, they then apply it to the tips of their arrows so that it will paralyze any animal that they shoot for food.

BELOW LEFT In spite of their wide-angle vision and keen hearing, unwary frogs and toads still fall prey in great numbers to birds and snakes. They form a major part of the diet of water snakes that creep up stealthily and capture them from behind, swallowing them whole.

fertilized eggs around his hind legs and carries it to the water when they are ready to hatch.

In some cases, the young are born already well developed, so they are less at risk from the danger of being eaten by predators. Several caecilians give birth to fully formed young.

Social life

Amphibians are not generally social animals, although they will sometimes congregate in an area with the best conditions for survival. In such a situation, amphibians form a crowd rather than an organized group.

In areas habitually occupied by amphibians, the opposite is true. Here, each animal occupies its own territory—a few square inches, for example—and defends it against its neighbors, gaining the rights to any prey that strays into its area.

Tadpole togetherness

Certain groups of larvae, such as toad tadpoles, appear to be linked by simple forms of social behavior. They come together for environmental reasons alone, and move around in irregular formation. In other cases, tadpoles near the of their larval stage may form a simple, coordinated group. If stranded in a pond that is drying out, they will gather together at the center, moving their broad tails in unison so that the mud on the bottom of the pond is disturbed. The small hollows where water still remains become deeper and fill up with water from the surrounding slime. Provided that the small puddle does not dry up completely, the tadpoles will develop into frogs and hop to safety. Under these circumstances, all the tadpoles act in the same way for the common good, without observing a hierarchy.

LIMBLESS BURROWERS

Shaped like earthworms, the caecilians are little-known amphibians that burrow through surface soil and leaf litter in warm and tropical areas; they are carnivores, catching worms, insects and lizards in their large jaws

The caecilians are the most unusual and least-known group of amphibians. They live in water or under damp ground, in mud, sand and swamps—usually in forest areas within the tropics. Caecilians have cylindrical, elongated bodies with no limbs. They have stumpy, tapering heads and short, rounded ends. Only very primitive species have tails. Caecilians vary in length from 3 to 59 in. Many are ringed by numerous bands and resemble large earthworms, for which they are often mistaken. They may also be mistaken for worm-lizards—reptiles that belong to a separate order, but that lead a similar lifestyle. Caecilians, worm-lizards and earthworms all followed a path of parallel evolution, adapting to the same damp, underground conditions. Consequently, all three groups closely resemble one another.

LEFT **Stages in the development of the sticky caecilian of Sri Lanka: a cluster of eggs joined together (A); the female protects her eggs by coiling herself around them until they hatch (B); a larval caecilian, before hatching, is still attached to the yolk sac (C); the larva immediately after hatching, showing the** large, feathery gills (D).
BELOW **The map shows the geographical distribution of the caecilians.**
PAGE 1707 **The gray caecilian of the Central American rain forest is, like other caecilians, a secretive, earthworm-shaped amphibian that hunts small prey such as worms and insects.**

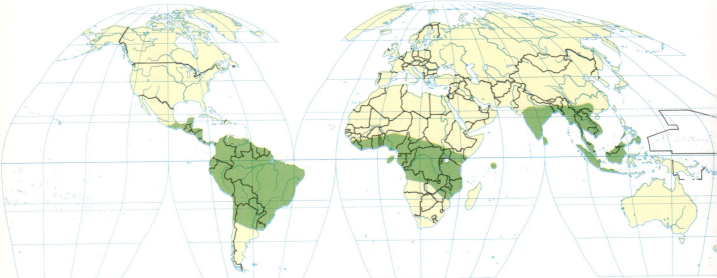

■ Caecilians

ABOVE Caecilians, such as this West African species, live mainly underground. They are either sightless (the name "caecilian" comes from the Latin *caecitas* meaning "blind") or have small eyes covered with skin and capable of sensing light. They lack limbs and have strong, heavily boned skulls that they use for burrowing.

Underground hunters

The more advanced caecilians have smooth skin, while others have patches of scales, some running the length of the body. The scales are similar to those of fish, except that they are embedded under the skin— an extremely primitive evolutionary feature.

The internal features of caecilians reveal the extent to which they have adapted to their environment. The skull is made up of large, compact bones that enable the animal to burrow merely by exerting pressure with its body and pushing forward. The rest of the skeleton is made up of only the central bone structure. When their bodies became elongated, the hip bones and limbs were lost. As with other snake-like animals, adult caecilians have one lung that is large and long and one that is reduced to a small lobe. Larval caecilians, like other larval amphibians, have gills.

Caecilians have a well-developed sense of smell, an adaptation to hunting for food underground. They are unique among vertebrates in possessing a pair of small, antenna-like extensions that lie in a groove between the eyes and nostrils. These extensions collect chemical information from the environment and pass it on to the nose. Caecilians are also able to find food by detecting vibrations in the ground through their lower jaw. Their hearing and sight are only poorly developed, since they are not important for a life spent underground or in the water. In some species the eyes are actually covered by the skull bone or by skin, so they cannot see at all.

Slow evolution

The high degree of adaptation to underground life suggests that caecilians evolved slowly over a very long period. However, the group is almost without fossil record. To date, only one fossil bone has been found, so the origin and evolution of caecilians must be established almost exclusively by examining the surviving species and their environment.

Caecilians were once considered to be extremely rare. In fact, they are rarely seen simply because of their secretive life-style. Although they are completely absent from some parts of the world, certain species are very common in some locations, while most are thinly scattered over a wide area.

Tropical inhabitants

Inhabiting vast areas of the tropics, caecilians live in areas ranging from sea level to 6500 ft. They are found in Central America, much of South America, equatorial Africa, the Seychelles, India, Indochina, part of the Indo-Malaysia archipelago, and the southern Philippines, but are absent from Madagascar and Australia. The origins of caecilians can, to some extent, be traced by studying the separation of the continental landmasses in tropical regions.

Rarely observed

Little is known about the biology of the caecilians, and even less is known about their behavior and courtship. However, some species that live in water have been observed performing an undulating, aquatic dance before mating. In all species, the male transfers sperm to the female directly and the eggs are fertilized internally. Until a few decades ago, it was believed that all caecilians laid eggs. Now it is known that although some species lay eggs, the majority give birth to live young.

More is known about the breeding behavior of egg-laying caecilians than any other group. In the most primitive species, females lay their eggs in the soil near streams. The larvae have gills and live in the water where they are free-swimming. They only come onto land when they have developed into adults. Some types spend their entire larval stage in the egg underground, and hatch as miniature adults.

All egg-laying caecilians show parental care, coiling themselves around their eggs to protect them. The sticky caecilian of Sri Lanka is typical. The female lays a string of eggs and wraps herself around them until they hatch. While they are developing, the eggs absorb moisture until they have almost doubled in volume.

The young are born in small, underground chambers leading off the parent's burrow. The passages usually connect to water, and the larvae head toward it as soon as they are free of the eggs' protective coverings. They lead an aquatic life until they develop into adults.

Unusual reproduction

Perhaps as many as half the species of caecilians have a most unusual form of reproduction for amphibians, shared only with a few frogs and salamanders. When the eggs hatch, the larvae do not leave the mother, but develop inside her, feeding from her for most of the time.

The hatched larvae remain in the female's oviduct—the tube leading from her ovary where the eggs are produced. Once they have consumed the egg yolk, they feed on a rich secretion called "uterine milk" that is produced by glands in the oviduct. The larvae have small teeth that they use to feed on the secretion. They acquire adult teeth shortly before they are born.

During this stage of development, the larvae breathe through their gills, exchanging oxygen and other gases through fine blood vessels in the mother's body. At the end of this period, which lasts up to 11 months, the female gives birth to 7-20 young.

Caecilian diets

Most caecilians are opportunistic feeders, preying on the small animals that share the same underground environment—for example, worms, burrowing crickets and termites. Some larger species also eat small vertebrates such as lizards, frogs, toads and young mice. Caecilians themselves are mainly preyed upon by birds and snakes—snakes may catch them inside their underground burrows. However, most vertebrates ignore caecilians because of the unpleasant and poisonous substance that some species secrete from their skin.

CAECILIANS CLASSIFICATION

The caecilians belong to the order Gymnophiona (or Apoda), and number 163 species grouped in 34 genera and five families. Most inhabit the moist soil and leaf litter beneath forests and plantations, and some occur in lowland rivers. Confined mainly to tropical regions, they occur in Central and South America, Africa, India, Southeast Asia, Indonesia and the Philippines. Because so little is known about the caecilians, few of the species have common names. Asian species include the sticky caecilian, *Ichthyophis glutinosus*, of Sri Lanka, while African caecilians include *Geotripetes seraphini* of Central and West Africa. Some of the New World species are *Caecilia thompsoni* of Colombia, *Gymnopis multiplicata* of Central America and the gray caecilian, *Dermophis mexicanus*, of Central America.

SMOOTH, SLENDER AND SECRETIVE

Known as the tailed amphibians, salamanders and newts lead quiet, mostly unseen, lives. While all newts and many salamanders enter water to breed, there are salamanders that live entirely in the water or on land

Pacific giant salamander

Hellbender

Red salamander

Red-spotted newt (j

Texas blind salamander

Long-tailed salamander

Greater siren

Mud puppy

Tiger salamander (adult)

Tiger salamander (larva)

Siberian salamander

SALAMANDERS AND NEWTS — CLASSIFICATION: 1 —

The salamanders and newts, or tailed amphibians, belong to the order Urodela (sometimes referred to as the Caudata). The 358 species are grouped in 60 genera, and occur over much of Eurasia, in northwest Africa, in North America, and in northern South America. There are nine families in the order: the Hynobiidae, the Asiatic salamanders; the Cryptobranchidae, the giant salamanders; the Ambystomatidae, the mole salamanders; the Dicamptodontidae, the Pacific mole salamanders; the Salamandridae, the newts, brook salamanders and fire salamanders; the Amphiumidae, the amphiumas; the Proteidae, which contains the olm, the mud puppy and the water dogs; the Plethodontidae, the lungless salamanders; and the Sirenidae, the sirens.

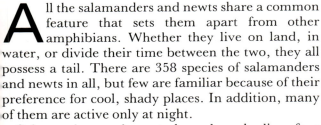

All the salamanders and newts share a common feature that sets them apart from other amphibians. Whether they live on land, in water, or divide their time between the two, they all possess a tail. There are 358 species of salamanders and newts in all, but few are familiar because of their preference for cool, shady places. In addition, many of them are active only at night.

Salamanders and newts have long bodies, four short but sturdy legs and a long tail. Unlike frogs and toads, they retain their tails throughout their adult life. Some species grow to an enormous size, reaching about 5 ft. in length, but the majority are relatively small, averaging 2-6 in.

The general appearance of these tailed amphibians is similar to that of the lizards, and they were once classified with the reptiles. However, the similarity is only superficial. In the structure of their bodies, they resemble the earliest known amphibian fossils more closely than any other living amphibians.

Delicate skin

Like all amphibians, salamanders and newts have delicate skin that makes them prone to water loss. They cannot survive long periods in dry conditions, and they have become extremely sensitive to changes in humidity. When climatic conditions are not

ABOVE The land-dwelling and nocturnal fire salamander of Europe only returns to the water when it is ready to give birth to its live young. The newly born larvae are already well developed with feathery, external gills. Fire salamanders may also produce juveniles that have fully formed lungs instead of gills.
PAGE 1711 Newts, such as this marbled newt of southwest Europe, spend most of their life on land. Each spring, they take to water for two or three months to breed.

favorable, some salamanders and newts survive by hiding away and remaining inactive for long periods until the weather improves.

Many species of salamanders and newts live in water throughout their lives, but the majority complete their larval development in water and then spend their adult lives on land—often under stones or rotting wood. They are largely confined to temperate climates, with most species living in the Northern Hemisphere—in Europe, Asia and North America. However, they can live in quite cold conditions, and one species—the Siberian salamander—has a northern distribution that crosses the Arctic Circle. There are species that live in the hot conditions of Africa, but only near the Mediterranean Sea. The lungless salamanders are the only species that thrive in truly tropical climates. They range through Central America and northern South America, reaching below the Equator.

ABOVE **Once the larvae of newts and salamanders have grown legs, they differ little in shape from the adults. The young smooth newt shown here** still has to lose its feathery, external gills.
FAR RIGHT **The map shows the geographical distribution of salamanders and newts.**

Salamanders and newts have varied means of reproduction. They usually have some form of courtship behavior, after which the male produces a jelly-like sac containing sperm. The female may deposit her egg cells with the sperm to have them fertilized outside her body, or she may pick up the sperm sac in her cloaca so that the egg cells are fertilized inside her body.

Most species lay eggs, depositing them in or near water. The resulting larvae resemble adults in appearance, but have external gills that are often large and complex. As the larvae develop into adults, they reabsorb their gills into their bodies ready for life on land. Unlike frogs and toads, salamanders and newts do not reabsorb their tails.

Staying youthful

Several species reach maturity without losing their gills and spend their entire lives in water. They even breed while they still have features typical of the larval stage. Other species that normally develop lungs and undergo a complete metamorphosis to the adult stage sometimes retain their larval features and life-style. Such cases are unusual, and are caused by specific environmental conditions, such as the lack of a particular chemical in the body. A well-known example is the Mexican axolotl, which keeps its larval appearance if it is lacking in iodine.

For most of the year, the males and females of a species are difficult to distinguish. In the breeding season, however, many salamanders and newts change their appearance, making identification easier. Males, in particular, often acquire more intense color markings. Some species develop outgrowths of skin along the line of the back or along the feet.

These changes in appearance not only make it easier to identify the sexes within a single species, they also make it easier to distinguish between different species and subspecies. Several European and American forms are difficult to identify outside the breeding season.

Prey and predators

Salamanders and newts are formidable hunters during both larval and adult stages of their development. They will eat any animal small enough to cope with, including worms, the larvae and adults of many types of insects, freshwater shrimps, water fleas, snails, frog spawn, and tadpoles. On the other hand, they also fall prey to many enemies, including water birds, owls and other birds of prey, carnivorous mammals, such as otters and shrews, and water snakes. Humans are not usually direct enemies, although certain salamander species are hunted for food in Central America and the Far East.

Salamanders and newts do not normally produce any sounds, unlike frogs and toads that have developed vocal sacs. However, some occasionally produce a faint croak when they are molested by predators.

Defensive secretion

Several land-living species of salamanders have developed a system of defense that makes them unappetizing to some of their predators. They secrete a mildly poisonous substance from their skins. The substance produces an unpleasant itching effect in the mouth of any attacker, and also serves the vital function of keeping the amphibian's skin moist and preventing it from drying out.

The secretion-producing ability of these salamander species has given them an unjust reputation for causing serious injury, if not death. At one time, it was even thought that they could bite and inject their poison.

Another legend suggested that salamanders were immune to fire and could walk through flames. The legend probably stemmed from their habit of hiding in wood. If a damp log was thrown on a fire, a frightened salamander may well have emerged, little harmed, because it was protected by its moist skin. In fact, the name "salamander" originally meant fire lizard, and asbestos was once called "salamander's wool."

Ancient amphibians

The giant salamanders and Asiatic salamanders are closely related, and are among the most primitive species of amphibians alive today. Apart from possibly the sirens, they are the only group of tailed amphibians to employ external fertilization. They do not use a spermatophore, the package of sperm produced by most other groups. Instead, after the eggs have been laid by the female, the male sheds his sperm over them. The eggs are normally laid in a jelly-like sac. Giant and Asiatic salamanders have a complex skull structure similar to that of fishes. As amphibians have become more advanced, the number of skull bones has gradually reduced. Some bones have disappeared and others have fused together.

The Asiatic salamanders

Members of the Asiatic salamander family are generally small in size, varying between 4 and 8 in. in length. They undergo complete metamorphosis, with the larvae turning into fully formed adults. Some species, however, do not develop lungs, and breathe mainly through the skin. Asiatic salamanders on the whole have small lungs, and live in fast-flowing streams where oxygen is abundant. A few types of Asiatic salamanders are unusual for tailed amphibians in that they have sharp, curved claws.

Distribution and hibernation

The area of the Asiatic salamanders' distribution extends from the edge of eastern Europe across to the Pacific, and from the Arctic south to the mountains of southwest Asia and southern China. Most species are found in Japan and eastern Asia.

The best-known species is the Siberian salamander, which is gray-brown with a broad golden-yellow back and variable black markings on the side of the body. The Siberian salamander measures about 4.5 in. in length and has a smooth, shiny skin. It is particularly well adapted to cold climates, and is found throughout most of Siberia and even within the Arctic Circle. In some areas, such as around Lake Baikal in eastern Siberia, it occurs in great numbers and is able to resist subzero temperatures without suffering.

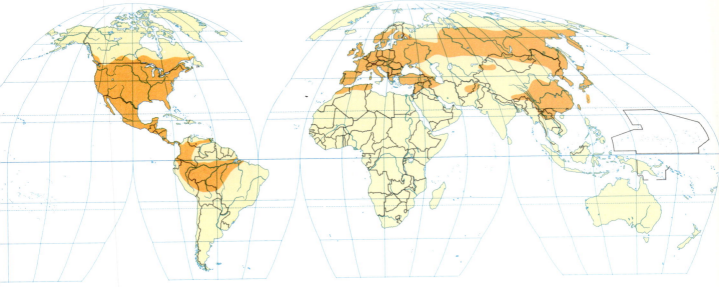

Salamanders and newts

SALAMANDERS AND NEWTS — CLASSIFICATION: 2 —

Asiatic salamanders

The family Hynobiidae contains the Asiatic salamanders of northern and eastern Asia. There are 33 species in nine genera, most of which inhabit fast-flowing streams. Species include the Siberian salamander, *Hynobius keyserlingii*, which is widespread in Siberia and other parts of northern Asia; *H. nebulosus* of Japan; and *Batrachuperus karlschmidti* of China.

Giant salamanders

The three species of giant salamanders make up the family Cryptobranchidae. The Japanese giant salamander, *Megalobatrachus japonicus*, occurs in Japan, and the Chinese giant salamander, *M. davidianus*, lives in eastern China. The hellbender, *Cryptobranchus alleganiensis*, is a New World species from the eastern and central USA. All three inhabit rivers and streams.

Siberian salamanders spend the long, rigorous northern winters asleep under the frozen mud, ready to emerge at the first signs of thaw. Siberian salamanders do not metamorphose until the third year and are not sexually mature until the fifth. Once the ice has melted in the spring thaw, the Siberian salamanders gather together in shallow pools. The mature female lays two long, thin, jelly-like egg sacs that she attaches to twigs, plants, or stones under the water. Each egg sac contains 50-60 eggs.

Once the eggs have been laid, the males waiting nearby come over to fertilize them. They shed their sperm while swimming back and forth over the egg sacs. The sperm penetrates the coating of the egg sacs to fertilize the individual eggs. Eventually the coating starts to disintegrate, so that when the eggs hatch in approximately three or four weeks, the larvae can escape easily. They measure only 0.4 in. long at this stage, and will immediately start to feed on small water creatures. The larvae grow rapidly during the spring, and by late summer have developed into juvenile salamanders.

One of the smallest Asiatic salamanders occurs in Japan and on several of its islands. Measuring under 4 in. in length, it is yellow-brown in color. More is known about its behavior in the wild than about any other member of its family. Males develop their courting colors in autumn when their color deepens, a white spot appears on the throat and a crest develops on the tail. They now lead an aquatic life throughout autumn to the following spring. The salamanders swim around until they find a place suitable for a female to lay her eggs. They will remain in the same spot for a long time, occasionally waving their tails from side to side in order to attract a female.

The tail movements help to distribute a cloacal secretion, which the female detects. The secretion also advertises the male's territorial rights to other salamanders. When a female approaches, the male attracts her attention by raising and lowering his lower jaw rhythmically to emphasize the white throat spot that develops during the breeding season. The female produces an egg case that the male fertilizes externally. The male stays with the eggs for a long time in order to protect them from predators.

One species of Asiatic salamander that measures up to 8 in. in length is distributed along the mountains east of Tibet, up to 13,000 ft. above sea level. It used to be worshiped by Buddhist monks on Mount Omei and was protected as a holy creature. If one of these salamanders were killed, fierce storms would follow, and the salamander was thus regarded as sacred. The species was considered to have healing properties, especially as the remedy for stomach-ache. It was used extensively in the preparation of folk-healing remedies.

Amphibian giants

The giant salamanders belong to a small family that contains the largest amphibians of any kind. They never leave the water, and retain larval characteristics throughout their lives. They keep their larval teeth, and do not possess eyelids (like all tailed amphibian larvae) even when they are adult. They do, however, lose their gills quite early in life. Their eggs are fertilized externally, as in the Asiatic salamanders. Two species of giant salamander occur in the Far East, and the only other species is found in the eastern states of the USA.

The general appearance of the giant salamanders is cumbersome and primitive. Their heads are broad,

RIGHT The Chinese giant salamander has extremely poor vision and relies on touch and smell to locate food—worms, insects, crayfish and smaller salamanders—in its underwater habitat. The average adult weighs 55-66 lbs.

BELOW RIGHT The Japanese giant salamander is the world's largest amphibian, and may grow to over five feet in length. Overhunting of this species for food has seriously reduced its numbers in the wild.

their limbs are short and thick-set and their relatively short tails are flattened vertically. The largest species is the rare Japanese giant salamander, found in restricted parts of central southern Japan. It can exceed 5 ft. in length and weighs over 220 lbs. The Chinese giant salamander of eastern China is slightly smaller. Both inhabit the waters of deep, strong-running rivers.

They are generally only active at night, spending the day asleep under rocks. Despite their large size and apparent slowness, they are successful predators. They feed on fish, frogs, crayfish, water-living insects, snails and other salamanders, which they ambush by hiding under large, submerged stones or in natural hollows along the banks.

Japanese and Chinese salamanders are restricted to flowing water with plenty of oxygen due to their size and lack of gills. A visible flap of skin runs along the sides of the body, to increase the surface area for skin respiration. They also breathe through their lungs, taking gulps of air from the surface when necessary. When kept in captivity, these giant salamanders surface for air every six to eight minutes.

Defense of the larvae

During summer, the female Japanese and Chinese salamanders lay several hundred transparent eggs, about 0.79 in. wide, that are attached in long, jelly-like strings. These are fertilized by the male. He remains near the eggs until they hatch in order to defend them from predators such as fish. When the larvae emerge from their eggs, they quickly learn to swim, however rough the water. They are less streamlined than the adults at first, but as they develop, they begin to resemble their parents more closely.

Both the Chinese and the Japanese giant salamanders have been actively hunted as a food source, and they are now very rare in the wild. They can live for an extremely long time. The first specimen caught in 1829 lived in captivity for 52 years, and died in 1881.

The only other giant salamander, the hellbender, measures up to 28 in. in length. It is distributed throughout the central and eastern states of the USA. It is very similar to the other species in form and habits in that it never leaves the water. However, the adults are distinct in that they preserve one pair of gill slits hidden within the folds of skin around the neck.

During the breeding season, the adult male hellbender selects a small hollow protected by an overhanging stone and defends it against other males. He turns away females that have laid their eggs. Only egg-bearing females are allowed to stop in the nest, and lay their eggs.

The female hellbender lays two long strings of eggs, up to 450 in number, held together by a sticky thread. The thread glues on to the rocks and hardens. The male then produces sperm that disperses in the water.

He beats his tail to guide the sperm toward the eggs, repeating the action several times, inviting several females to lay their strings of eggs in the same spot. He then stays on the nest for 10-12 weeks until the eggs hatch, defending them against any enemies. A few days after the eggs have exhausted their supply of egg yolk, the larvae hatch and swim away against the current to find a new place to live. They feed on small water creatures, such as insect larvae, worms and shrimps in the river's muddy bottom.

The mole salamanders

The mole salamanders are so named because of their burrowing habits—they spend most of their lives underground. They are normally only seen in the breeding season, when they make their way to ponds in order to mate and lay their eggs. Most adult mole salamanders live on land. However, some remain in the larval form even when they are sexually mature (paedomorphic). The most well-known example of the group is the Mexican axolotl.

Mole salamanders have flattened bodies, broad heads and smooth skin. Many have bright, colorful markings on their bodies. They are found in southern Alaska, southern Labrador, and over wide areas of North America as far south as the Mexican highlands.

Spring migrations

The spotted salamander is a well-known species that migrates in vast numbers to breeding grounds in the spring. Over a period of a few days, the spotted salamanders mate, lay their eggs (approximately 200 per female), and then return to their life on land. The eggs hatch and develop into adults by the autumn. Other mole salamanders breed at varying times of the year. Some guard their eggs until they hatch.

The largest and most widespread species is the tiger salamander. It can grow to 9 in. in length and is dark with yellow markings. These markings vary greatly, and may consist of a series of broad, irregular stripes or, more frequently, patches of various sizes.

As with other members of the family of mole salamanders, the tiger salamander ranges throughout North America. It has a sturdy body, a broad head and a wide, flat tail. After reaching adulthood, many tiger salamanders will retain their larval gills. In color and markings, the tiger salamander shows great variation over a large range. It usually inhabits semi-

arid sagebrush areas, damp mountain woods and meadows—appearing at altitudes of 9800 ft. The tiger salamander eats insects, slugs, snails and some vertebrates. As the world's largest terrestrial amphibian, it will not hesitate to attack other amphibians and small rodents.

Burrowing for food

The tiger salamander often lives underground, in soft ground. During hot, dry periods, it spends long periods beneath logs or stones near water. Rather than digging its own burrow, the tiger salamander may occupy the burrows of squirrels, tortoises, crayfish and other animals. It is the burrowing habit of the tiger salamander which earns the family of mole salamanders its name.

As a nocturnal amphibian, the tiger salamander mainly appears in the open at night, especially after rainfall. It also surfaces regularly during the breeding season. Breeding occurs in lakes, ponds and puddles, especially in watery areas where the fish predators that eat the larvae are scarce. The tiger salamander lays its eggs between December and February in the southern parts of its range in North America (including Mexico and parts of Central America). At high altitudes and in northern regions of North America, the tiger salamander lays at a later date.

Neoteny

The larvae of the tiger salamander species grow rapidly until they metamorphose into the adult form. Following metamorphosis, subadult individuals lead a largely terrestrial life. However, some tiger salamanders retain larval structures into adulthood. The failure to fully metamorphose is called neoteny. When neotenous tailed amphibians reach breeding age, they still retain their external gills. Unlike adult salamanders, they lack eyelids.

Neoteny may be temporary, occurring in species that lack a particular nutrient. A probable cause of neoteny is iodine deficiency. Iodine is essential in the synthesis of the hormone thyroxin—the production of increasing amounts of thyroxin in the thyroid gland triggers metamorphosis. As a result, there must be sufficient amounts of iodine in the water for successful metamorphosis to take place. Experiments demonstrate that there are insufficient levels of iodine in the watery areas where tiger salamanders are neotenous. The

same areas also suffer a high frequency of goiter in cattle—a swelling of the thyroid gland that also derives from iodine deficiency. The aquatic nature of neotenous tiger salamanders enables them to thrive in areas that enjoy rainfall throughout the year. But in times of drought they become stranded and die.

Neoteny is particularly common in the Mexican axolotl, which inhabits Lake Xochimilco in Mexico. The adult Mexican axolotl retains its larval gills if deprived of the iodine it needs to produce the hormone thyroxin. Almost all Mexican axolotls fail to metamorphose. They are generally neotenous and totally aquatic in behavior—indeed "axolotl" is a local name meaning "water monster." The low level of iodine in the waters of Lake Xochimilco is almost certainly responsible for the larval features of the axolotl, although the cold waters of the lake also limit the effects of thyroxin. The Mexican axolotl has reputed healing powers, and is also in demand as a culinary delicacy. As a result, it is now endangered and has international protection to prevent its extinction.

Breeding ponds

The 10-in.-long spotted salamander is a secretive, ground-dwelling amphibian that ranges throughout the eastern half of North America. During the warm,

ABOVE The tiger salamander of the northern USA may be barred, spotted, plain olive-green, or black, according to its locality. It lives mainly underground, emerging at night to hunt insects, slugs and snails. After the early spring rains, tiger salamanders gather in temporary pools to court and lay their eggs.

BELOW A pair of mole salamanders perform their courtship "waltz," gripping the base of each other's tail (A). A female Jefferson mole salamander lays her eggs on an underwater branch (B).

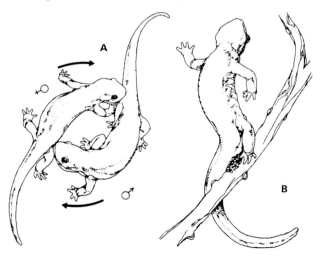

ABOVE Few salamanders have been as well studied as the spotted salamander of the eastern USA. When the warm rains arrive in early spring, the spotted salamanders make mass migrations to woodland ponds where they engage in vigorous mating for two or three days. After the females have laid their eggs, they return to their land-dwelling way of life until it is time to return to the ponds the next year.

damp nights of early spring, it migrates to breeding ponds, estimating the precise time for the journey from the heavy rains and increased climatic temperatures. Male and female salamanders migrate to their chosen breeding ponds in great numbers. For several days in mid-March, mass mating occurs. During breeding, the salamanders thrash around so violently in their breeding ponds that the water appears to boil.

Brilliant yellow spots speckle the blue-black bodies of the spotted salamander, heightening the effect of this mating spectacle. Fertilization occurs internally—the male produces the sperm in a small capsule known as a spermatophore. The spermatophore consists of a broad base, surmounted by a sperm-filled cap, which the male deposits for the female to collect in her cloaca. The female lays her eggs in batches of about a hundred eggs. She attaches the eggs to submerged vegetation or twigs before returning to dry land.

The young spotted salamanders hatch in three to six weeks. At birth, the larvae are tiny, gilled creatures but they grow rapidly. When the larvae metamorphose and leave their watery habitat in the autumn, they are 2.4 inches in length. They will return to the water in the second spring of their adult lives to carry on the reproductive process. The spotted salamander spends most of its time underground.

Feeding mainly on earthworms and soft-bodied insects, it rarely appears on land other than during the breeding season.

Heavy head

The mole salamander lives underground in burrows dug by other animals. Brown or gray in color with blue-white markings, it lives among logs, bark and stones in woods and low-lying areas. It reaches 3-5 in. in length and is a stocky amphibian, with a large, heavy head and stubby limbs. If in danger, the mole salamander "head-butts" predators such as small mammals, using poison glands on its head to repel predators.

The Jefferson salamander grows to 8 in. in length and is gray-brown in color, often with a scattering of blue spots over its body. It is a long, slender amphibian, with a large, wide snout and particularly long toes. Its head is large and its body is proportionately very short, giving it a strange appearance. Early in spring, the adults make their annual migration to their preferred breeding pond. After fertilization, the female lays 200 eggs in groups of 15 eggs at a time. The eggs are produced in cylindrical clumps that adhere to twigs or other submerged objects or vegetation. After 30-45 days, the 0.5-in.-long larvae hatch. The process of metamorphosis lasts 3 to 6 months. Newly metamorphosed young leave their watery habitat between July and August to start their life on land, where they live under debris in woodland near ponds and wetlands.

Woodland amphibian

The attractive marbled salamander is a handsome, shiny-black amphibian with broad, uneven spots and bands that are silver-gray in color. A woodland species, the 4.5-in.-long marbled salamander breeds in the autumn. Courtship occurs on land, and the female deposits her eggs singly, in a hollow under a rock or fallen log, until she has formed a small mound of eggs. She then curls herself around the mound, incubating her eggs until the rains come. The first rains of winter cause the eggs to swell up, and hatching takes place a few days later. The larvae develop in the temporary pool that forms in the hollow.

The Californian tiger salamander inhabits arid environments, where it lives underground near ponds. It has a blunt head and is dark in color, with creamy, round spots similar to those of the tiger salamander.

ABOVE The Mexican axolotl reaches sexual maturity without changing from a larval state to that of a normal salamander. It remains in the water and keeps the external gills and broad tail characteristic of salamander larvae. In spite of its undeveloped appearance, the Mexican axolotl breeds successfully and usually completes the whole of its life cycle underwater.

The breeding season of the 8-in.-long Californian tiger salamander lasts from December to February. Mating usually occurs in temporary pools caused by rainfall. The female lays her eggs singly and attaches them to slender stems or the leaves of aquatic vegetation. The larvae measure 0.4 in. in length when they emerge from the egg. By the time that they complete their four-month-long period of metamorphosis, they are 2 to 3 inches in length.

The secretive northwestern salamander, inhabiting the northwestern USA and southwest Canada, is brown in color and has parotid glands that form a large swelling behind each eye. Parotid glands, common in the salamanders, are collections of small glands that produce poisonous or noxious chemicals used to deter predators such as shrews.

A sticky deterrent

Finding its home in damp meadows, woods and forests, the 9-in.-long northwestern salamander thrives at altitudes of up to 10,000 ft., where it hides under stones and fallen logs. Female northwestern salamanders lay their eggs in ponds, lakes and streams from January to July, depending on the climate and altitude of the breeding area. The larvae take up to two years to develop in the cool mountain waters, and neotenous individuals are frequent. When an adult is disturbed, it raises its tail and secretes a sticky, toxic fluid as a deterrent to predators from the skin glands on its neck, back and tail.

SALAMANDERS AND NEWTS — CLASSIFICATION: 3 —

Mole salamanders

The family Ambystomatidae contains the 35 species of mole salamanders grouped in four genera. Most live on land, at least during the adult stage, and all are confined to North America. The genus *Ambystoma* is the most well known, with species such as the tiger salamander, *A. tigrinum*, of the northern USA; the Mexican axolotl, *A. mexicanum*, which survives only in Lake Xochimilco in Mexico; the Jefferson salamander, *A. jeffersonianum*, of the northeastern USA and Canada; the spotted salamander, *A. maculatum*, of the eastern USA; the mole salamander, *A. talpoideum*, which occurs in the central and southeastern states of the USA; and the northwestern salamander, *A. gracile*, of the northwestern USA and southwest Canada.

Pacific mole salamanders

The family Dicamptodontidae comprises the three species of Pacific mole salamanders: the Pacific giant salamander, *Dicamptodon ensatus*; Cope's giant salamander, *D. copei*; and the Olympic salamander, *Rhyacotriton olympicus*. Terrestrial as adults, the three species occur only on the Pacific coast of North America.

Pacific giant salamanders

Once thought to belong to the mole salamanders, the three species of Pacific giant salamanders have now been given their own family. Similar in form to the mole salamander family, they are restricted to the west coast of North America. The Pacific giant salamander is the largest land-living salamander, growing to 11 in. in length. It is reddish brown in color with a marbled network of irregular, very dark patches. Despite being heavily built and having an ungainly appearance, the Pacific giant salamander is actually very agile and can climb tree trunks, bushes and even rocky outcrops.

The Pacific giant salamander inhabits the oceanic forest that extends along the west coast of North America, from British Columbia (Canada) to central California. Humid climatic conditions in these areas enable it to remain active all year, and it can sometimes be seen out and about during the day. During the spring, adults can be found in streams and clear lakes.

The female lays a series of single, whitish, eggs in different places below the surface of the water. The larvae that hatch are slender in shape and adapted for a life spent in running water. They generally hide under stones on the bottom of the stream, where they hunt small invertebrates. The adults hunt larger prey that includes snails, worms, crustaceans, insects, other amphibians, and even small reptiles or rodents. A distinctive feature of the Pacific giant salamander is its vocal cords, which can produce sound.

Cope's giant salamander is closely related to the Pacific giant salamander, but retains its larval characteristics throughout life and lives in water. The only other species in the group is the Olympic salamander. It is small in size, growing to no longer than 4 in., and is easily recognizable by its disproportionately large eyes. The belly color of the Olympic salamander is a characteristic and handsome bright yellow or orange, with a varying amount of spots. It occurs in cool places on mountains that border the sea. The adults live on land, returning to water to breed. The diet of the Olympic salamander consists mainly of small, freshwater crustaceans and aquatic insects or larvae.

Newts, fire and brook salamanders

Fire salamanders, brook salamanders and newts form a diverse family that ranges throughout North America, Europe and parts of Asia. The proportion of life spent in water and on land varies considerably with the different species. The adult fire salamander only returns to water to breed. In contrast, newts spend almost half the year in water.

During their long and elaborate courtship, members of the family usually breed in water, often returning to the same breeding pond in successive years. Fertilization takes place internally. Often, the male grasps the female in a firm grip from beneath. He then places his forelimbs over those of the female and holds her, sometimes with the aid of his tail. The male maintains the position, known as amplexus, until he produces a spermatophore (a sac of sperm) that the female collects with her cloaca. In most species, the female will lay her eggs below water, where they develop into larvae. Typically, fire salamanders, brook salamanders and newts have slender bodies with long tails. They possess lungs and movable eyelids, and their underparts tend to be more brightly colored.

Amphibian of the mountains

Anderson's Japanese salamander is a thick-set, flattened salamander that grows to 6 in. in length. It has a flat, triangular head with obvious parotid glands on each side. Two rows of tubercles run from the shoulders to the sides of the tail. One row runs along a line of projections created by the tips of the ribs—the ribs protrude at these points without piercing the skin. The other line of tubercles runs above the ribs. The skin of Anderson's Japanese salamander is rough and granular in appearance and brown-black in color. Found on only a handful of Japanese and Chinese islands, it probably inhabits mountain forests where the vegetation is dense and the humidity high. Nothing is known of its general behavior and breeding habits.

The rice-field salamander or crocodile newt, as it is more commonly called, of Asia is a hardy amphibian that grows to 8 in. in length. In color, the upperparts of the amphibian are reddish brown to black. It has orange underparts and pale brown-black lips, snout and lower jaw. Usually, the crocodile newt lives in flooded rice fields.

Protruding ribs

The sharp-ribbed salamander of Spain, Portugal and Morocco grows to a length of 12 in., making it the largest of the European tailed amphibians. It is strong and squat in shape, with a flattened, toad-like head and small eyes. The tail of the sharp-ribbed salamander is flat and wide, and grows to the same length as the body. Skin coloration in younger sharp-ribbed salamanders varies between dull-yellow and olive-green. As the amphibian reaches adulthood, its skin assumes a dark-gray tone.

The male sharp-ribbed salamander has several distinctive features, particularly a reddish hue to its body color. It also has a longer tail than the female and pads on the underside of the forelegs that it uses to grasp the female during courtship. A row of yellow warts along the sides of the body runs above the tips of its needle-sharp ribs, which protrude through pores in the skin if the animal is grabbed. As an additional

ABOVE The sharp-ribbed salamander is well protected against predators. Its needle-sharp ribs project through its skin and into the mouth of any attacking predator.

BELOW During mating, the males of many species of salamanders tightly grasp the females under the forelimbs—an action known as amplexus.

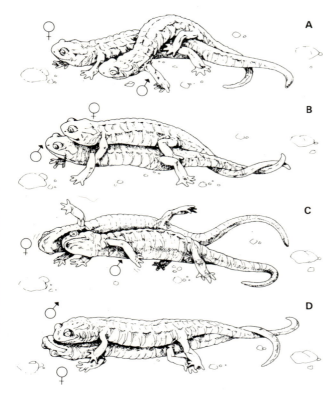

A

B

C

D

LEFT Courtship and mating rituals in the sharp-ribbed salamander. A male chases and jostles a female (A), and then moves beneath her body (B). Having released a spermatophore (a sac of sperm), the male moves out of the way (C) to allow the female to pick it up. On rare occasions, the animals mate in a face-to-face position (D).

or stones. The larvae metamorphose after about four months, when they are approximately 4 in. in length. The rate of larval metamorphosis depends on the warmth of the weather—growth and metamorphosis occur more quickly in warm conditions—and the young are fully grown after three years. They are nocturnal and aquatic animals, and feed on insects and other invertebrates.

During the mating season, the males compete for the female's attention and may attempt to steal a female from a competitor. They may also interrupt the mating, or cover the rival's spermatophore with mud. Males also grapple for the possession of a female, and a mating male will chase his rivals away. When he has the female in a firm grip, the male can transport her by swimming with his tail and walking on his hind limbs. Even at this point another male may grab the male's hind limbs or attempt to seize the female.

Black and yellow

Although a member of the same family, the fire salamander is physically quite distinct. Its vivid black and yellow markings make this secretive amphibian very striking in appearance. Growing to a length of 11-12.5 in., it inhabits damp woods, springs and streams. The fire salamander has a stout body and broad head, with a noticeable fold of skin across its throat. It has a short, flat tail and warts on each side of its body.

Internal fertilization

Courtship takes place on land, and the mating couples often return to their original breeding sites. During the courtship ritual, the male fire salamander emits a faint mating call, butting the pursued female and sometimes biting her, before clasping. Unusual for salamanders, the male transfers the spermatophore directly into the female's cloaca by twisting his body. Following the first mating, the male will release the female and repeat the procedure several times.

The female retains the 15-25 eggs inside her body until they are fully formed larvae. She then enters the

defense against predators, the sharp-ribbed salamander also has poison glands on its tail. If threatened, it thrashes its tail in a threat display, attracting a predator to the part of its body that tastes repulsive.

The sharp-ribbed salamander is a slow-moving creature that lives in well-vegetated, still water. It feeds on insects and also takes amphibian larvae, including those of its own species. It rarely leaves the water, and when the drought comes, it will often bury itself in the mud until the next rains come.

Rapid sexual maturity

The sharp-ribbed salamander reaches sexual maturity only six months after metamorphosis, and breeds between September and March, during the rainy season. Following courtship, the male clasps his mate in a tight grip known as amplexus. Immediately after depositing his spermatophore, the male frees a forelimb and swings his body around to face his mate, who then collects the spermatophore. Altogether, the male may produce up to six spermatophores.

The female lays her eggs singly or in clumps of 200-300, and attaches them to submerged vegetation

ABOVE The alpine salamander is unusual as it produces fully formed young rather than laying eggs or giving birth to larvae. The two to four offspring have the same physical structure as the adults, since they complete their metamorphosis inside the female's body. The advanced development of the young is probably an adaptation to the high altitudes at which the animals live. During the winter most of the water turns to ice, and there are few places where eggs could be laid and aquatic larvae could survive.

shallow water of a pond or stream to give birth. The female initially immerses her tail in the water, and gradually backs in, until she is almost entirely submerged.

Aquatic young

The larvae are 0.8 inches in length at birth and already have four fully developed legs and three pairs of external gills. Sometimes the newborn young have a thin envelope of skin around them, but break free almost immediately. Their tails, unlike those of their parents, are broad and crested and are ideal for swimming in water. The larvae are brown in color with darker underparts.

Initially, the young fire salamander has a yellowish tinge on the flanks and speckles of shiny black dots over its body. As it metamorphoses, the body becomes stouter, the tail thickens and the gills disappear as lungs develop. Eventually the 2.4-in.-long young salamander acquires the scattering of yellow markings that decorate the adults. It leaves the water a few weeks after birth if the weather has been warm but will remain in its watery environment until the following spring in colder conditions. Fire salamanders only return to the water to give birth.

The alpine salamander is an amphibian of high altitudes. It lives in the Alps, the French Jura and the mountains of western Yugoslavia and Albania. It is commonly found at heights of between 2600 and 6500 ft., and as high as 10,000 ft. above sea level. It is bluish black in color and has an orange abdomen with light blue sides covered in dark blue dots. The alpine salamander has distinct parotid glands—wartlike glands on the shoulder or neck—and has a ribbed appearance with marked vertical grooves running up and down the sides of its body. It is slender, reaching a length of up to 5 in., and of all the salamanders the alpine is the least dependent on an aquatic environment. The alpine salamander is active in the evening or at night.

Alpine salamanders are unusual in that they give birth to fully developed young. The larvae develop inside the female, who usually gives birth to two

THE FIRE SALAMANDER
— WARNING COLORS —

The bright black and yellow or black and orange coloration of the fire salamander sets it apart from the other European salamanders, all of which have rather dull, spotted or marbled skin. Though the precise pattern of the fire salamander's markings varies from one individual to another, most populations have their own characteristic color schemes. Fire salamanders from northern Spain, France, West Germany and western Switzerland tend to be striped, while animals from other parts of the range are more often spotted. In Portugal and western Spain, the markings are red, and the Italian fire salamanders have red spots on their bellies.

In spite of its striking appearance, the fire salamander is difficult to spot in the wild because it only emerges when the conditions are just right. Only when the air is very humid does it leave its hiding place and wander through the woods and bushy areas of hillsides with its slow, sure-footed tread.

Such conditions most often occur at night or in the early morning, particularly after several hours of rain, and during summer storms. During the cold season, from October to March, fire salamanders congregate in large numbers in frost-free places such as old mine shafts and quarries.

The coloration of most salamanders enables them to blend in with their surroundings and escape from predators. The markings of the fire salamander, however, are not intended as camouflage but as a warning. Predators can recognize it easily among other potential prey and many of them will avoid attacking it, for the fire salamander possesses a very effective battery of defensive weapons. The skin contains numerous glands that secrete a sticky fluid. The fluid can affect the nervous system of an attacker, but its main defensive value is in the irritant effect it has on the skin—especially the mucous membranes of the mouth. Its effects can be more than just irritating—a bite from a fire salamander can even kill a small lizard.

Europe's main amphibian-eating snakes—the grass snake, the viperine

1726

snake and the dice snake—all avoid eating the fire salamander, even though they are little affected by the poison. As far as humans are concerned, the fire salamander's poison is mild, and the only risk to a human being is a painful itch. Despite its warning colors and poison glands, the fire salamander still has plenty to fear in the wild: it is food for many larger creatures such as owls, crows and badgers.

Myths and legends

A number of popular legends have grown up around the fire salamander. It gains its name not from its bright coloration, but from the erroneous belief that it can walk unharmed through fire. Such a myth originated in the days when wood was the main form of fuel in the home. People in Europe would collect branches from the forests to burn as fuel. The wood they collected from the ground may well have contained fire salamanders hiding in it. In winter,

when the locals needed more wood to burn, the chances of finding fire salamanders were greater, since the animals seek out old wood as a place in which to hibernate.

When the wood was put on the fire, the salamander, roused from its slumbers by the unexpected warmth, would probably have made a dash for safety. People would therefore catch their first glance of the amphibian as it emerged from the fire onto their hearth.

A symbol of power

The fire salamander has been attributed with other extraordinary powers. The legend arose that it could put out fires, and dried specimens were sold in markets to ward off the danger of fire in the home. Ever since, the fire salamander has been used as a symbol of power, or as a symbol of a force of nature that cannot be controlled or dominated by man.

FAR LEFT AND BELOW LEFT The fire salamander's glossy yellow and black coloration varies so much that no two individuals are precisely the same. While some are predominantly black with scattered yellow spots, others are mostly yellow. Fire salamanders inhabit broad-leaved woodlands and areas rich in ground vegetation, and they seldom stray far from running water. In such habitats they can hide away in damp places, emerging at night to walk slowly through the undergrowth in pursuit of insects. BELOW Successive phases of courtship in the fire salamander: the male chases the female (A), crawls beneath her (B) and grasps her from below in amplexus (C); he then deposits a spermatophore (marked by the arrow) and moves aside to allow the female to take it up in her cloaca (D and E).

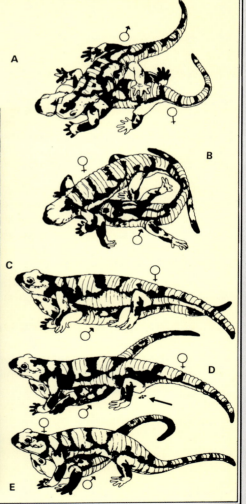

ABOVE Though some fire salamanders that live at high altitudes are aquatic, the only time that an adult usually enters the water is when a female is ready to give birth. She gradually lowers herself backward into the water until all but her head is submerged. The young emerge as well-developed larvae.

offspring. Their unusual breeding behavior is an adaptation to living in a cold climate with long periods of cold, dry weather, where much of the water is locked up in the form of ice. Although small lakes and pools are quite numerous at high altitudes, the effective period for larval development in the water is very much reduced since the small pools may still be covered with ice in June or even later.

Development of the eggs and larvae

Alpine salamanders mate in late summer. The male climbs onto the female, lies along her back and hooks his forelegs over hers. The female can retain the fertilized eggs within her body for one year, and in colder climates, where the adults hibernate for longer periods, for as long as two to three years. As many as 60 eggs are fertilized, but only the first two in each oviduct will develop. If either of these fails, one of the later eggs develops instead. As these eggs develop, the mass of other eggs break down to form a fluid around the developing eggs, giving them sustenance.

The larvae have all the usual amphibian features including gills, that grow up to half as long as the whole larva. At this stage the gills press against the uterus walls, and may act as a primitive form of placenta, passing food and oxygen from the mother to the young. The tissues of the uterus produce a nutritious material of fats and protein that is absorbed by the fetus. When the larvae are mature, the female gives birth to the fully formed young on land.

Habits and habitat

The alpine salamander is a secretive animal, only leaving its haunts at night. It is an expert climber around the rock faces of the high mountains as much of its range is above the tree line. Though the alpine salamander does not require water for breeding, it does need moisture. It makes its home under rocks and stones, and among moss and grass. At lower altitudes, the alpine salamander inhabits beech woods where it forages in the rich leaf litter for soft-bodied invertebrates such as worms and slugs.

Prominent eyes

The spectacled salamander grows to a length of 2.5-4.5 in. It has a slender body, a narrow head with prominent eyes and a thin tail that is longer than its body. It has prominent ribs, which give the body its segmented appearance, and its skin is quite rough. The tail has a sharp ridge above and below. The spectacled salamander is the only European salamander to have only four toes on the hind feet—the others having five. The animal's coloration is quite distinctive. Its upperparts are generally blackish, with a yellowish patch over its eyes. Its belly is pale with dark areas, and its throat is black with a white patch. The lower surfaces of its legs and tail are brilliant red in the adults. When the spectacled salamander is threatened by a predator, it turns its tail up toward it, to reveal the red underside. It will also play dead, if disturbed, as another means of defense.

Food and environment

The spectacled salamander lives in mountainous areas in humid habitats, such as damp woods near water. It takes to the water only in the breeding season. For the rest of the year the adults are terrestrial, and are rarely seen in daylight. During the breeding season in early spring, the female lays her eggs in small

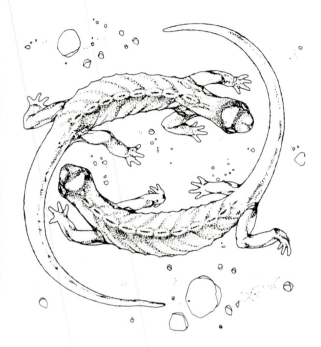

LEFT **During courtship, a male spectacled salamander chases a female before depositing a spermatophore, which the female picks up with her cloaca. The female enters a stream in the spring to lay her eggs among rocks, and the larvae normally** hatch about three weeks later.
BELOW **When threatened, an adult spectacled salamander curls up its tail to expose the bright red warning color on its underside. It may also feign death in an attempt to deter predators.**

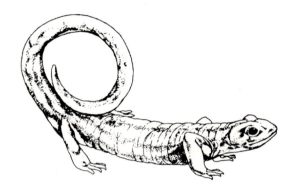

SALAMANDERS AND NEWTS
CLASSIFICATION: 4

Fire salamanders, brook salamanders and newts

The family Salamandridae contains the 53 species and 14 genera of fire salamanders, brook salamanders and newts. They occur in western and eastern North America, in Europe, northwest Africa, western Asia, Southeast Asia, China and Japan. Most live on land, but return to the water to breed.

Anderson's Japanese salamander, *Tylototriton andersoni*, occurs only in the Ryukyu Islands of Japan and on Hainan Island in China. The sharp-ribbed salamander, *Pleurodeles waltl*, is found in Morocco, Portugal and much of Spain, while the gold-striped salamander, *Chioglossa iusitanica*, is restricted to northern Portugal and northwest Spain. Many well-known species belong to the genus *Salamandra*, including the fire salamander, *S. salamandra*, which ranges through southern, central and Western Europe, and extends into northwest Africa and southwest Asia; the alpine salamander, *S. atra*, of the Alps and parts of Yugoslavia and Albania; and the spectacled salamander, *S. terdigitata*, which is confined to the mountains of western Italy.

Many of the newts belong to the genus *Triturus*, including the smooth newt, *T. vulgaris*, which is widespread in Europe and also occurs in western Asia; the palmate newt, *T. helveticus*, of western Europe; the great crested or warty newt, *T. cristatus*, which ranges over most of Europe and extends east to Central Asia; the marbled newt, *T. marmoratus*, of Portugal, Spain and southern France; and the alpine newt, *T. alpestris*, which occurs in much of western, central and eastern Europe. The Californian newt, *Taricha torosa*, occurs only in the far west of the USA, but the eastern newt, *Notophthalmus viridescens*, is widespread in eastern North America. The Sardinian brook salamander, *Euproctes platycephalus*, is restricted to Sardinia.

ABOVE The gold-striped salamander from the mountains of northern Portugal and northwest Spain feeds on flies, small worms and spiders. It stalks them over rocks and damp vegetation and catches them by shooting out its long, sticky tongue. It usually lives near streams and springs, and is a strong swimmer that scuttles into the water when disturbed.

clusters attached to the rocks in a stream where the current is not too swift.

The spectacled salamander feeds on small insects that it catches on its sticky tongue. Its lungs are very much reduced in size, and it probably obtains most, or all, of its oxygen through its skin or through the lining of its mouth.

Similarities to a lizard

The gold-striped salamander is an agile, slender salamander with a long tail and bulging eyes. Uniform brown or gray below, it is black or brown above and has a pair of orange or copper-colored stripes along its back that join to form one line down the tail. The tail, which may account for more than half of the animal's total length of up to 6 in., makes the gold-striped salamander distinct from any other European salamander. In the male the base of the tail is noticeably swollen.

The gold-striped salamander is found throughou Spain and Portugal and lives in high, moist, rock places, near springs and streams. It is most activ during dusk hours. As well as being lizard-like i appearance, it can also move quickly. If pursued, i will scuttle rapidly for cover or run toward a strean and throw itself into the water, where it can swim well Another lizard-like characteristic is its ability to shee its tail if it is seized, allowing it to escape, leaving the predator with the lashing tail. The tail will regrow but as with lizards, it never reaches its original length

The Caucasian salamander

The Caucasus salamander lives in the grassy area above the forests of the Caucasus mountains, a heights up to 10,000 ft., although it can be found a lower altitudes near the sea. It grows up to 7.5 in long, and has a flat head and a slender, slightl flattened body. It is blackish brown above, with tw rows of irregular yellowish patches along the back merging to form one row on the tail. Its underpart are dark reddish brown to gray, sometimes with whit spots. The Caucasian salamander is a nocturna species, and captures small prey such as spiders an millipedes. It feeds in the water as well as on land, an preys on small invertebrates such as mosquito larvae

The newts

Newts make up a compact, uniform group of amphibians. All newts spend a good part of the year in the water, even when adults. They need moisture, as they dry out easily if exposed to drying conditions. Newts breed in the water, and when they return there each year they undergo a partial reverse metamorphosis. The tail becomes wide and flat as an adaptation for swimming, and lateral line organs—sense organs embedded in the skin that respond to water-borne vibrations—develop on the back and on the head, and are useful for sensing prey in water. At the same time, the skin becomes thin and permeable to the oxygen dissolved in the water. When the animals are not in the water, outside the breeding season, the skin is much rougher and drier.

Regeneration and shedding of skin

Newts are able to replace lost or damaged parts of their body by "regeneration." All newts shed their skin from time to time. The skin splits around the lips, and then rolls back, releasing the limbs and the body. The newt may rub itself against the ground or vegetation to help remove the skin, and it peels off the last bit with its mouth. It then eats the shed skin, which is thin and nutritious. Newts do not have parotid glands—wartlike glands on the shoulder or neck—though they may produce poisonous secretions from numerous

ABOVE A smooth newt makes its way to its breeding pond. The most common and widespread of all the European newts and salamanders, it prefers to breed in still, shallow water such as weedy ponds and ditches.

BELOW The courtship ritual in the smooth newt: the male moves toward the female and positions himself slightly to one side of her (A); the two make brief physical contact (B); and the male bends his tail, vibrating it to waft scent toward the female (C). He deposits a spermatophore (D) and the female collects it in her cloaca (E).

PAGES 1732-1733 During the breeding season, the male smooth newt (top) differs markedly in appearance from the female. A continuous crest develops along his back and tail, large, dark spots appear on his body, and the lower edge of his tail turns bright orange.

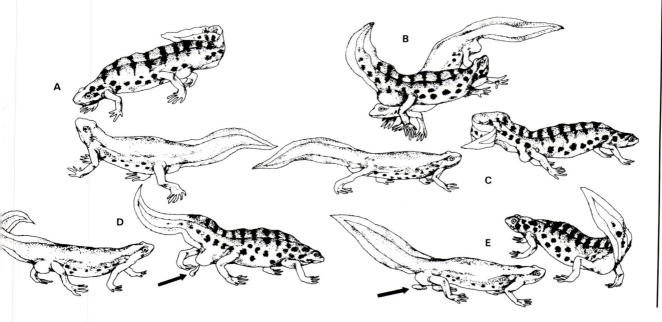

THE GREAT CRESTED NEWT
— PREDATOR IN THE POND —

The great crested newt is far from common, but it is certainly one of the most widespread, and one of the most eye-catching of the European amphibians. It lives in ponds, where it comes to the surface for a gulp of air on a hot summer's day, when oxygen levels are low in the water. But the best time to see great crested newts is at night, when these mainly nocturnal amphibians can be observed feeding and courting in the water.

The great crested newt is a large species—males reach a length of about 5.5 in. and females as much as 7 in. It is fairly sturdy in shape, and brownish or grayish in color, with darker spots. It takes its name from the impressive crest that the male grows during the breeding season, and which runs from the top of his head to the end of his tail. During the mating season, the male's tail also bears a silvery band down the middle with bluish highlights. The female does not have a crest, but both she and the male have a bright orange belly with black blotches that contrasts strongly with the rest of the body. The skin of both sexes is covered with tiny white raised spots that give this amphibian its alternative name—the warty newt.

Aquatic dragons

Great crested newts are often described as little aquatic dragons. While they are harmless to people, they are voracious predators of virtually any aquatic invertebrate. In the water, they are usually slow and lazy, floating off the bottom and moving gently around among the vegetation. But as soon as a newt becomes aware of some small animal moving nearby—a worm, for example—it becomes attentive and alert. With its trunk slightly bowed and its head near the bottom, it slowly approaches its potential prey. As soon as it is within striking distance, it pounces on its victim with unexpected speed, seizing it, and often shaking it vigorously from side to side to stun it. Great crested newts will often battle over a worm—if one animal catches the prey, another may move in to grab the other end. The fight usually ends with both newts taking a piece each.

BELOW LEFT During the mating season, the adult male great crested newt develops a large, spiky crest along his back and the length of his tail. Great crested newts are now uncommon, as a result of the destruction and pollution of village ponds, but they are protected by law throughout Britain. **RIGHT** Great crested newts lay their eggs and spend the larval stage of their lives in ponds. Most larvae leave the ponds by August, having lost their external gills, but those that hatch late from their eggs may overwinter in the water, completing their metamorphosis the following spring. **BELOW RIGHT** Adult great crested newts spend much of their time in the water, feeding on a variety of aquatic vertebrates, including water beetle larvae, water fleas, freshwater shrimps, leeches and worms. They hunt their prey by using their acute sense of smell.

Out of hibernation

Great crested newts spend the winter months in a torpid state in a damp place—under a log or a stone, for example—where they are sometimes joined by other species of newts. As the winter retreats and warmer weather approaches, the newts gradually awake and emerge from hibernation into the spring sunshine.

Courtship takes place in April. The male performs an elaborate and enthusiastic courtship dance, displaying to the female with a series of twists and turns in the water. He chases her around the pond, then darts in front of her to arch his back and display his crest and bright underparts to full effect. He wafts his scent toward her with his tail, and if she is receptive he will deposit a spermatophore—a packet of sperm— in the water. Fertilization takes place internally, with the female picking up the spermatophore in her cloaca. She lays up to several hundred eggs, securing them to the leaves of submerged vegetation, and by bending parts of leaves over them she attempts to hide them from predators.

After egg-laying, the adults stay in the pond for another few weeks, feeding on aquatic invertebrates from the muddy bottom of the pond, and on the spawn and tadpoles of other amphibians. They eventually leave the breeding pond in June or July, by which time the male has lost his colorful crest.

Their larvae, meanwhile, begin to develop. They eat tiny aquatic animals at first, but graduate to larger invertebrates as they grow. They measure 1.5-2 in. in length at the beginning of July, and soon afterward, when they near the completion of their metamorphosis, their gills are reabsorbed and their lungs develop. The young great crested newts can then leave the water to start their life on land. They are not ready to breed until they are two years old or more, and do not usually return to their ponds until they reach breeding age.

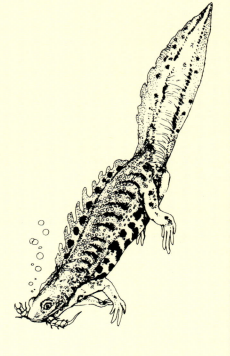

ABOVE The marbled newt grows up to 5.5 in. long and is one of Europe's most strikingly colored amphibians. For most of the year, the males and females are difficult to tell apart, since the males lack the crest that they grow on their back during the breeding season.

BELOW During the courtship of the palmate newt (an event that occurs in shallow water), the male stands in front of the female and vigorously lashes his tail (A); he then turns and deposits a soft sac (a spermatophore) containing sperm for the female to pick up in her cloaca (B).

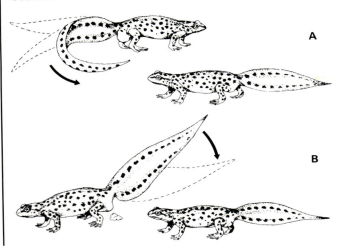

small glands on the back. They have four toes on the forelimbs and five on the back.

The ideal newt habitat is a medium-sized pond surrounded by woodland and grassland. They do not like the deeper water of lakes, partly because it is too far for them to surface for air, and partly because fish prey on both adults and larvae. Many are bottom feeders that have to come up to gulp air in low-oxygen conditions, such as on hot summer days. Most newts are nocturnal, spending the day under stones, where they also hibernate, though some bury themselves in mud for the winter.

Mating and fertilization

Unlike the European salamanders, newts do not mate in amplexus (the position in which the male clasps the female with his limbs). The male newt usually displays to the female using visual and tactile stimuli. He also gives out chemical signals, such as scent signals, during courtship. In a typical courtship display, the male places himself in front of, or beside, the female, and presents one side of his body to her, curving his body and lashing his tail to transmit his odor—comprised of chemical communicants known as pheremones—toward her. If she is interested, she will remain where she is, and the male will deposit a spermatophore—a mass of sperm cells covered in a gelatinous envelope. She picks this up in her cloaca, and the sperm cells are released, to be stored until the eggs are ready for fertilization.

Breeding and metamorphosis

Breeding takes place in spring, the newts preferring well-vegetated ponds and pools. The female lays her eggs singly and often wraps them in the leaves of water plants, or attaches them to a stone. The larvae hatch two or three weeks later. By the time they metamorphose in late summer, they look similar to the adult female. The adults leave the water in early summer, and the earliest metamorphosed larvae leave soon afterward, though late-hatched larvae will remain in the water over winter and do not metamorphose until the following spring. Some species have external gills, and their tails are crested to aid swimming.

Hunting for food

All newts are carnivorous. The larger species eat large slugs and worms, seizing and gulping them with

vigorous shakes of the head and body. The smaller
species do the same with smaller worms, and some
also catch insects on their sticky tongues.

Varieties of newts

The smooth newt is often the most common
amphibian in its range. It is an adaptable animal,
occurring in a variety of habitats from field borders
and woods to town parks and gardens. It can be found
in most stagnant pools, from western Europe to the
Ural Mountains. It can reach a length of about 4.5 in.
(but is usually smaller), and is typically an olive-green
or brown color above, and blotched with a central
stripe of orange below. In the breeding season, the
male develops a fine crest, many dark spots and a blue
band above the orange on the lower side of the tail.

In the water, the smooth newt hunts by sight—
unlike the great crested and alpine newts, for
example, that find their food on the bottom by smell.
The smooth newt eats insects, worms, tadpoles and
spawn, and will even feed at the surface. Out of the
water, they eat small, soft-bodied insects such as the
greenfly, as well as worms and slugs. Smooth newts
are more active than most other newts, and are often
the first to colonize new areas of water. They are agile,
and can even climb over walls.

TOP **The dull upperparts
and bright underparts of
the alpine newt are a
warning to predators that
its body is covered
in poison glands.**

ABOVE **Alpine newts,
like other amphibians,
are unable to drink with
their mouths and must
absorb liquid through
their skin.**

ABOVE The California newt occurs in forest ponds, though when these dry up, the animal will take refuge in leaf litter or in rodent burrows. The poison produced by the California newt is highly potent and occurs in both the adult and its eggs. Scientists believe that just 0.0003 oz. of the poison found in the California newt's eggs would be enough to kill 7000 mice.

From the south of Italy

The Italian newt is the smallest European newt. Found only in southern Italy, it rarely grows to more than 3 in. in length. It is a soft brownish color above and is lighter below, often with dark spots. Its throat is yellow or orange. During the breeding season, the male develops a crest on its tail, and both sexes develop golden spots on their sides and behind their eyes. The Italian newt is a secretive species out of water. It breeds in still waters, such as ponds. In permanent areas of water, neotenous forms of the Italian newt occur.

The great crested newt is widely distributed throughout the same area as the smooth newt, and is divided into several subspecies. In southwest Europe, it is replaced by its close relative, the marbled newt, which has bright, mossy-green marbled upperparts and a duller body. The great crested and the marbled newts behave in a similar way, but the marbled newt is probably more terrestrial. The two species hybridize across a band of France where their ranges overlap.

Coping with the cold

The alpine newt occurs across almost all of Europe. Flame red or bright orange below, it is dark gray or black above, often with spots on its sides and a bluish tinge in the breeding season. The females grow to about 4.5 in. in length, but the males are smaller. Very adaptable, the alpine newt can be found in a range of habitats. It tolerates cold conditions well and occupies small areas of water, from mountain pools to woodland ponds. It never wanders far from water, and is often active earlier in the day than most of the other European newts that share the same range. Unlike other newts, it does not skirt around water outside the breeding season, but walks straight in.

Courtship takes place as soon as the ice has thawed in spring. The female lays about 150 eggs in early spring, and the larvae hatch in two to four weeks. They either metamorphose after about three months, or overwinter if conditions are cool. Neotenous populations of the alpine newt are quite common.

Warning colors

The rough-skinned newt is 5-8 in. long, with a warty skin. It has large eyes, dark-colored lower eyelids, and is dark brown above and yellowish or orange below. The females only breed every two to three years. In the breeding season, as well as developing the smooth skin and compressed tail of many newts, the male rough-skinned newt develops a horny layer at the tips of the toes. The rough-skinned newt is believed to produce toxic skin secretions that make it unappetizing to predators. If threatened, it may use another form of defense—it exposes the bright colors of its underside in a display that is thought to warn predators of its unpleasant taste. It lives in ponds and slow-moving, well-vegetated streams.

The red-bellied newt, as its name suggests, has a blood-red belly, which is marked with green. Its upperparts are black or greenish black. It has large eyes and orange lower eyelids. The tail of the red-bellied newt is strongly compressed, with a fine tip. It lives in streams, ditches and ponds.

Its breeding habits are similar to those of the European newts. The male does not grab his prospective mate at any stage of the proceedings. Instead, he nudges her along her body before swimming around to block her path. He then rubs her head with his snout and performs a fanning movement with his tail. He may restrain her to a degree by hooking his hind legs over her neck. The male moves in front of the female to expose his cloaca—a gesture probably linked to a form of chemical communication. Finally, while moving slowly forward in front of her, he deposits a spermatophore, which she picks up. A few days later, the female lays her eggs, and the larvae leave the water later in the season, having metamorphosed. Sexual maturity is reached after two or three years.

A vivid red

A most interesting North American species is the eastern newt, which is also unappetizing to predators, at least in its immature, terrestrial or "eft" stage, when it is colored a vivid red. The adults, which tend to be predominantly aquatic, are greenish or brown above with red spots and stripes, and are yellowish below. When the young metamorphose in the ponds where the adults go to breed, some of them leave the water as red efts, to live a terrestrial life for one to three years

ABOVE The eastern newt of North America lives in ponds, lakes, and quiet backwaters. It shows variation in color throughout its life; although the adult (seen here) is brown or olive-green, the immature eastern newt — called an eft during its terrestrial stage — is bright red, warning predators of its deadly poisonous skin secretions.
BELOW Before mating, a male eastern newt clasps the female with his hind legs and rubs her face with his cheek glands.

LEFT The red-bellied newt, found throughout Japan, is a close relative of the European newts. It is notable for its tolerance of temperature changes. **BELOW LEFT AND BELOW** Various positions held by male and female brook salamanders during their courtship ritual: the male holds the female's tail in his jaws as well as gripping her body with his tail and hind legs.

until they are sexually mature. Others—especially in coastal populations—bypass the eft stage, retain their gills and become sexually mature in a neotenous form.

A long metamorphosis

The three brook salamanders—the Corsican, Pyrenean and Sardinian—occur in well-defined, isolated highland areas in Europe. The Sardinian brook salamander is fairly typical of the three. It is flat-headed, grows to 4.5-5.5 in. in length and has a slender body. It is drab in color, with a brownish, marbled back marked by a yellow line, and a pale yellow underside patched with black. It lives in the high mountains of Sardinia, at 5900 ft. or more above sea level.

The breeding season lasts right through the summer, during the few months when the habitat is free of snow. Mating occurs in water. The male approaches the female, moves beneath her and grasps her with his tail near her hind limbs. He often uses his hind legs as well, and will grasp her tail in his jaws. They hold this position for some hours, and mating is concluded with a spermatophore being passed directly from the male to the female's cloaca. The eggs are attached to the underside of stones in the water. The streamlined larvae that hatch are more active than the adults, which are rather sluggish and feed on slow-moving invertebrates in the water or on land. The Sardinian brook salamander survives the winter by burying itself deep in the ground.

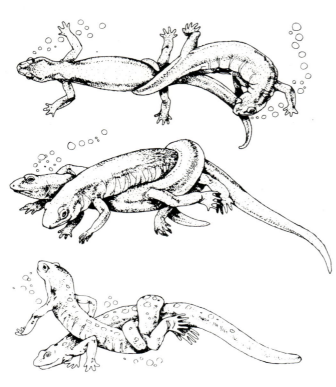

SLENDER, SMOOTH AND SECRETIVE

The Corsican brook salamander has a brown to greenish skin color. Because it lacks lungs, it exchanges oxygen mainly through its thin, moist skin. It is restricted to the mountainous Mediterranean island of Corsica, where it lives in or near rocky streams from sea level up to 6900 ft. However, it is usually found at 1960-5000 ft.

The Pyrenean brook salamander is the largest member of the brook salamander genus, growing up to about 7 in. long including the tail. Found only in the Pyrenees, between Spain and France, it lives in and around the mountain lakes and rivers, preferring water that never rises above 59°F in temperature.

Amphiumas

The amphiumas belong to the smallest family of salamanders. The three species all live in the muddy waters and swamps of the southeastern United States. They are popularly known as congo eels because their tapered heads and long, cylindrical bodies give them a superficial resemblance to eels. However, unlike eels—which are fish—all amphiumas have two pairs of tiny, weak limbs with one, two or three toes on each, depending on the species.

Amphiumas spend most of their lives in the water, where they swim well with sinuous movements of their flexible bodies. During the day, they rest in dense stands of waterweed or in burrows in the mud. The three-toed amphiuma sometimes digs its own burrow, but often uses the abandoned burrows of crayfish for a daytime retreat.

At night, amphiumas hunt for food. They prey on both invertebrates—for example, worms, crayfish and insects—and vertebrates—fish, snakes, frogs and even small amphiumas. Amphiumas hunt by sticking their heads out a short distance from their burrows to seize passing prey.

Congo eels are well supplied with mucus glands that make their skin extremely slippery and difficult to handle. Local fishermen dislike them because they eat fish, are difficult to remove from their nets, and can inflict nasty bites with their sharp teeth.

The largest and best-known species is the two-toed amphiuma. Ranging in size from 18 to 46 in., it is grayish brown with lighter underparts. It can wriggle,

TOP The Corsican brook salamander occurs only in Corsica. Adults may grow to up to 4.5 in. in length but are usually smaller. They often become dormant in hot, dry weather—a phenomenon known as estivation.

ABOVE The Pyrenean brook salamander is a close relative of the Corsican brook salamander. It is most common in cold mountain streams and lakes where it is mainly active at night and suffers from being hunted by trout.

eel-like, from one area to another, and does so if its usual wetland is in danger of drying up. It also wanders overland during wet weather in search of food or a new swampy habitat.

A slightly smaller three-toed amphiuma is dark brown with light gray underparts and a dark throat patch. It inhabits lowland wetland areas and faster-flowing upland streams. The smallest of the three species, the 12-in.-long one-toed amphiuma, occurs only in northern Florida and southwest Georgia. It was only discovered in 1950, and appears to spend more time burrowing than its relatives.

Courtship and reproduction

Courtship among amphiumas takes place in the water, and unlike most salamanders the female takes an active role. Several females may compete for the attention of a single male by rubbing their noses against him and wrapping their bodies around his. The male transfers sperm—stored in a packet resembling a string of beads and called a spermatophore—directly into the female's cloaca while she is wrapped around him.

Females produce about 200 eggs, with larger females producing more than smaller ones. They lay their eggs in a single long string under rotting pieces of wood in shallow water or on moist land. The female coils her body around the eggs, guarding them for up to five months until they hatch.

The larvae are about 2 in. long when they hatch, with short, white gills and tiny limbs. Adult

amphiumas lose their external gills, but keep the gill covers and one gill slit on either side of the head. Adults also retain the lidless eyes of the larval form.

The olm, the mud puppy and the water dog

The family of proteid salamanders includes the olm, the mud puppy and the water dogs. The olm is neotenous, retaining its larval characteristics. Even though it has lungs, it keeps its large, feathery gills in its adult state and spends all its life in the water.

The olm lives in a world of permanent darkness—in underground lakes, rivers and streams in the limestone regions of Austria, Italy, and Yugoslavia. It is virtually blind, although the position of its eyes can be seen as small dark spots beneath the skin.

Its body is a dull white with a pinkish, grayish or yellowish tinge. However, when the olm is exposed to light for long periods, its color darkens—becoming first violet and then black. If an olm returns to the dark, the process reverses and it changes back to its original pale color.

Burrowing in the mud

The olm is long and thin—measuring up to 12 in. from its snout to the tip of its tail, with about a third of its length consisting of the tail. Its limbs are small in relation to the size of its body, and it uses them to support itself, rather than for moving around. Each limb bears short, stumpy toes—three on the front and two on the hind limbs. It has a broad, down-turned snout that it uses to burrow in mud or sand in search of freshwater worms and crustaceans. It also has three distinctive large, dark red tufted gills on each side of its neck. Its tail, which it uses for swimming, is flattened from side to side with a smooth-edged crest.

It is not known how the olm breeds in the wild. In captivity, the female gives birth to live young. A number of eggs start to develop within the female's oviduct, but most break down in the early stages. They form a liquid that nourishes the one or two remaining eggs that go on to complete their development. The newly born larvae resemble miniature adults, but have well-developed eyes.

LEFT The two-toed amphiuma is almost totally aquatic, and swims by sinuous movements of its body. It feeds on a variety of prey, including frogs and smaller amphiumas.

Spade-shaped heads

The water dogs and the mud puppy belong to the family of North American proteids. They are all quite similar in appearance, with large, broad, spade-shaped heads that taper to short, strongly flattened tails. They have stouter limbs than the olm and bushy, deep-red gills. Their bodies are grayish brown, with dark brown to blue-black spots.

Proteids' gills vary in length according to their habitat. Those that live in cold, fast-moving and well-oxygenated water have small gills. Those that live in warmer, more stagnant water with less oxygen have large, well-developed and constantly moving gills.

The mud puppy is the largest and most widespread of the proteids, measuring 7.5-12 in. long (and occasionally nearly 16 in.). It ranges from southern Canada to the southern United States. It lives in lakes, rivers and streams and has been found at depths of 89 ft. in the Great Lakes. The mud puppy tends to be nocturnal, feeding on aquatic worms, insects, crustaceans and small fish and their eggs.

The four species of water dogs live in slightly different habitats. The Alabama water dog inhabits streams and rivers lined with leaf litter and other vegetable debris, and hides under stones and logs. The heavily spotted Gulf Coast water dog mainly inhabits clear, spring-fed streams with sandy bottoms. The dwarf water dog prefers slow-moving streams and muddy bottomed ditches, and the Neuse River water dog lives only in two large, deep river systems in North Carolina—the Neuse and the Tar.

ABOVE The limbs of the two-toed amphiuma or Congo eel are unusual in having two fingers and two toes. It hides during the day among aquatic plants, crustacean shells and other hidden recesses. Normally, the amphiuma becomes active three or four hours after sundown.

BELOW The adult olm regularly rises to the surface of the water to take in oxygen (A). It can also live on land for short periods (B), where it will feed. Females show their readiness to mate by sniffing the male's cloaca (C), and the female lays 12-70 fertilized eggs under a stone (D).

A

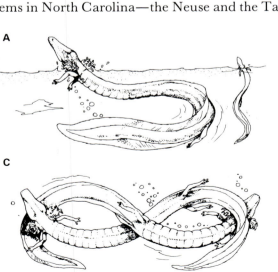

B

C

D

Lungless salamanders

Lungless salamanders form the largest family of tailed amphibians, with over 200 species making up 60 percent of all salamander species. They live in a variety of damp habitats, with a distribution that centers in North America—particularly in the southern part of the Appalachian Mountains. These mountains have provided them with stable, humid conditions for the last 250 million years. The isolation of their mountain retreats over such a long period has led to the evolution of many species that are limited to a particular mountain range. In cases where two species occur on the same mountain range, they occupy different habitats at varying altitudes.

Lungless salamanders also extend from southern Canada through Central America to northern South America. There are only two Old World species, both confined to parts of Italy, and the extreme southeast of France and Sardinia.

Many species live under stones near swiftly flowing mountain streams, where an overhang of tree cover provides cool conditions. Others live on rockslides, near caves. Species from Central and South America often live among the trees of humid tropical forests, under bark and around mosses and other plants that grow on trunks and branches. They are generally nocturnal.

ABOVE The North American mud puppy can be identified by its fuzzy edged, dark blue spots, though its body color may vary from a rusty red to gray. The mud puppy lives in lakes, rivers and streams. It is generally nocturnal, although it may be active during the day in muddy or weed-choked waters. The feathery maroon gills are larger in individuals that live in warm stagnant water where there is little oxygen.

Lungless salamanders breathe through their skin and throats, both of which have a good supply of blood vessels. The floor of the mouth moves up and down, pumping air into the throat in much the same way that it is pumped into the lungs of most other amphibians.

Varied breeding habits

The many species of lungless salamanders show a range of reproductive behavior. Some lay eggs in water where they hatch into larvae. Some larvae, such as those of the blind cave salamander, do not develop further. Instead, they remain in the larval state, rather like the olm. Other species lay eggs in damp places near water to which the larvae migrate. In other lungless salamanders, the eggs hatch out directly into small replicas of the adults. Females that lay their eggs on land generally guard them until they hatch.

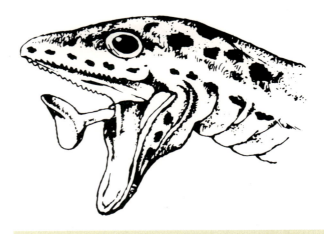

RIGHT The tongue of the Italian cave salamander is unusual in that it darts out from the mouth (up to 0.5 in.) to catch small prey. When not in use, it lies concealed in a sheath-like groove in the floor of the mouth. The stalk and mushroom-shaped disk on the end of the tongue is visible when it is extended.

Courtship behavior is well-developed in lungless salamanders, and usually involves the male rubbing and nudging the female. Male salamanders have glands on the head, body and tail, and their secretions stimulate the female to breed. The thin groove between their upper lip and nostril is thought to transfer water-borne secretions from glands on the chin to the nose.

Some species belonging to the large group of woodland salamanders perform an elaborate courtship display. The male raises and lowers his limbs while he nudges the female with a gland on his chin. As he moves along her side, he grasps her lightly between his jaws. Then he vibrates his tail, which the female straddles, and the pair move off together in the "tail walk" position. Next, the male deposits his packet of sperm and leads the female over it, so that she can pick it up with her cloaca. The couple then separate.

Nearly all lungless salamanders lay large, heavily yolked eggs, depositing them in damp locations. Brook salamanders lay their eggs singly and attach them by stalks to the underside of stones, in or near brooks and small streams. Usually, they lay a whole batch under one stone. Woodland salamanders lay separate eggs that stick together like a bunch of grapes, while dusky salamanders lay their eggs in elongated clusters.

Dwelling in caves

The cave or web-footed salamanders are a small group of lungless salamanders that live in rocky limestone areas, often inside caves. Three species inhabit the mountains of northern and central California, and two European species are limited to north-central Italy, the island of Sardinia and a small area in the extreme southeast of France.

Superficially, cave salamanders may not appear to be specialized, but close investigation reveals some unusual features. For example, the cave salamander has a sticky tongue that consists of a disk on a stalk. Normally, the tongue lies in a sheath on the floor of the mouth, but it can protrude rapidly, extending about half an inch, when the cave salamander wants to catch

SALAMANDERS AND NEWTS — CLASSIFICATION: 5 —

Amphiumas

The amphiumas belong to the small family Amphiumidae, with only three species, all in the genus *Amphiuma*. Animals of swamps and still water, they are confined to the southeastern USA. The two-toed amphiuma, *A. means*, ranges along the coastal plain from Virginia south to Florida and east to Louisiana. The three-toed amphiuma, *A. tridactylum*, ranges from Texas and Louisiana north up the Mississippi Valley to western Kentucky. The one-toed amphiuma, *A. pholeter*, occurs only in northern Florida and the extreme southwest of Georgia.

Water dogs, the mud puppy and the olm

The family Proteidae (or Necturidae) contains six aquatic species of proteid salamanders placed in two genera. The genus *Necturus* contains the mud puppy, *N. maculosus*, of the eastern and central USA and parts of southern Canada, and the four species of water dogs from the eastern and central USA. These include the Alabama water dog, *N. alabamensis*, of Alabama, western Georgia and eastern Missouri, and the Gulf Coast water dog, *N. beyeri*, of Missouri, Louisiana and eastern Texas. The other member of the family is the olm, *Proteus anguinus*, which lives in underground lakes and streams in southern Austria, northeast Italy and western Yugoslavia.

Great crested newt
(breeding male)

Smooth or common newt
(breeding male)

Olm

Alpine newt
(breeding male)

Marbled newt (breeding male)

Corsican brook salaman

Fire salamander

Italian cave salaman

Spectacled salamander

small invertebrates such as flies, beetles and centipedes on its sticky surface.

Cave salamanders are skillful climbers and can ascend wet rock faces with ease, aided by the expanded surface of their webbed toes. They also use their blunt, cylindrical tails when climbing. When cave salamanders walk uphill, the tip of the tail swings from left to right and curls down for use as a "walking stick." When they walk downhill, the end of the tail presses against the surface on which they are moving and serves as a brake.

The Italian and Sardinian cave salamanders both have slender trunks and relatively long legs. They also have flattened, roughly hexagonal-shaped heads and exceptionally large eyes. Their bodies are dark brown with lighter marbled markings. In some subspecies, the basic dark body color is obscured by yellow or reddish brown blotches.

ABOVE An inhabitant of the high rain forests of Central America, this 5.5-in.-long lungless salamander spends most of its time crawling about the leaves of trees. Having no lungs or gills, it breathes through the lining of its mouth and through its thin, moist skin.

The Californian cave salamander lives only in mountainous regions, and remains active even when temperatures approach freezing. The Mount Lyell salamander of the central Sierra Nevada mountains lives at altitudes of 4260-11,500 ft., on wet rockslides and in damp crevices of granite rock, which it resembles in body color and pattern. It usually feeds at night on spiders and small insects. The Mount Shasta salamander prefers limestone localities in the Mount Shasta region of northern California. It was only discovered in 1953, living near a cave entrance. Apart from rocky places, it also inhabits humid areas of coniferous forest.

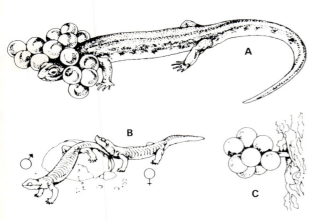

ABOVE The North American red salamander is a stout-bodied, short-limbed species that lives under moss and stones in or near springs or trickles of water that flow through open land and through wooded areas. The bright coloration is more intense in younger individuals. Old adults are a dull, brownish purple with larger spots that often run together.
LEFT Breeding behavior of some lungless salamanders: a female dusky salamander guards her eggs (A). The female Italian cave salamander rests her throat on the male's tail during courtship (B). Lungless woodland salamanders of North America attach their eggs to rotting tree trunks by stalks (C).
FAR LEFT California slender salamanders climb trees during the rainy season. For the rest of the year, they live on the ground.

The limestone salamander, which is entirely brown in color, inhabits wooded limestone outcrops of the central Sierra Nevada mountains. It is reputed to climb up tree trunks with great agility and roll up its body when disturbed.

Sticky and slimy

The largest group of lungless salamanders includes the 34 species of small, slender-bodied woodland salamanders. They are generally dark-colored with fine freckles, but the many subspecies all have slightly different markings. Some have bright-colored, often reddish stripes, cheek patches or large blotches on the limbs. Most species live in the forested highlands of the Appalachian Mountains in the eastern United States.

During the day, woodland salamanders hide under rocks and logs, although they can often be seen searching for food after heavy rainfall, especially in the spring and autumn. They eat a range of invertebrate food that many other predators find distasteful, including hard-shelled beetles and stinging ants. Woodland salamanders have sticky skin-gland secretions that make them unpleasant to predators. These secretions may also serve to glue together the jaws of rats, snakes and other attackers. The females lay their eggs in clusters, depositing them in damp places such as the hollows of rotting logs. The eggs hatch directly into small adult forms.

One of the most common species of woodland salamander is the red-backed salamander, which ranges from the coastal areas of eastern Canada to North Carolina in the United States. It is very adaptable, having expanded from its original woodland range. As long as there are plenty of trees, it will visit suburban gardens and city waste plots. It grows to 3.5 in. or more, and occurs in two distinct color phases. In the lead-backed phase, it is gray or black, flecked with lighter markings; in the red-backed phase, it has a broad, colored stripe running the length of its back and narrowing toward the tail. The stripe is usually red, but it may be orange or yellow.

The slimy salamander is another common and wide-spread species throughout uplands of the eastern and southern United States. It grows to 6 in. or more, has large, bulbous eyes, and is black with silvery white speckles. The slimy salamander inhabits moist, wooded ravines with moss-covered rocks and sprouting ferns.

The zigzag salamander has a more restricted range that includes the east-central highlands from Indiana south to Alabama. Although it is predominantly a woodland species, it also lives on rock slides and at the entrance to caves. It is 2.5-3.5 in. long and can be identified by the yellow, orange or red wavy stripes on its tail region.

Some woodland salamanders are restricted to a particular mountain range, including the Cheat mountain salamander from the moist forests and ravines of Cheat Mountain, Virginia, and the Caddo mountain salamander of the Caddo Mountains of western Arkansas. Six of the seven woodland salamanders of western North America occupy the humid forests of the Pacific coastal region, from northern California to southern British Columbia in Canada. The seventh one is the Jemez mountain salamander, which is limited to a single mountain range in the southwestern United States and lives at altitudes above 8500 ft.

Zoologists divide lungless salamanders into two groups according to the way in which they open their mouths. In the smaller group, known as the

SALAMANDERS AND NEWTS
CLASSIFICATION: 6

Lungless salamanders

The family Plethodontidae, the lungless salamanders, forms by far the largest of the salamander families, with 209 species in 24 genera. They occupy a variety of damp habitats in North, Central and northern South America and in a small region of southern Europe. Most species, however, occur in the eastern USA.

The dusky salamanders of the genus *Desmognathus* occur in southeast Canada and the eastern USA, while the shovel-nosed salamander, *Leurognathus marmoratus*, is confined to the extreme west of North Carolina and adjacent parts of neighboring states. The woodland salamanders of the large genus *Plethodon* occur in both eastern and western North America, and include the slimy salamander, *P. glutinosus*, of the eastern USA, and the red-backed salamander, *P. cinereus*, of southeast Canada and the eastern USA. The spring salamanders of the genus *Gyrinophilus*, the red and

mud salamanders of the genus *Pseudotriton* and the American brook salamanders of the genus *Eurycea* are all distributed over the eastern and southern USA. The slender salamander, *Batrachoseps attenuatus*, lives in the western USA.

The grotto salamander, *Typhlotriton spelaeus*, lives in southern Missouri and parts of adjacent states, and the Texas blind salamander, *Typhlomolge rathbuni*, is confined to the San Marcos area of Texas. The climbing salamanders of the genus *Aenides* include many western North American species, such as the arboreal salamander, *A. lugubris*, from California, and the green salamander, *A. aenus*, of parts of the central and south-central USA. The ensatinas of the genus *Ensatina* and the slender salamanders of the genus *Batrachoseps* all live in the western USA. The cave or web-footed salamanders of the genus *Hydromantes* occur in California and parts of southern Europe, and include the Italian cave salamander, *H. italicus*, from north and central Italy and southeast France.

desmognaths, the animals have a rigid and relatively immovable lower jaw. They open their mouths mainly by raising the upper jaw. They use the lower, spade-shaped jaw like a shovel or spade, digging and turning over earth and vegetable debris in search of food. Desmognaths include the group of dusky salamanders, the shovel-nosed salamander with its short, stout body and the red-hills salamander, a long, slender-bodied form that burrows in sandy soil.

There are some 15 species of dusky salamander that take their name from their dark body color (although the young tend to have yellow, chestnut or red spots). Dusky salamanders live in or near small mountain streams or in the seepage area of springs where the ground is waterlogged. During wet weather, some species, such as the Allegheny mountain salamander, forage into neighboring wooded areas. Dusky salamanders are extremely agile, and can jump several times their body length.

The largest of the dusky salamanders, the black-bellied salamander of the southern United States, grows to 6.5 in. or more. Although it is most active at night, it can sometimes be seen near streams during the day, resting on water-splashed rocks near waterfalls. The smallest of the group, the pygmy salamander, is less than 2 in. long. It lives under rotting

ABOVE Many of the North American lungless salamanders have a number of subspecies that differ slightly in their coloration and body markings. There are three subspecies of the North American red salamander. The black-chinned red salamander has a concentration of black pigment on its chin. Another subspecies, the southern red salamander, is a more purple-red color flecked with white, especially on its snout and the sides of its head.

logs on the forest floor in the Great Smoky Mountains. At night, especially during wet or foggy weather, it can be seen on tree trunks hunting small invertebrate prey.

The shovel-nosed salamander can be distinguished from dusky salamanders by its more wedge-shaped head and smaller eyes. Both species live in and near streams, their mottled colors camouflaging them against the stony bed of streams.

Clear water or muddy homes

Three different groups that include the spring, red and mud salamanders are all similar in appearance and life-style. Most are red or pink with black spots, and the young adults have particularly brilliant colors. Spring and red salamanders prefer clear, cool waters, while muddy salamanders like soft, muddy bottoms and saturated seepage areas. The Tennessee

ABOVE The arboreal salamander lives in oak woodland along the Californian coast and is usually most active at night. It is an expert tree climber and has been found as high as 59 ft. above ground. During the late spring and early summer, these salamanders congregate underground or in hollow trees (in one case, 35 individuals were found together), and emerge after the first autumn rains. The females lay grape-like clusters of eggs on the ground.

cave salamander of the spring salamander genus is one of several blind, aquatic, cave-dwelling salamanders that live in limestone caves in the southern USA.

See-through salamanders

The other aquatic cave-dwelling salamanders have more slender bodies and are grouped under a general heading of blind salamanders. They resemble the olm, and all live in the southern United States. Blind salamanders have ghostly white or pinkish skin, often with an iridescent sheen. The skin is so translucent (light shines through it) that the outline of the darker internal organs is often visible.

The Texas blind salamander retains larval features throughout its life. It generally grows to 3-4.5 in. in length, and has a flattened, duck-like snout that it uses to rummage through mud and silt for small aquatic invertebrates. The Georgia blind salamander is a smaller aquatic larval form, usually 2-3 in. long, with a broader and much less flattened snout. It is known from only a few specimens found in well water at a depth of over 196 ft., and in a few caves in southwest Georgia and Florida.

The grotto salamander lives in the Ozark plateau in the central United States. It has two distinct phases: in the larval phase, it lives in mountain brooks and springs. It has pigmented skin of a brownish purple color with yellow flecks, and well-developed eyes. Later on, in the second phase of its life, the grotto salamander moves to underground waters of caves and grottos. It loses its colored pigmentation, its eyes become smaller and cease to function, and it develops tiny feet and legs.

Dwellers in darkness

Brook salamanders are more closely linked with water than other groups of lungless salamanders. They include permanent larval types that live in underground waters, such as the 2.5-3.5-in.-long Cascade Cavern salamander that inhabits one small area of Texas. Others, such as the dark-sided salamander, often live in the dim light near the entrance of caves.

Most species of brook salamander have yellow skin, especially on their undersides. The northern two-lined salamander is the most common yellow-colored salamander of the American northeast. It has a broad yellow, brownish green or almost orange stripe down its back and narrow dark lines on its sides.

Tree-climbing types

Tree-climbing salamanders belong to several groups. The arboreal salamander of the Californian coast region is a stout-bodied species, up to 3 in. long. It has a prehensile tail, and the end of its toes form suction pads. It climbs trees during the wetter winter months, but during the dry summer it rests—either underground or deep within the hollows of trees.

The green salamander of the eastern and southern United States belongs to the same group. It has a lichen-like, yellowish green mottling over its body. Both its head and body are flattened—an adaptation that allows it to squeeze into and move around inside small crevices. It is another excellent climber of cliffs and, occasionally, trees.

ABOVE Several species of slender salamanders live in the Pacific coastal region of the United States, in a variety of habitats from desert regions to mountains up to 6500 ft. above sea level. They are often found in small groups, hiding beneath rocks during the day. RIGHT **A female slender salamander guards her string of eggs as they hatch. She lays 4-20 eggs under logs or rocks and these hatch in the spring. The larvae do not undergo an aquatic stage.**

Sirens

Sirens are neotenous amphibians (they retain their larval characteristics throughout their lives). There are three species of sirens, ranging throughout the southern and central USA to northeastern Mexico. They are slender and eel-like in appearance, with bunches of feathery external gills behind their small heads. They have small, weak front legs but lack hind limbs. Sirens live in the shallow waters of streams, ponds and muddy irrigation ditches. Hunting at night, they feed on crayfish, worms and mollusks. While eating their prey, the sirens also swallow quantities of aquatic vegetation.

The greater siren is one of the largest of the tailed amphibians and ranges from Washington, D.C., to Florida. Growing to a length of 20-29.5 in., it is olive-green in color with lighter green or yellow spots on the undersides. Each forefoot of the greater siren ends in four blunt toes. In contrast, the adult lesser siren reaches 7-27 in. in length and is brown to blue-black in color. It ranges throughout the southeastern USA, Texas and Mexico.

Surviving drought

During droughts, the lesser siren survives by entering a state called "estivation." As the ponds and ditches in which it lives dry up during summer, the lesser siren buries itself in mud. The slimy mucus covering on its skin then hardens to form a parchment-like cocoon that enables the amphibian to survive the period of dry weather. It can remain in this state of dormancy for two months until heavy rains return, when it breaks out of the cocoon and resumes a normal life in creeks and other waterways.

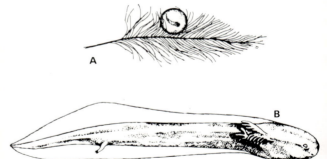

being able to vocalize a wide range of sounds. The greater siren makes a yelping distress call when disturbed, and the lesser siren produces clicking sounds as it gulps air at the surface and when it approaches another individual of the same species. It also has a shrill distress call.

Certain aspects of their anatomy distinguish sirens from other salamanders. Internally, they lack any remnants of a pelvic girdle, making their bodies extremely flexible—the only other group of amphibians to share this feature are the wormlike caecilians. Sirens also have very few ribs and their hearts have finger-like extensions that increase the volume of blood that can be pumped around their long bodies. The three species of sirens lay eggs that they attach singly to the roots of water plants. The aquatic larvae that hatch from the eggs have well-developed tail fins.

ABOVE Sirens are eel-like amphibians that live in freshwater areas of the southeastern USA. The greater siren is the largest species, measuring over 3 ft. long. Sirens lack both pelvic bones (making their bodies very flexible) and hind legs, though they do have small and weak front legs.
ABOVE RIGHT Two stages in the greater siren's life cycle: an egg that the female has laid on a feathery, underwater leaf (A). The greater siren larva can reach a length of 6 in. (B).

The dwarf siren varies in color from brown, gray and green to greenish black. It is a small North American amphibian that reaches only 4-7.5 in. in length. Each forefoot of the dwarf siren has three toes, and the front legs are smaller than those of the other two species. Several subspecies of dwarf sirens exist, each with a distinctively colored pattern of stripes that provide camouflage against the muddy bottom of a pond. The dwarf siren is especially abundant among the roots of the water hyacinth in Florida, but also ranges through South Carolina.

Mythical creatures

The common name of the sirens derives from the female water spirits of Greek mythology that sang and lured sailors to their doom on rocky shores. Indeed, the sirens are unusual among tailed amphibians in

SALAMANDERS AND NEWTS — CLASSIFICATION: 7 —

Sirens

The sirens make up the family Sirenidae, with three aquatic species from parts of the southern and eastern USA. The dwarf siren, *Pseudobranchus striatus*, occurs in Florida, southern Georgia and the extreme south of South Carolina. The greater siren, *Siren lacertina*, is found over much of the eastern coastal plain, from Washington, D.C., to southern Alabama. The lesser siren, *S. intermedia*, has a more extensive distribution, occurring along the eastern coastal plain from North Carolina to Texas and north up the Mississippi Valley to Lake Michigan.

JUMPING AND CROAKING

Dazzling in their variety, frogs and toads are the most numerous amphibians on earth. Their long hind legs give them great leaping power, while their deafening choruses may be heard from over half a mile away

Frogs and toads form the largest order of amphibians with nearly 3500 species, ranging worldwide from northern Scandinavia to the high mountains and tropical rain forests of South America. They are extremely adaptable amphibians, and their habitats include the cold northern tundra where they hibernate in mud to survive the cold, and hot, dry deserts where they avoid the heat by burrowing. Desert species of frogs and toads usually emerge at night when the climate is cooler and more humid. They also synchronize their breeding activity with the length of daylight, temperature and rainfall. The tadpoles of desert species develop at an extremely fast rate before the areas of temporary water dry out.

Most frogs and toads range from 0.8 to 5 in. in length. The largest known species of frog is the goliath frog of West Africa, which grows to over 31 in. in length and weighs over 6 lbs. 8 oz. Of the many small tropical frogs, the smallest is a species of poison-arrow frog from Cuba, which grows to an average length of just 0.4 in.

Bulbous bodies

Many species of frogs and toads are similar in appearance. They have short, bulbous bodies and lose their tails after reaching adulthood, an adaptation that allows them to jump more easily. The forelimbs and larger hind limbs of toads and frogs are well developed and muscular and are used to propel the amphibian forward. Their heads are large and merge directly into the bodies which have no distinct necks. They have large eyes that protrude forward, and their upper eyelids are fixed. The lower eyelids consist of two movable transparent membranes called nictitating membranes. As they sweep across the eye, these membranes clear away particles that would otherwise interrupt vision. Secretions from tear glands keep the surface of the eye moist.

In contrast to most amphibians, frogs and toads have a well-developed sense of hearing. They have prominent eardrums that lie flush with the side of the head, and they are the most primitive vertebrates to have a middle-ear cavity where the sound is amplified. The acute sense of hearing is associated with the wide repertoire of calls that frogs and toads make.

Although both sexes of frogs and toads are able to make sounds, males make them more frequently to attract and stimulate females during the mating ritual.

FROGS AND TOADS CLASSIFICATION: 1

The frogs and toads of the order Anura form by far the largest of the amphibian orders, with 3494 species in all. They occupy a great range of habitats throughout the temperate and tropical regions of the world. They are divided into 20 families, the largest of which are the Ranidae, the true frogs; the Dendrobatidae, the poison-arrow frogs; the Rhacophoridae, the Old World tree frogs; the Hyperoliidae, the sedge and bush frogs; the Microhylidae, the narrow-mouthed frogs; the Bufonidae, the true toads; the Hylidae, the true tree frogs; and the Leptodactylidae, the leptodactylid frogs.

As many as two dozen males may call at the same time, creating a deafening chorus audible over half a mile away. The calls originate as the amphibian inhales air into the mouth through the nostrils. Flaps of skin close the nose, and the exhaled air from the lungs causes vibrations of the vocal cords situated in the larynx. In males, the air then passes into a pair of vocal sacs lying underneath the throat that have the effect of amplifying the sound. Apart from the spring breeding chorus, male frogs use sounds in crowded breeding ponds to avoid mistakenly mounting another male. Similarly, females have a distinct call that they make to indicate that they are unwilling to mate. Many species also use territorial and distress calls.

Breeding behavior

Although many frogs and toads live on land, certain species return to water to breed. During mating, frogs and toads migrate to suitable breeding ponds in large numbers. The male clings to the female by a nuptial pad that develops as an extra digit on the hand and clasps the female in an amplexus grip. The male fertilizes the female's eggs by releasing sperm as she lays them. Female frogs and toads lay from one to several thousand eggs.

Females lay their eggs in still, shallow water. A jelly-like casing protects the eggs from predators and also insulates them from extremes of temperature. The fertilized eggs grow by cell division within the jelly

ABOVE AND LEFT During the breeding season, male frogs and toads attract the females by producing a range of calls that vary between species. The sounds are produced by the air vibrating elastic tissue in the voice box, and this is amplified by the vocal sacs that lie underneath the chin and act as resonant chambers. PAGE 1755 The European stripeless tree frog climbs well using the sucker-like adhesive disks on its fingers and toes.

ABOVE **Common frogs mate in the water of shallow ponds. The male holds the female in a tight grip (called amplexus) under her forearms and fertilizes the eggs as they are** laid. **The female lays approximately 5000 eggs each season.**
ABOVE RIGHT **The tadpoles that emerge from the eggs have well-developed external gills and long tails.**

BELOW LEFT **Stages in the development of the tadpole: inside the egg (A); with feathery, external gills (B); and with developing mouth and eyes (C). The tail develops into a strong** propelling organ (D). **At eight weeks, the tadpole's hind legs are well developed (E); and at three months, it has almost changed into a frog—it has all its limbs but still retains a tail (F).**

covering and develop into aquatic larvae called tadpoles that have tails with well-developed fins. Most tadpoles have short backs and almost spherical bodies. Their mouths consist of a pair of fleshy lips with rows of horny teeth arranged on them. Most tadpoles feed by scraping plant matter from algae and other water plants. They can also filter-feed from algae that they find in water.

Stages of change

As the tadpole stage progresses, the young undergo a slow metamorphosis. The tadpoles lose their tails and develop hind legs. Internally, there are modifications to the blood circulation, and the development of lungs takes place at the same time as the external gills are reabsorbed. Lungs are essential in enabling the tadpoles to breathe above water. The young frogs that emerge onto land are vulnerable to predators

ABOVE During the final stage of a tadpole's metamorphosis into a frog, when the animal is about three months old, it reabsorbs its tail into its body.
ABOVE RIGHT The common frog leaps across the surface of the pond by suddenly straightening its powerful hind limbs. As it lands, the forelimbs break the fall and the chest hits the water surface. The common frog jumps primarily to escape from enemies.

particularly larger frogs and toads, snakes and birds. In those frogs and toads that lay large numbers of eggs, most of the young perish at the egg, tadpole or subadult stage of development—only a few individuals reach maturity.

Some frogs and toads lay a few, large eggs and incubate them rather than leaving the eggs to develop by themselves. Parental care is a good protection from predation. The tadpoles that hatch on land will either wriggle into nearby water or enter it on the backs of their parents. Certain species build foamy nests suspended from vegetation that overhangs water. After hatching, the larvae drop directly into the water.

New Zealand frogs and the tailed frog

Adult frogs and toads can be distinguished by their lack of a tail, which would make jumping difficult. The tailed frog of the northwestern USA and the New Zealand frogs do not actually have true tails, but possess two tiny, tail-wagging muscles from their tadpole stage. The three species of New Zealand frogs live on forested mountainsides where water is scarce. Reaching a length of less than 2 inches, these nocturnal frogs prefer to ambush their victims when hunting, rather than actively pursuing their prey. Fertilization takes place externally, and the females lay clusters of up to 11 eggs in dark, damp crevices under stones or logs, and in water-logged soil. The young use their tails to break out of the eggshells. They retain their tails for up to one month after hatching—they are then reabsorbed into the body.

Hochstetter's frog is the most common species of New Zealand frog, distinguished by its strongly webbed toes. It lives near small, cold-water streams in the mountain forests of the North Island. Archey's frog only inhabits the Coromandel mountain region of the North Island, ranging through mist-covered forests and along the stony ridges of subalpine grasslands. The rarest species is Hamilton's frog that, until 1958, was only known to exist on a small (0.6 acre) area of rockside on a single island in the Cook Strait, but has since been found in a more extensive rocky area of a second nearby island.

New Zealand frogs are unique amphibians that originally ranged over a wider area of New Zealand. The introduction of predators, such as rats, has now reduced their numbers. In addition, the greater number of pigs and goats on the islands has altered the vegetation of their upland habitats. All three species receive protection as endangered species throughout their range.

The 2-inch-long tailed frog ranges throughout the northwestern USA. It inhabits fast-flowing mountain streams with mossy banks that receive shade from forest vegetation. The adult frog is a dark olive-gray color, often with a yellow triangular patch on the snout. Like the New Zealand frogs, the skin surface of the tailed frog has a covering of small warts and projections called tubercles. The toes are long and slender, and the outer toes of the hind feet are noticeably thicker than the others.

The tailed frog's "tail" is cylindrical and measures 0.16 to 0.24 inches in length. Functioning as an extension of the cloaca, it allows the male to fertilize the female internally. No other species of frog or toad is known to use this method of reproduction. The introduction of sperm into the female's cloaca may be an adaptation designed to ensure fertilization of the eggs in fast-flowing water.

Mating occurs in the autumn, and the female stores the sperm in her body until the following spring, when she lays a jelly-clad string of 30-50 eggs under stones in the water. The tadpoles take a month to develop before emerging from their eggs, probably due to the low water temperature. The tadpoles that emerge from the eggs have large suckers that they use to cling to stones and water plants in the fast water currents, and to climb up wet rocks above water level to feed on algae. The low water temperatures in these streams reduce the rate of metamorphosis. As a result, the tadpoles take two to three years to reach adulthood.

Disk-tongued toads

The disk-tongued toads are a small family of 14 species distributed across Europe, northwest Africa, parts of the Far East, the Philippines and Borneo. Unlike most other frogs and toads, disk-tongued toads cannot extend their tongues to grab their prey; instead, they catch food with their mouths. They also differ from the adults of other species by retaining their ribs after metamorphosis.

The common midwife toad of central western Europe is the most well known of the disk-tongued species. A land dweller that rarely goes near the water, it measures some 2 inches long and has a brownish gray coloration. It owes its fame to its breeding behavior, in which the male is responsible for hatching the young. On warm spring and summer nights, the male common midwife toad utters a soft bell-like call that attracts females from some distance away. When a female approaches, he immediately clasps her around the waist, and begins caressing her cloaca with his hind feet to encourage her to lay her eggs. Some 40-80 large eggs emerge in a long string joined together by jelly. The male fertilizes them and instead of leaving them where they are, wraps the ribbon of eggs around his hind legs.

FROGS AND TOADS CLASSIFICATION: 2

New Zealand frogs and the tailed frog

The family Leiopelmatidae contains just four species of frogs. The three species of New Zealand frogs belong to the genus *Leiopelma* and are confined to New Zealand, while the tailed frog *Ascaphus truei* occurs in western North America. (The tailed frog is sometimes placed in a family of its own, the Ascaphidae.)

Disk-tongued toads

The family Discoglossidae consists of the disk-tongued toads, with 14 species in five genera. They range over Europe, western Asia, northwest Africa, parts of the Far East, the Philippines and Borneo. The common midwife toad, *Alytes obstetricans*, lives in Western and central Europe, while the painted frog, *Discoglossus pictus*, occurs along the Mediterranean coasts of France, Spain and North Africa, and in Sicily and Malta. The fire-bellied toads belong to the genus *Bombina*, and include the yellow-bellied toad, *B. variegata*, which ranges from France through central and southern Europe to the Black Sea, and the red-bellied toad, *B. bombina*, which ranges from West Germany through Eastern Europe to the western USSR and Turkey.

Taking care not to lose any of the eggs, the male common midwife toad retreats into his hiding place —a burrow that he has dug, or a hole under a log— and stays there until the eggs are fully developed. By staying put, the male ensures that he keeps the eggs at the correct humidity. However, he does sometimes emerge in dew or during a damp night to allow the eggs to absorb the evening moisture. When the young are ready to hatch, the male finds a pond and backs into the water, submerging his rear end together with the ribbon of eggs. The tadpoles promptly break free and swim away. The drab coloration of the common midwife toad serves as excellent camouflage in its dark woodland or stony habitat.

A fiery warning

The upper surfaces of most fire-bellied toads—also members of the disk-tongued toad family—are usually dull gray-brown or green to disguise them as they sit still among the plants in ponds or streams. But they have striking red or yellow underparts that they reveal when predators threaten them. The colors probably warn their enemies that they are not to be tampered with, since all fire-bellied toads secrete a foaming, toxic fluid that can cause great irritation to an attacker's mouth.

ABOVE Among midwife toads, it is the male who takes responsibility for looking after the eggs. He drapes the spawn around his hind legs and carries them around with him until the tadpoles hatch, occasionally dipping them into water to keep them moist.

BELOW As the female midwife toad produces the strings of eggs, her mate fertilizes them (A) and entwines them around his hind legs (B-C). When the eggs are ready to hatch, he takes to the water and finds a suitable pool where he leaves them to develop.

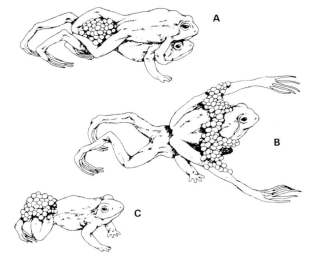

ABOVE AND LEFT The darkish, mottled upper surface of the yellow-bellied toad makes it difficult to spot when it is swimming or sitting quietly on the mud at the edge of a pond or stream. However, when a predator attacks the toad, it lies on its back and raises its head and legs to reveal the bright coloration of its belly and undersurface of the limbs. The flash of yellow may startle the predator and drive it away.

In spite of this toxic defense, other frogs and some snakes still eat large numbers of fire-bellied toads. If a predator attacks it, a fire-bellied toad will arch its back and cover its eyes with its front legs so that the yellow palms face outward. It then folds its hind legs over its back to display the vividly colored soles of its hind feet.

Fire-bellied toads are widely distributed throughout the Old World. Most are small animals that measure one to one and a half inches in length, with slightly flattened bodies and warty skins. They spend much of their time in pond and ditchwaters and are active by night, often betraying their presence with short, soft calls.

The upperparts of the yellow-bellied toad are grayish or brown, and the animal is usually difficult to see when it sits motionless on the ground. Its underparts are lemon yellow or orange, with bluish black marbling. It occurs in central southern Europe, where it prefers to stay near muddy pools, springs, ditches and swamps.

The red-bellied toad has orange or, more rarely, bright red underparts, again with dark marbling. The oriental fire-bellied toad of eastern Siberia and China displays the most eye-catching colors—a bright green back spotted with black, and a flame-red belly with black marbling.

European cousins

The two species of painted frogs occur only in the Mediterranean region. One of them, the Israel painted frog, is considered to be the rarest amphibian in the world. Since 1940, only five have been seen in the Hula Valley, northeast Israel. Its relative, the painted frog, lives along the southern coasts of France and Spain, and in North Africa, Sicily and Malta. It occurs around still or running water and is particularly common in areas where irrigation schemes have created a network of channels and pools. Active during the day and night, it can often be seen sitting with its head poking just above the surface of the water.

Clawed and Surinam toads

The 26 species of clawed and Surinam toads constitute a family that occurs in Africa and Central and South America. They spend most of their lives in the water and have no tongues, since these are organs that other amphibians developed as a means of moistening and swallowing dry food on dry land. They all have flattened bodies with splayed limbs and small, flattened, triangular heads. Their eyes are tiny and face upward, since they spend most of their time lying on the bottom of ponds, peering up through the water for prey. The clawed and Surinam toads are drably colored to match the ooze on the beds of the pools they inhabit, and their bodies may be covered with slime.

The Surinam toad is one of the oddest-looking species in the family and lives in the Amazon and Orinoco rivers of South America. It is roughly square in shape with broad, webbed hind limbs and slender forelimbs, each ending in four sensitive, thread-like toes. The Surinam toad uses its toes to sift through the mud for food, enabling it to find prey when the water is so thick with silt that it is unable to see properly.

The breeding behavior of the Surinam toad is unusual and distinctive. Instead of leaving her eggs to develop of their own accord, as the common frog does, the female Surinam toad carries them around in special pockets in the skin on her back.

Mating somersaults

Getting the eggs onto the back of the female Surinam toad involves a complex mating ritual. During courtship, the male clasps the female's back and the two perform a series of somersaults in the water, rising toward the surface. As they float upward the pair turn over, so that they float with their bellies facing upward. When the female lays her eggs, they fall onto the male's belly and he fertilizes them. As the couple turn over again and swim downward, the fertilized eggs roll across the female and slide into the special pockets on her back. The process is repeated several times, and although many eggs fall to the bottom of the pond and are lost, the female eventually ends up with a full load.

ABOVE The painted frog occurs along the Mediterranean coast of France, Spain and North Africa and around Sicily and Malta. Despite its resemblance to the common frog it is actually one of the disk-tongued toads, a primitive family with simple, disk-shaped tongues that cannot be extended to catch prey. The painted frog spends much of its time in the water, squatting in the shallow parts of rivers, streams and pools with only its eyes jutting above the surface.

Each of the Surinam toad's eggs develops in its own pocket in the female's skin. The tadpoles' tails are "plugged in" to the mother's system, so that they act like the placentas of mammals, exchanging nutrients and gases. In these favorable conditions, the tadpoles develop fast, and undergo metamorphosis while still entrenched in their pockets. Once they have transformed into perfectly formed though still miniature frogs, they break free of their pocket walls to begin independent lives.

Unique claws

The African clawed toad is similar in shape to the Surinam toad, with its flattened body and head, and a covering of evil-smelling slime that may act as a deterrent to predators. It is named for the three black claws on the toes of each hind limb. Its

Tailed frog

Panama golden stub-footed frog

Golden Man

Dish backed tree frog

Giant toad

Ornate horned frog

Surinam toad

African clawed toad

hindlimbs are long, webbed and powerful, but the forelimbs are slender and weak and are unable to support the toad's weight when it is out of water. As a result, it moves overland in a series of clumsy, belly-flopping leaps.

On the bottom of the pool, where the African clawed toad spends most of its time, it uses its forelimbs to feed itself with prey. It feeds on aquatic insects, worms, crustaceans and fishes, ambushing them as they swim past. It will often burrow into the mud so that it is almost invisible, but it has to emerge at regular intervals to breathe. The African clawed toad prefers stagnant, deoxygenated pools, which means that it cannot absorb much oxygen from the water through its skin, like other frogs and toads. Instead it relies on its extra-large lungs, gulping large amounts of air from the surface and returning to the bottom to keep a lookout for prey.

The tadpoles of the African clawed toad are distinctive in shape, with broad, flattened bodies and slender tails. Their most remarkable feature, though, is the transparency of their body tissues: the bones and internal organs can be clearly seen through the muscles, making them fascinating creatures to study.

The burrowing toad

The burrowing toad of Central America is the only member of its family. Similar in many ways to the clawed and Surinam toads, it has adapted to life on dry land and has developed a tongue so that it can eat dry food. As its name suggests, it spends much of its time digging tunnels. It is specially equipped for this job with a horny, spade-like outgrowth on the first toe of each hind foot. The burrowing toad uses these outgrowths to dig into the nests of termites that form its main food. Measuring some 3.5 inches long, it is olive-brown or blue-gray in color with irregular yellow spots that often join together to form a vertical line down its back.

Spadefoot and horned toads

The spadefoot toads, like the burrowing toads, have developed a digging apparatus on their hind feet. Spadefoot toads occur in both Eurasia and North America, where they have become particularly well adapted to arid climates. In Europe they inhabit a broader range of habitats, but they prefer dry areas with sandy soils.

ABOVE The primitive Surinam toad travels across a pond with her eggs developing in special pits in the soft hollow of her back. The eggs have a translucent covering that later opens when the female molts. In some Surinam toads, the tadpoles develop directly into froglets.

BELOW Mating Surinam toads swim in a series of loops. At the top of each loop, the female lays some eggs that fall on the belly of the male who fertilizes them (A); as the couple dive down, the eggs slip onto the female's back where they later develop into froglets (B). The cycle is then repeated (C).

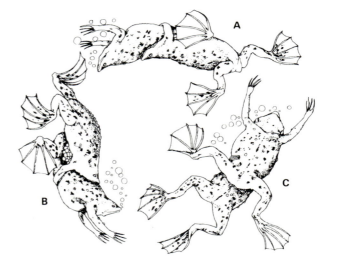

THE AFRICAN CLAWED TOAD
— AN AQUATIC HUNTER —

Half-buried in the ooze at the bottom of a stagnant pool, the African clawed toad lies quite still, invisible to both its prey and the predators that might want to eat it. Though motionless, it is not asleep. The small, beady eyes mounted on top of its flattened head keep careful watch, monitoring the other occupants of the pool as they move through the lukewarm water. Occasionally a fish or crustacean comes too close, and with a snap and swirl of water it vanishes into the toad's mouth. When the water clears the toad is back on the bottom again, watching for another victim.

Measuring two to three inches long (excluding the legs), the African clawed toad has a flattened, mucus covered body and large, webbed hind feet that splay out on either side. It takes its name from the short, black claws on the inner three toes of each hind foot that the animals use to dig out tiny animals from the bottom of pools. The male African clawed toad has a further use for the claws—they help him hold onto the slippery female during mating.

The African clawed toad lives in the swamps of tropical southern Africa where it spends nearly all its life submerged in the stagnant waters. It is almost helpless on dry land, and will emerge only if its pond or stream has dried up. Even then it often prefers to burrow down into the mud beneath the pool until the next rains come, entering a state of dormancy. In this condition it uses so little energy that it needs no food. Although it is much weakened after emerging from dormancy, its rapid rate of eating soon brings it back to peak fitness.

A meal of mosquitoes

The African clawed toad eats a range of food, including fishes, crustaceans, aquatic insects, larvae, dead animals and even its own tadpoles. It fills its mouth with food and pushes the meal down its throat using its slender front toes. Because it also eats vast quantities of mosquito eggs and larvae, it is especially useful to humans since it reduces the spread of mosquito-borne diseases like malaria.

The start of the rainy season heralds the mating season for African clawed toads. During this period the male croaks from morning to evening to attract females. After mating, each female lays a batch of 500-2000 eggs on underwater plants. The tadpoles emerge from the eggs after about a week and spend another week immobile in the water, nourished by the remains of egg yolk enclosed within their bodies. Once they develop mouths, the tadpoles start to move around in large groups, filtering the water to trap the microscopic floating animals that flit among the vegetation.

LEFT The white "stitches" along the flanks of the adult are sense organs that detect the movements of prey. ABOVE AND RIGHT The tadpoles of African clawed toads are pale and partly transparent. The sequence shows a tadpole that has just grown hind limbs (A); a tadpole with all four limbs (B); and a young toad that has reabsorbed its tail (C).

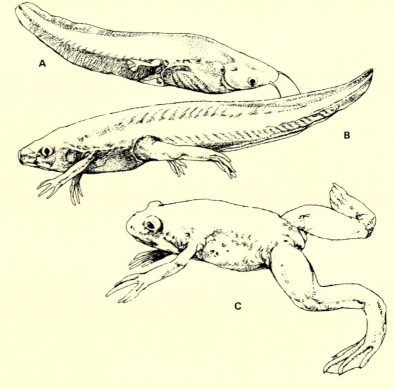

The European common spadefoot lives on dry plains throughout most of Europe and western Asia. It favors scrubland, relatively sparse woodland and sandy heaths. It is a small toad, measuring a little under two inches long, and is gray to olive-green in color with numerous brown blotches. It has protruding eyes with vertical pupils—a characteristic of nocturnal animals. Unlike many toads, it has a smooth, fine skin without any surface wrinkles or bumps, and has a somewhat rounded body. When it crouches down, its shape is rounded, an adaptation to dry climates; when resting like this, the toad exposes only a comparatively small surface area to the air, reducing moisture loss through evaporation.

Swift diggers

Like the burrowing toad, the European common spadefoot and its relatives have sturdy, horny processes (outgrowths) on the insides of their hind legs that they use to burrow swiftly into the ground. They dig deep, vertical tunnels that they stay in throughout the day and during long, dry periods. At night, the toads emerge to forage for insects, spiders and other small creatures. They are particularly active during the spring breeding season, but less so during the rest of the year when they stay near their burrows.

European common spadefoots mate in April, usually after heavy rain. The male lies on the bed of a pond for several days, awaiting the arrival of a female. When a willing female appears, he mates with her by clasping her round the waist and fertilizing the eggs as they emerge. Each female may lay as many as 1000-3000 eggs. The eggs are joined together in long strings that wrap themselves around the stems of swamp plants.

The North American spadefoots are similar to the European species both in their appearance and breeding habits. They occupy hotter, drier regions, and their breeding cycle is dependent on the periodic rains that form short-lived pools where they can lay their eggs. The most widespread species on the central plains of the USA, such as the plains spadefoot and the western spadefoot, base their whole life around these temporary pools.

When it rains heavily, all the spadefoots in the area emerge from their burrows, find partners, mate, and the females immediately lay their eggs. The tadpoles emerge from the eggs within a few hours and begin to grow. Since the pools can dry up within a few weeks or even days, the tadpoles have to develop extremely quickly if they are to survive. They normally eat plant matter, such as algae and debris, that they filter out of the water. A great mass of tadpoles will often swirl around together in a circle, disturbing food from the bottom of the pool so that it rises up toward the surface where they can reach it.

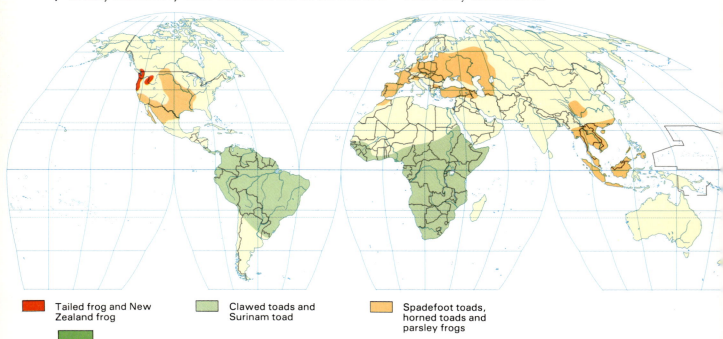

| | Tailed frog and New Zealand frog | | Clawed toads and Surinam toad | | Spadefoot toads, horned toads and parsley frogs |

FROGS AND TOADS CLASSIFICATION: 3

Clawed and Surinam toads and the burrowing toad

The family Pipidae contains 26 species of toads grouped in four genera that range over Africa and parts of Central and South America. The Surinam toad, *Pipa pipa*, inhabits the Amazon and Orinoco river basins in northern South America, while the African clawed toad, *Xenopus laevis*, ranges widely over East, Central and southern Africa. The family Rhinophrynidae contains just one species, the burrowing toad, *Rhinophrynus dorsalis*, which occurs in Mexico and Central America.

Spadefoot toads, horned toads and parsley frogs

The family Pelobatidae contains 88 species in 10 genera that are distributed over North America, Europe, western Asia, Southeast Asia, Indonesia and the Philippines. They include the European common spadefoot, *Pelobates fuscus*, of most of Europe and western Asia; the plains spadefoot, *Scaphiopus bombifrons*, of the central and western USA; the Malaysian horned toad, *Megophrys monticola*, of Southeast Asia, Indonesia and the Philippines; and the common parsley frog, *Pelodytes punctatus*, of Western Europe.

The cooperative feeding behavior of the spadefoot tadpoles is unusual, but even more extraordinary is the way that some species develop into carnivores if normal food sources fail. A small, virtually dried-up pool will often contain just a few enormous tadpoles that have survived by eating several hundred of their brothers and sisters. As the pool dwindles in size, it becomes crucial for the tadpoles to develop lungs, and often less than a dozen adult air-breathing toads emerge from a muddy puddle that had once been a clear pool holding several thousand tadpoles.

The horned toads of Southeast Asia are also ground dwellers, but they live in forests where their mottled brown coloration makes them almost

TOP Strictly nocturnal, the European common spadefoot spends its day in a deep, damp burrow that it digs with the "spades" on the outer edges of its hind feet. If attacked, it produces a garlic-smelling secretion that deters its predators.

ABOVE Similar to its European relative, the western spadefoot of North America prefers to live in slightly drier regions, and breeds in temporary, rain-filled ponds.
FAR LEFT The map shows the distribution of three families of frogs and toads.

invisible among the litter of dead leaves on the forest floor. They take their name from the horn-like flaps of skin that protrude from their snouts and eyebrow ridges. They lay their eggs in mountain streams, and the tadpoles are equipped with lips whose sucking action enables them to hang on to submerged objects and resist the fast-flowing currents.

Parsley frogs

The parsley frogs of Europe resemble common frogs in shape and skin texture, and owe their name to the green, spotted patterning on their backs that, in some individuals, looks like chopped parsley. The common parsley frog is one to two inches long with a slightly flattened body, a rounded snout and long, slim limbs.

During the day, the common parsley frog hides in crevices in rocks and walls, or in burrows that it digs in loose soil, but at dusk it emerges to search for small invertebrates. In summer, it emits a characteristic call—a repeated high-pitched note resembling the creaking of a leather shoe. The frogs breed once or twice a year (more frequently in the south of their range); they mate and lay their eggs in quite small patches of water including ditches, dew ponds and the small pools remaining along the courses of partially dried-up

ABOVE The common parsley frog is a close relative of the spadefoot toads but is rather more advanced, with slender hind limbs that are well adapted for jumping. It is found throughout France and much of southern Spain in damp habitats. Hiding in burrows and crevices during the day, it emerges at night to feed on small invertebrates, often climbing into bushes to capture its prey. It derives its name from its speckled "parsley" green coloring.

streams. Each female lays 1000-1500 eggs. The eggs of the second brood, laid in autumn, overwinter as tadpoles and complete their development during the following spring.

True frogs

The true frogs have the widest variety of habitats of any frog family. Varying in length from 0.6 to 14 in., the adaptable true frogs occur throughout the world with the exception of the polar regions, Madagascar and New Zealand. They have slender bodies and long, muscular legs, both perfectly adapted for jumping and swimming. Their skin is usually smooth and often brown or green in color. Most species of true frogs are aquatic and lay their eggs on leaves above water. Certain species are tree dwellers and have adhesive pads on their feet—an adaptation to forest life.

Edible frogs

One of the most familiar of the true frogs is the edible frog, found throughout central Europe. It usually lives in colonies near the banks of ditches, along the shores of lakes fringed with swamp vegetation and beside slow-moving canals.

The 3.5-inch long adult edible frog is usually olive to bright green in color with dark blotches and paler, longitudinal stripes. Using its green coloration for camouflage, it hunts along the waterbanks, waiting for winged insects to fly within range. It leaps out of the water to catch its prey, propelled by its powerful hind legs. The edible frog also hunts on land, usually at night or after a downpour of rain. Its diet consists of large ground beetles and earthworms that emerge from their burrows to forage on the soil surface.

During the summer months, the edible frog basks in full sunlight on floating lily leaves, waiting for its prey. At the warmest times of the day, it alternates between periods of basking and immersion, thereby replacing the moisture lost through evaporation.

Nocturnal chorus

The loud, croaking chorus of edible frogs is a familiar nighttime sound beside their watery habitats. The male edible frog amplifies his voice by inflating the vocal sacs that adorn the sides of his head, often in response to the noise of trains and planes in the area. It usually reaches a peak of intensity on moonlit nights during the breeding season.

In Europe, the breeding season of the edible frog begins in May or June when males and females gather in ponds to begin mating. The edible frog reaches sexual maturity after two years. If a number of males occupy the same pond, the frog chorus continues uninterrupted for five to ten days. When a male and female form a pair, the male clasps the female under her forelegs, stimulating her to produce her eggs (up to 10,000 each season). As the eggs emerge, the male coats them with sperm to fertilize them, and they fall to the bottom in small groups and spread out among the swamp vegetation.

Rates of metamorphosis

The female lays her eggs when the water temperature is rising in late spring. As a result, the edible frog tadpoles develop quickly. They grow to a considerable size—approximately one inch long—and become very

ABOVE The widespread and flourishing edible frog is a hybrid of the pool frog and the marsh frog, and like them is seldom found far from water. If two edible frogs mate, they usually produce sterile offspring, so in order to breed successfully, they must mate with one of the parent species. Despite this, the edible frog has been in existence for 8000 years or more, and shows no signs of declining in numbers.

broad, particularly just before metamorphosis to adulthood when they are three and a half months old. The rate of metamorphosis is slower in cooler weather.

Predators of the edible frog include swamp birds such as herons and bitterns, and mammals such as otters, rats and weasels. Humans also regard their legs as a delicacy—hence their common name. The closely related marsh frog, a large species that originates in southeast Europe, is also in demand as a culinary delicacy. It has now been introduced into many other areas including southeast England, where it is known as the Romney Marsh frog. Its habits are almost identical to those of the edible frog.

Voracious hunters

The bullfrog of North America is one of the largest members of the true frog family. It grows to 8 in. in length (excluding the legs). Ranging through the

Common tree frog

Marsh frog

Green toad

Yellow-bellied toad

European common toad

European common spadefoot

Common midwife toad

European common frog

eastern USA and the northern borders of Mexico, it has also been introduced to the west coast of the USA, Cuba and Canada. The bullfrog is similar in appearance to the smaller edible frog of Europe. It has a thick-set body and large, exposed eardrums that are particularly obvious in the male. The upperparts of the bullfrog are dark green to black, sometimes with dark spots, and the underparts are whitish with tinges of yellow. The females are browner than the males and have a larger scattering of spots.

"Jug o'rum"

The bullfrog rarely ventures out of water. It lives near ponds, marshes and slow-moving streams, lying idle along the water's edge under the shade of shrubs and weeds. In winter, the bullfrog hibernates near the water under logs and stones. It takes its common name from its distinctive, booming mating call. The extraordinary call occurs every three to four seconds and sounds similar to a throaty shout of "jug o'rum," from which it has gained its popular name.

Humans often hunt bullfrogs for their flesh, which is regarded as a delicacy. In Cuba, bullfrogs are numerous and locals hunt them on a large scale to sell as food. American bullfrogs have been imported to Europe where they now flourish, often at the expense of the native wildlife. The bullfrog is a voracious species that eats mice, shrews, birds, amphibians, large insects and fish. It even preys on snakes, including the garter and coral snake.

Frog-jumping competitions

In many parts of the USA, bullfrogs are pitted against one another in frog-jumping contests. After placing the competing frogs on pads, the owners encourage them to leap. The distance is then measured, and the contest is judged on the distance traveled by the frog over three consecutive jumps.

Wrestling green frogs

North America is the home of several green-skinned, aquatic species that resemble the bullfrog and edible frog in appearance and behavior. Known collectively as the green frogs, they include the leopard frog, which ranges throughout the USA and Canada, the green frog of the northeastern USA and the pig frog of the southeastern USA. Male green frogs are territorial and engage in ritualized fights where two males rear

ABOVE The marsh frog is the largest frog to occur in Europe. It is more aquatic than the common frog and rarely strays far from water. In summer, it can be seen basking in the sun at the edge of pools, streams and drainage ditches, but it quickly dives into the water if disturbed. In winter, it hibernates at the bottom of pools, absorbing what oxygen it needs through its skin. The marsh frog feeds underwater and on land.

up on their hind limbs and wrestle with each other.

Certain species of the true frog family have red-brown markings on a range of body colors. These act as camouflage in habitats where the brown, moist ground and brown plant stems prevail over green foliage. In general, true frogs that are brown in color are less aquatic than green species, and spend much of their lives among damp vegetation. They only return to swamps and pools to find mates and to lay their eggs, and the tadpoles develop in the water. Once metamorphosis is complete, the adult frogs mainly forage on land.

Colorful in cold climates

The common frog has an extremely wide range of body colors—gray, brown, pink, olive or yellow, usually with darker orange or red blotches and a scattering of black spots over the back. The powerful

ABOVE The slender build of this young American bullfrog gives little clue to the massive proportions of the adult. A full-grown bullfrog can measure about 8 in. and leap more than 3 ft. in pursuit of prey such as insects, frogs and even snakes.
BELOW The map shows the distribution of the true frogs and Old World tree frogs.

hind legs of the common frog have dark, transverse bars. Robust in build, it is particularly tolerant of cool climates—for example, it occurs north of the Arctic Circle in Scandinavia—and this enables it to live in a broad range throughout central and northern Europe and across Asia as far as Japan and parts of China. It prefers cooler climates, and in Greece and Albania it inhabits mountainous country at altitudes above 4900 ft., where the air temperature is comparatively low.

The 4-inch-long adult common frog is largely terrestrial. The female, in particular, often inhabits cool alpine meadows strewn with boulders and also appears at the edge of beech woods. The males occur near water, often close to small mountain streams and lakes at the relatively high altitudes of 7800-8500 ft. Being largely carnivorous, the adult common frog preys on invertebrates such as insects (mainly grasshoppers, moths and beetles), small slugs and snails, spiders and often tadpoles and froglets of their own species.

In cooler climates, the common frog adapts to the cold by bringing its breeding season forward to take advantage of the short northern summers. The groups of common frogs that inhabit the Alps at altitudes of up to 6500 ft. usually breed in mid-March when the snows melt. They gather in ponds and small alpine lakes or in the artificial pools provided for grazing cattle. In the lowlands, they often breed in garden ponds, particularly in areas where the natural lakes

True frogs   Old World tree frogs

and ponds have become polluted. Mass mating occurs, and the pools often seem to boil with the thrashing of breeding frogs. Each female may lay as many as 4000 eggs, each surrounded by its own sphere of jelly that both protects and insulates it.

Wriggling in jelly

Four weeks later, the small tadpoles emerge, attaching themselves to the jelly mass or neighboring underwater vegetation for a few days before swimming off into the pond. In small mountain lakes and pools, the developing tadpoles form compact groups close to the bank where the water is shallower and where waterweeds arrest the strength of the current. Each group consists of several thousand individuals and is visible from some distance as a large black mass in the water.

In the shallows, the tadpoles take advantage of the sun as it heats up the water. By gathering in these warmer parts of the pool, they raise their metabolic rate and complete their metamorphosis before the end of the alpine summer. If they fail to reach full adulthood before the water temperatures drop at the end of summer, they perish in their larval forms as winter approaches.

A sprightly amphibian

The agile frog prefers higher temperatures than the common frog and ranges throughout Mediterranean Europe, but is absent in the Iberian Peninsula. There are also isolated colonies in northern Germany, Denmark and southern Sweden. The agile frog normally occurs in fairly damp habitats at lower altitudes, but is surprisingly tolerant of dry conditions. It lives in sandy coastal regions, vineyards, olive groves and broad-leafed woodland. The agile frog has a less variable coloration than the common frog. It usually has yellow-buff or pinkish brown upperparts with a few black spots, and measures 3.5 in. long.

Although it favors relatively high temperatures and will even remain active at temperatures of 86°F if humidity is high, the agile frog needs conditions similar to the common frog for breeding. It is one of the first species to lay its eggs in spring, and will even lay in late winter, usually choosing lakes with swampy shores. Occasionally agile frogs and common frogs share a common breeding pond and mate at the same time.

In northern Italy, the agile frog lives side by side with the very similar Italian agile frog, found in the

ABOVE The common frog of Europe takes to water during the breeding season. The female lays one or two thousand eggs, ejecting them from her cloaca to be fertilized by the male. The jelly around the eggs then swells up in the form of the familiar frogspawn; the developing tadpoles do not eat the jelly around them, since it is meant to protect them from predators and from the cold.

broad-leafed woods in the foothills of the Alps. The Italian agile frog has reddish brown upperparts and a pink flush on its limbs and underparts. Despite their similarity in habits and appearance, the two species are distinct and never interbreed. Both species forage at night, hunting insects, mollusks and other small creatures. Neither displays the cannibalism that is common among other frog species because their sense of smell is acute, allowing them to discriminate between their own young and those of other amphibians.

A West African forest giant

Other species belonging to the true frog family range throughout the eastern and southern parts of Africa. They include the South African bullfrog and the enormous goliath frog. Measuring up to 16 in. in length from snout to vent (or 31 in. with its legs outstretched), the goliath frog is the largest of all the

ABOVE Each measuring less than 0.4 in. long, these two newly metamorphosed agile frogs have yet to reach their full adult size of 2-3 in. Although small, the adults have long hind legs, enabling them to jump distances of 6 ft. 6 in.

FAR RIGHT The moor frog occurs in damp meadows in eastern Europe and western Asia. It differs from its relative, the common frog, in having a more pointed snout and a quiet voice that resembles the sound of water running down a drain.

frogs and toads. Because of its enormous size, the goliath frog is a heavy, slow-moving animal that is unable to jump over any distance. When danger threatens, it usually hides itself among vegetation or in mud. It also retreats to deep depressions in rivers. The goliath frog is hunted by the local people of its native West African forests, who believe that the bones of its mighty hind legs bring good luck.

Tunneling to reach water

Ranging through Africa from the Sahara to South Africa, the African burrowing frogs are members of the true frog family. They are recognizable by the hardened tips of their small heads, which protrude well beyond their mouths. They inhabit dry regions, and the females lay their eggs in underground chambers not far from water.

After a female has laid her eggs, she will stay with them until the embryos emerge. She then digs a tunnel between the egg chamber and the pond, through which the hatched larvae pass to reach the water. In the water, they continue to develop as larvae.

Found throughout much of Africa south of the Sahara, the mottled burrowing frog is a distinctive creature with a squat, stout body. Reaching 1.5

inches in length, it has short legs that are poorly adapted for jumping but quite efficient at digging. As with other African burrowing frogs, the mottled burrowing frog uses its pointed snout to tunnel through light, sandy soil. Its ability to dig deep tunnels is crucial to the frog's survival, since it lives in arid country where the risk of dehydration and death is ever-present. In a long tunnel, deep below the surface, the temperature and humidity remain almost constant, enabling the frog to survive moderately severe droughts.

Several members of the narrow-mouthed frog family (see pages 1783-1786) use the same methods to avoid the dehydrating effects of the equatorial sun. They dig deep burrows to shelter during the worst of the midday heat. Several species, known as the rain frogs, only appear above ground after heavy rain, and advertise their presence with bellowing calls similar to those of a bullfrog.

Poison-arrow frogs

Although almost all frogs and toads have a trace of poison in their skin glands, several brightly colored Central and South American species are notorious for the extreme potency of the poisons that their skins secrete. These small, brightly colored terrestrial frogs inhabit rain forests.

The venom of the kokoi poison-arrow frog of Colombia is one of the most powerful of all known poisons—as little as 0.0000003 oz. is enough to kill a full-grown man. The local Choco Indians take advantage of this and collect the frogs for their poison. The tribesmen impale several frogs on a piece of wood and hold them over a fire. The heat causes the poison to ooze out of the skin glands, and it is collected in wooden cups. After the poison has fermented, the tribesmen smear it on the tips of their arrows—as many as 50 arrows can be treated with the poison from just one frog—and use them to hunt birds and monkeys.

The poison takes effect almost instantaneously. When it comes into contact with the victim's blood, the animal is paralyzed before it can make any attempt to escape. All poison-arrow frogs are very small and brilliantly colored—the kokoi poison-arrow frog is bright red with black spots. Others are pink, green, purple and even gold in color. The bright colors serve as a warning to predators, which learn to avoid the vivid colors. The defense mechanism certainly works and these frogs are very common in the equatorial forests of tropical South and Central America.

LEFT The mantellins of Madagascar measure only 0.8 to 1.2 inches. Their vivid colors suggest that they do not need to fear potential predators, since their skin glands produce defensive poisons.

BELOW LEFT Like many species that live in hot, dry regions, the mottled burrowing frog of Africa spends much of its time underground, and lays its eggs in a hole to prevent them from drying up.

Carrying the young

Poison-arrow frogs have a highly developed system of caring for their offspring. The male carries the eggs on his back, and the tadpoles hatch and remain there until they have nearly completed their metamorphosis. The male then carries the larvae to the water where they must fend for themselves. They complete their transformation into adults in the water.

Males are strongly territorial, and will defend their own patches of ground vigorously with ritual displays.

FROGS AND TOADS CLASSIFICATION: 4

True frogs

One of the largest families in the order Anura is the Ranidae, or true frogs. It contains 611 species grouped in 40 genera that are distributed over much of North and South America, Eurasia, Africa and Indonesia. The large genus *Rana* contains many of the more familiar species, including the edible frog, *R. esculenta*, which ranges over much of Europe; the marsh frog, *R. ridibunda*, of eastern and southwest Europe (it has also been introduced into England and Italy); the American bullfrog, *R. catesbeiana*, of eastern North America; the green frog, *R. clamitans*, of the northeastern USA; the common frog, *R. temporaria*, which occurs in all but the far south of Europe and ranges through the western USSR to Siberia and northern China; the agile frog, *R. dalmatina*, which ranges from France through central Europe to the Black Sea; and the wood frog, *R. sylvatica*, of Canada, Alaska and the northeastern USA. Other genera include a number of African species, including the South African bullfrog, *Pyxicephalus adspersus*, of southern Africa; the mottled burrowing frog, *Hemisus marmoratus*, of much of sub-Saharan Africa; and the goliath frog, *Conraua goliath*, of West Africa.

When a neighboring male approaches, the territorial male stands on all fours and issues a warning call. He then jumps toward the intruder and begins to wrestle with him while standing on his hind legs. Males of the red-and-blue poison-arrow frog of Central America engage in prolonged bouts of ritual combat before the females' eggs have been laid. The function of territorial behavior establishes local dominance and rank. The loser gives way and relinquishes his territory to the victor, together with all breeding rights.

Old World tree frogs

Many species of the Old World tree frogs family have adapted to meet the demands of a life spent in the trees. They have flattened bodies, adhesive disks on each toe and loose skin on their bellies that clamps on to a branch and acts as a sucker.

Famous for their ability to "fly" they inhabit the upper tree canopy of rain forests in India, Southeast Asia down to Indonesia and Japan. A number of these flying frogs, such as Wallace's flying frog, have heavily webbed feet that they use as parachutes in a controlled descent from tree to tree. The frogs glide laterally for a distance of 49 ft., holding their bodies and limbs rigidly outstretched. Their ability to "fly" means that they need not risk predation by descending from the high forest canopy to the ground in order to reach other trees. Growing from 1 to 5 inches in length, the flying frogs are brightly colored in shades of green or brown, with bright webbing between the fingers and toes. The webbing appears as a flash of color when the frogs leap into the air.

Foam nests

The breeding habits of flying frogs reflects a life spent in the trees. The females lay their eggs in the branches of trees, usually overhanging ponds or swamps. They keep the eggs moist by surrounding them with a nest of liquid beaten to a foam. By laying their eggs in the trees, the females never need to descend to ground level to find a nest site in a pool or stream, so they avoid the risk of predation. During the mating ritual, the female assumes a characteristic signaling position by flattening her body. The male then mounts her and climbs back far enough for his hips to rest between those of the female.

When mating begins, the female secretes a fluid that she beats into a bubbly foam with her hind legs. The

ABOVE The goliath frog is the largest frog in the world. It lives in the humid forests of West Africa. A fully grown specimen can weigh over 6 pounds—heavier than a brick—and reaches a length of more than 13 in.
BELOW The poison-arrow frogs of tropical America jealously guard their territories against intruders, whether male or female. Living on the forest floor and in the trees, their aggressive behavior includes calling (A), and wrestling (B).
PAGES 1780-1781 The brilliant colors of poison-arrow frogs warn predators of their toxins.

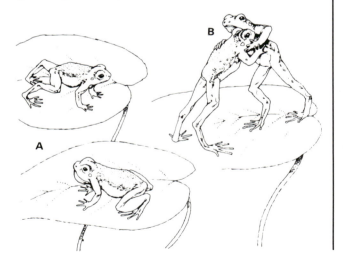

male presses his cloaca into that of the female and fertilizes the eggs as she lays them into the foamy mass. After fertilization of the eggs is complete, the exterior of the foam mass hardens to retain the moisture and turns yellowish brown in color. The hardened foam only returns to being a liquid once the larvae are ready to hatch. Eventually the hard coating cracks and the fluid within drips out into the pond below, carrying the tadpoles with it. They then continue their development into miniature frogs.

A frog of the cloud forest

The Malaysian hill froglet lives in mountainous cloud forest where standing water rarely occurs. It lays its eggs in huge sheets of damp moss that hang from the trees. The moss remains damp as a result of mists that swirl round the tree-tops of the upland forests. Other species of Old World tree frogs lay large eggs that develop directly into miniature frogs without an intermediate tadpole stage.

The gray tree frog of the Central African savannah is one of the largest frogs in the family, growing to a length of 3 in. Unlike other species typical of moist rain forest, it can adapt to life in hot, dry conditions. To conserve moisture, it is most active at night, when it hops from one leaf to another to catch the winged insects that make up its staple diet. By day, it sits motionless on tree trunks where its speckled brownish coloration makes it almost invisible against the bark.

Sedge and bush frogs

The sedge and bush frogs range throughout Africa south of the Sahara and also occur on the island of Madagascar, inhabiting a wide variety of habitats from equatorial forests to swamp reeds. They are small to medium-sized tree-dwelling frogs, growing to a length of 0.8 to 2 in. Many species in the family resemble the true tree frogs in appearance and have sucker disks on their fingers and toes. The clinging force of these disks derives from friction and wet adhesion.

Sedge and bush frogs display a variety of brilliant colors and distinct markings—from red, yellow and orange to black and white. The colors and patterns vary considerably between individuals and between different populations, and frogs from one area are often different from those in another part of their range. Body coloration also changes as a result of internal stimuli (body temperature and mental state), as well as external factors such as light intensity and humidity.

Leafy envelopes for eggs

Sedge frogs occur among tall swamp grasses or in the dense tree canopy of equatorial forests. Most species of sedge frogs lay their eggs in a dense mass of jelly that they deposit in vegetation overhanging water. The golden leaf-folding frog has refined the process—after laying her eggs, the female folds leaf edges around the egg mass and uses sticky secretions from her oviduct to seal them and prevent the eggs from losing moisture.

The running frog of Senegal and southern Africa is a silver-gray ground-dweller that grows to a length of 1 to 1.5 in. It has the distinctive characteristic of running across ground on four legs when predators threaten, instead of hopping away. The running frog lives on savannah grassland, camouflaged among the grass stems by its unmistakable coloration of yellowish white and brown stripes. The males have vocal sacs on their throats and the sounds they produce can be heard over a distance of 1640 ft. Their characteristic call resembles the sound of a bottle being uncorked. As a ground dweller, the running frog lays its eggs singly or in small groups on plants beneath the water of temporary pools.

A hairy frog

The curious hairy frog derives its name from the thick hair fibers that adorn the body and thighs of the male during the breeding season. The hairy coating consists of thin-walled skin filaments that are richly supplied with blood vessels and are thought to function as external gills. However, if the hairs serve a respiratory function, it is curious that the male should possess them while the female does not. It is also surprising that the respiratory feature should develop in a species that seeks out fast-moving and therefore well-oxygenated streams for breeding.

The hairs are thought to serve a number of purposes. For example, as points of attachments for eggs that the female lays, as secondary sexual characteristics, or as camouflage against the aquatic vegetation. The most probable explanation is that the male needs extra oxygen during the breeding period, when he spends much of his time underwater looking for mates and tending eggs.

Seychelles frogs

The Seychelles islands of Mahe and Silhouette are the home of three frogs that together make up one of the smallest families of frogs. The best known is the one-inch-long Seychelles frog, which occurs on moist, mountainous areas where the water tumbles down to the sea in fast-running streams and waterfalls.

Because there are no still breeding pools normally essential for the development of the tadpoles, the adults have developed their own method of rearing the young. The female lays her eggs in gelatinous heaps of 15, on damp ground, and the male initially guards the eggs. As soon as the tadpoles emerge from the eggs, they squirm across the ground until they reach the male's body and climb up onto his back and sides. The male then secretes a sticky substance that moistens the larvae and glues them securely to his skin. Because of their position, the tadpoles are unable to feed as they develop, and have to rely on the nutrient provided by the egg.

Narrow-mouthed frogs

The family of narrow-mouthed frogs consists of 281 species. Ranging throughout the Old and New World, the family includes terrestrial and arboreal species. Narrow-mouthed frogs have stout, egg-shaped bodies

ABOVE The sedge frogs of Central and southern Africa have a variety of colors and patterning, and the colors change day by day according to temperature, humidity, and the frogs' nervous condition. The different species are often difficult to identify, and the best way to tell them apart in the field is by their calls.

with short limbs. They have small, tapered heads, narrow mouths and a pointed snout that they use to lever up the earth when digging. Most species burrow into the ground and also use burrows that have been abandoned by other animals. During the day, they often lurk under the leaf litter on the forest floor, camouflaged by their brown coloration. In Madagascar, where there are few tree-dwelling frogs, narrow-mouthed frogs have developed circular, adhesive disks on their feet for climbing, like those of true tree frogs.

The Asian painted frog of the narrow-mouthed frog family lives in close proximity to man, inhabiting city parks and the outskirts of villages—indeed it rarely appears in different habitats and extends its range in many places by moving into areas that man has colonized. Growing to 3 inches in length, the Asian painted frog is gray to chocolate-brown in color with a cream head and a cream stripe

ABOVE **The bold stripes on the running frog's back and limbs provide excellent camouflage among the grasses of its African savannah home. Its hind legs have not developed powerful jumping muscles, so at night, when it hunts, it runs across the ground like a lizard in search of insects, spiders, slugs and snails.**

running down each flank from behind its eyes. It is similar to the spadefoot toads in that it has a horny foot process on each hind limb that it uses to dig and burrow in the ground.

The normal breeding sites for the Asian painted frog are puddles, pools, ditches and streams after heavy rain. During the courtship ritual, the male calls from the bank of a pond as evening draws in, inflating his throat sacs. The series of calls resembles long, prolonged moans. Breeding occurs throughout the year if climatic conditions are suitable. After laying her eggs, the female returns to her concealed terrestrial life. She often lays the eggs in temporary pools that form after showers, and many of the tadpoles do not survive to become mature frogs because the pools dry up too quickly.

Known locally as the sheep frog, owing to its bleating call, the Mexican narrow-mouthed frog grows to a length of 1-1.5 in. It inhabits arid regions,

usually living in the undergrowth where it hides under rotting trunks, bark and dead plants. The Mexican narrow-mouthed frog is olive-green in color with dark spotted markings over its body. On each hind foot, the frog has a horny "spade" that it uses to dig a daytime shelter in the ground. It can mate throughout the year, and only requires a heavy downpour of rain to initiate breeding. The fertilized female lays 700 eggs that form a film on the water surface. Like all narrow-mouthed frogs, it is timid and takes flight from larger animals with a series of short, rapid hops.

The Carolina narrow-mouthed frog is another North American species that ranges through the south-eastern USA. Growing to a body length of 1.4 in., it mainly spends the daylight hours in hidden recesses in the undergrowth and only emerges on rainy nights to hunt for ants. During the breeding season, the male selects a small depression near running water and calls softly to attract a female. When she arrives, he grasps her under her forelimbs and produces a sticky fluid that effectively glues the pair together until all the eggs have been laid and fertilized. The eggs float off into the water and spread out on the surface to form a uniform film. When they hatch, the tadpoles each have two adhesive organs near their mouths that allow them to hang on to submerged rocks and plants.

RIGHT A male marbled rush frog, one of the sedge frogs of Africa, fully inflates his huge vocal sac while calling. Sedge frogs gain most of their food by catching flying insects such as mosquitoes that haunt swamps and reedbeds.

FROGS AND TOADS CLASSIFICATION: 5

Poison-arrow frogs

The family Dendrobatidae comprises the 116 species of poison-arrow frogs grouped in four genera. They all occur in tropical South America and parts of Central America, and include the red-and-blue poison-arrow frog, *Dendrobates pumilio*, and the kokoi poison-arrow frog, *Phyllobates bicolor*.

Old World tree frogs

There are 184 species in the family Rhacophoridae, the Old World tree frogs. Grouped into 10 genera, they are distributed throughout much of tropical Africa and Asia. Nearly a third of these are the flying frogs of the genus *Rhacophorus*, such as Wallace's flying frog, *R. nigropalmatus*, of Borneo and Sumatra. The gray tree frog, *Chiromantis xerampelina*, ranges over parts of Central and southern Africa, while the ground-dwelling species, *Aglyptodactylus madagascariensis*, occurs in Madagascar.

Sedge and bush frogs and the Seychelles frogs

The 292 species of sedge and bush frogs form the family Hyperoliidae and are divided into 23 genera. They are all found in sub-Saharan Africa and the adjacent islands. They include the running frogs of the genus *Kassina*, which range widely over the African savannahs; the sedge frogs *Hyperolius* of much of sub-Saharan Africa; the Seychelles Islands tree frog, *Tachycnemis seychellensis*, of the Seychelles; and the hairy frog, *Trichobatrachus robustus*, of West Africa. The Seychelles Islands are the home of the Seychelles frogs that form the family Sooglossidae. There are only three species in two genera, one of which is the Seychelles frog, *Sooglossus seychellensis*.

A rubbery skin

Rubber frogs inhabit southern Africa and derive their common name from the smooth, dark-skinned, rubbery appearance of their skin. They are good climbers, using the adhesive pads on their toes to scale rocks and rotting tree stumps. They are also great burrowers, often entering the nests of termite colonies to feast on the insects inside. If in danger, they defend themselves by producing a toxic, sticky fluid that is also damaging to other amphibians. They breed in ponds, the males attracting the females with strident whistles that are audible from a distance of over half a mile. The eggs are attached to water plants in groups of 1000-1500, or they fall to the bottom of the pond.

Pseudid frogs

The four species of pseudid or shrinking frogs of South America comprise a strictly aquatic family of frogs. They feed by stirring up the mud on the bottom of shallow lakes and preying on the small animals that they disturb. These frogs rarely leave the water, although one subspecies lives in areas where the pools evaporate each summer. The frog survives by burying itself in the mud and lying dormant until the next rains. Pseudids lay their eggs in the water, in a frothy mass that floats on the surface.

The paradoxical frog of Trinidad and the Amazon River is one of the better-known members of the pseudid frog family and gains its name from the fact that it actually grows smaller as it matures. The tadpoles of the paradoxical frog are enormous, measuring up to 10 in. long. After metamorphosis, however, the adult frogs rarely reach more than 3 inches in length. Even so, the paradoxical frog is the largest species in its family. The smallest pseudids measure under one inch long.

True toads

The true toads belong to one family and are among the most widespread of all amphibians, occurring naturally throughout the world except for Australia and New Zealand (where they have been introduced by humans), Madagascar and some of the Polynesian islands. Most toads have thick-set bodies, often of considerable size, and short legs that are ill adapted for jumping. Their dry skins are richly endowed with glands, giving the surfaces of their bodies an uneven, gnarled appearance.

True toads have two prominent glands behind and above their eyes (sometimes even on their thighs) that secrete a pungent, sticky, white fluid used for defense. When a predator seizes the toad, the glands secrete their fluid, seriously burning the predator's mouth and forcing the animal to drop the toad.

The active ingredients of the toad's toxic skin secretion have been studied in depth over the last few decades. One of them was found to be similar to digitalis, the drug derived from foxglove leaves, and traditionally used to treat heart disorders. The ancient Chinese also used toad skins as an ingredient in a drug employed to treat problems with blood circulation.

Feasting on insects

Toads catch and eat a wide range of food, including young frogs, newts, snakes and even young toads. They use their forefeet to fill their mouths with prey. They have even been seen sitting near the entrances to beehives in order to catch returning worker bees.

FROGS AND TOADS CLASSIFICATION: 6

Narrow-mouthed frogs

The family Microhylidae, the narrow-mouthed frogs, is a large group of 281 species in 61 genera. They range over eastern and southern Asia, Indonesia, northern Australia, sub-Saharan Africa, South America and southern parts of North America. They include the Asian painted frog, *Kaloula pulchra*, of Southeast Asia and Indonesia; the Carolina narrow-mouthed frog, *Microhyla carolinensis*, of the southeastern USA; and the Mexican narrow-mouthed frog, *Hypopachus cuneus*, of northern Mexico. The family also includes the four African rubber frogs of the genus *Phrynomerus*, although these are sometimes classified in a family of their own, the Phrynomeridae.

Pseudid frogs

The pseudid or shrinking frogs form a small South American family, the Pseudidae. There are four species in two genera, the most well-known of which is the paradoxical frog, *Pseudis paradoxa*, of northern South America.

Toads have large appetites and will eat a vast number of insects each night. During the day, they usually shelter under stones or in crevices, often continuing to feed on whatever small animals they can find.

During the winter, toads hibernate under logs or large stones, or in underground holes. At the end of winter, they emerge from their shelters and begin to make their way to the shallow ponds and lakes where they breed. These breeding sites are traditional, and the toads follow the same routes to them year after year, often in large numbers. The males are the first to make the trek, sometimes traveling several miles and all heading in the same direction. They will climb any obstacle in their path, and even walk straight across busy roads. In some places, underpasses (or "toad crossings") have been built on toad migration routes, and nets guide the animals into them.

Once the male toads reach the breeding pools, they squat in the water and produce a series of short, sharp croaks to attract the females. The females are larger than the males and as each one arrives, a waiting male will pounce on her and try to mate with her. Sometimes four or more males will seize the same female, while some desperate suitors will try to mate with other males, fish and even driftwood. When stimulated by the male, the female produces a string of jelly 6 ft. 6 in. or more long containing 4000-7000 eggs (spawn), each of which is less than 0.08 in. in diameter.

Toxic tadpoles

The toad's eggs hatch after 10-12 days, and the tadpoles often move around in large groups in the pond or lake. Like their parents, the tadpoles can secrete a toxic fluid that saves them from being attacked by predators that habitually feed on the larvae of other amphibians.

Once they have metamorphosed, the young toads, some 0.5 in. long, emerge from the water and begin their new life on land. Feeding on small prey such as springtails (leaping insects), mites and ants, the toads grow slowly, taking from three to five years to reach sexual maturity. They take another few years to achieve their maximum size. Although captive toads often live to over 20 years old, those in the wild rarely survive for more than ten years.

Despite their chemical defenses, toads are preyed on by owls and, during their brief breeding season, by

ABOVE The green toad is common in eastern Europe, and is found as far north as southern Sweden. It is smaller than its close relative, the European common toad, reaching about 4 in. in length. Though mainly nocturnal in its habits, it is often active during the day and regularly appears near human settlements.

BELOW A male European common toad calls, inflating his vocal sac (A); and a female carries a smaller male in the mating position (B). A natterjack toad eats the skin it is shedding during one of its regular molts (C); and a natterjack toad crouches forward and raises his hindquarters in a defensive posture (D).

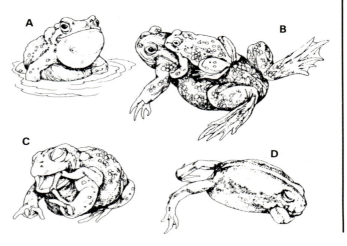

ABOVE Dwarfed by his mate, a male European common toad clasps a female under her armpits, fertilizing the long ribbons of eggs as they emerge from her cloaca. There may be more than 4000 eggs in a single ribbon, and it takes several hours for the female to release all her spawn. The toads secure the ribbons underwater by stretching them out and entwining them around plants. BELOW The female toad arches her back as she produces each batch of eggs, allowing the male to shed his sperm directly over them.

day-flying hawks such as kites and buzzards. Snakes will also eat toads if they can, but the toad has evolved a tactic to foil a hungry snake. It inflates itself and rears up on all fours; the snake cannot then grip the toad's almost spherical body and has to abandon the attack.

One of the most familiar species in the true toad family is the European common toad. Occurring throughout most of Europe (except Ireland and some Mediterranean islands), it is unusually tolerant of the cold and can be found as far north as the Arctic Circle.

The European common toad can sometimes be seen during the day when conditions are damp, but it is most active at night. It walks slowly and rather clumsily and often prefers to lie in wait for prey, ambushing it when it comes within range of its long, sticky tongue. The tongue is anchored at the front of the toad's mouth, and the toad flicks it out to scoop up worms, slugs, insects and spiders.

RIGHT Most toads live in warm climates, but the western toad ranges as far north as southern Alaska—a few hundred miles from the Arctic Circle. It also lives at high altitudes in the Rocky Mountains, where snow cover persists for much of the year. It spends the coldest months in hibernation, and needs only one month of warm weather to complete its breeding cycle.

Raining toads

The green toad is another species with a wide distribution, ranging from southern Sweden to the eastern Mediterranean and further east. Growing up to 6 in. long, it is particularly common in coastal areas where it can be very noisy in the evenings. At dusk, green toads sometimes gather in groups of several hundred. Rainfall during the day may tempt them out of their shelters, and the sudden appearance of large numbers of toads after heavy rain used to be regarded as a miraculous phenomenon: people believed that they fell from the sky—that it literally "rained toads."

The natterjack toad is a fairly small animal (usually 2.5 to 3 inches long) that ranges from Portugal and Spain across northern Europe to the Baltic states. It can be identified by the fine yellow line that runs down the middle of its back. The natterjack is an adaptable species, with a high tolerance to environmental changes, enabling it to live near human settlements where conditions change frequently. It is a rare animal in Britain, where it is confined to sandy heaths and coastal dunes.

The breeding season of the natterjack is unusually long for a true toad. Most natterjacks breed between April and July, but some pair up and lay their eggs as late as September. Late breeding may minimize the risk of the whole clutch being lost when pools dry up during prolonged hot, dry periods. If threatened, the natterjack adopts the same defense tactics as the common toad—it inflates its body and presses its head against the ground so that the poison glands behind the eyes become more prominent. A predator attempting to grab the toad will then receive a mouthful of the unpleasant secretion—an effective deterrent.

A saltwater toad

Several species of toads live in North America. These are similar to European toads in their structure, but some have interesting habits. The salt toad (a subspecies of the western toad), for example, derives

FROGS AND TOADS — CLASSIFICATION: 7

True toads

The family Bufonidae, the true toads, comprises 339 species grouped in 25 genera. They are one of the most widespread of all the frogs and toads families, occurring in Eurasia, Africa and the Americas. The largest genus is *Bufo*, which includes the European common toad, *Bufo bufo*, which is found through most of Eurasia and in northwest Africa; the green toad, *B. viridis*, which ranges from Eastern Europe to Central Asia; the natterjack toad, *B. calamita*, which ranges from Spain through Western Europe to the Baltic region; the marine or giant toad, *B. marinus*, of Central and South America and the southern USA (which has been introduced into Puerto Rico, Australia and New Guinea); and the square-marked toad, *B. regularis*, which occurs over much of Africa. The West African live-bearing toad, *Nectophrynoides occidentalis*, occurs in Guinea, while the harlequin frogs of the genus *Atelopus* range over Central and South America.

its name from its ability to breed in natural or artificial pools with high salt concentrations. It is an almost unique ability among amphibians, since most species occur only rarely in brackish water and never in salt water. Another race of the same species has adapted to life at high altitudes: its area of distribution extends up to 10,000 feet above sea level in the Rocky Mountains. In some low-lying areas the toads delay the breeding season until early summer to escape the danger of torrential floods during the spring thaw.

The marine toad is one of the largest species in the true toad family. Originally of tropical America and the southern USA, it may grow to 9 in. long, and it has an appetite to match, eating vast quantities of insects. In the 19th century, this fact came to the notice of sugarcane growers who were suffering the effects of plagues of insect pests in the Caribbean, on Pacific islands and in Australia. The toads were introduced to the cane fields to eat the pests, but as is so often the case with such introductions, the plan backfired.

In Australia, the introduced marine toads took a dislike to the cane fields and migrated to nearby farmlands and gardens. There they multiplied to form a plague of their own. The problem of the sugarcane pests, meanwhile, remained unsolved. Today, the marine toads compete with the native frogs and toads, driving them out of their traditional habitats and even eating them. Predators have little effect on marine

toads, since the toads have particularly well-developed poison glands behind their eyes that are capable of squirting their toxic secretions through the air for three feet or more, with devastating effect.

The square-marked toad is widely distributed throughout Africa. It is an adaptable creature that has extended its range to include dry, but not arid, areas, as well as moist swampland. It often breeds in temporary pools, and many tadpoles die when the pools dry up. To offset this loss, the square-marked toad is extremely prolific: it is estimated that a female can produce up to 24,000 eggs each year (from August to January). In Senegal and various parts of East Africa, in savannah areas with seasonal swamps, it gathers in such numbers that hundreds can be seen in just a few minutes during a night-time walk.

The West African live-bearing toad and its relatives have unusual characteristics. Of the eight species in the genus, four lay eggs in the usual toad fashion, but the other four fertilize their eggs internally, like mammals, and the developing young stay in the female's oviduct until they are self-sufficient. Two of these species are ovoviviparous—the female retains the eggs and the embryos draw their nourishment from yolk sacs. The other two species, which include the West African live-bearing toad, are viviparous: the young live freely in the uterus and take in food through their mouths, feeding on a substance

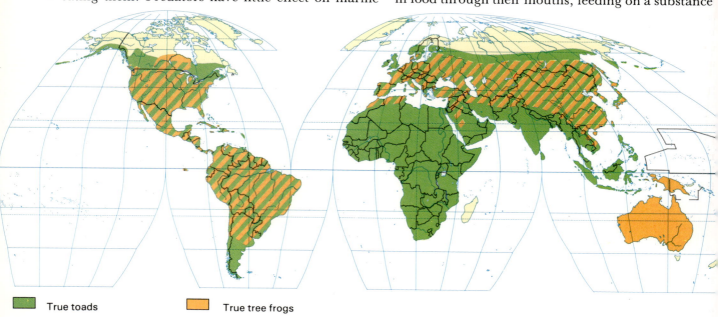

■ True toads   ■ True tree frogs

produced by the inner wall of the uterus. When they have developed into miniature toads, the mother pushes them out with great effort, using pressure exerted by the lungs. The gestation period lasts some 270 days, but it coincides with the dry season when the toads lie dormant for several weeks and the development of the young comes to a halt.

The harlequin frogs are included among the true toad family. They are often brilliantly colored—most frequently in combinations of red, yellow and black. Since they are also poisonous, it is likely that their startling colors warn potential enemies to keep away. One of the most eye-catching species in the harlequin frog genus is the golden frog of Panama. Colored orange-yellow with black blotches, it is so distinctive that it has become a tourist attraction and a symbol of the country.

A frog of gold

The gold frog of southeast Brazil—not to be confused with the golden frog of Panama—is one of only two species in its family. Just 0.8 in. long, the gold frog has a brilliant orange back and a yellow underside. Its most curious feature is a cross-shaped, bony shield that appears to be embedded in the skin of its back, but is actually fused to the animal's backbone. The gold frog lives on the ground in forested areas, or conceals itself among the spiny leaves of bromeliads (plants of the pineapple family). The tadpoles develop in seasonal pools; like those of the paradoxical frog, they are much larger than the adult and may measure about two inches long.

True tree frogs

The true tree frogs are an extremely large family containing over 600 species. They are flattened, lightly built frogs with long, slender limbs and—in most cases—adhesive disks on the ends of their toes. True tree frogs closely resemble the Old World tree frogs—an example of how a similar way of life results in similar adaptations (convergent evolution).

Most true tree frogs live in South and Central America, but they also occur in North America, Australia, eastern and Central Asia and Europe, where the most common species is the European tree frog. Measuring 2 in. long, it has smooth, brilliant green skin and lives near water in trees, bushes, tall grasses and reeds. It feeds on insects such as beetles,

TOP The marine or giant toad is native to the Americas, but was introduced into Australia in the 1930s to combat an infestation of grayback cane beetles in sugarcane fields. The toads thrived and rapidly increased in number, so much so that they are now considered pests themselves.

ABOVE Female West African live-bearing toads do not lay eggs like most other frogs and toads. Their young develop inside their bodies, and are born as fully formed, miniature adults.
FAR LEFT The map shows the geographical distribution of true toads and true tree frogs.

ABOVE The bright yellow coloration of the golden frog of Panama acts as a warning to predators to keep clear—for like the poison-arrow frogs, this species is highly toxic.

Glands in its skin produce a poison that is dangerous to any animal that attacks it. Made bold by its lethal defense system, the golden frog can often be seen in broad daylight.

butterflies and smooth-skinned caterpillars, as well as spiders and the occasional small fish. A good swimmer, the European tree frog also jumps and climbs with agility, using the adhesive pads on its toes to cling to leaves and stems.

The European tree frog belongs to a widespread and numerous genus that includes species distributed throughout North America. The Pacific tree frog can adapt to an even greater range of habitats than its European relative. It lives on the arid, sun-baked plains of California and Oregon just as readily as on the Rocky Mountains, at altitudes of up to 10,000 feet. The 2.5-inch-long canyon tree frog is specifically adapted to rocky environments and is particularly suited to life in the deep canyons cut by streams and rivers. It assumes the same color as the rocks to blend in perfectly with its background. The majority of species in the genus lay their eggs in small clumps on aquatic vegetation.

One of the most common of the Australian tree frogs is White's tree frog, a creature with a bloated, flabby appearance that occurs in and around houses and breeds in wet grassland.

Although most tree frogs have a similar life-style and behavior, some differ significantly. The male of one species in southern Brazil and Argentina builds a shallow basin that it scoops out of the mud or sand at the edge of a pond or stream. Water seeps in through the walls to fill the basin, making an ideal nursery for the eggs and tadpoles. The male then sits inside the basin and calls to the females, in the hope of attracting one of them to enter his basin and mate. The basin enables the tadpoles to develop in water while keeping them isolated from the main pond where they would be exposed to attack by predators.

Stagnant pools

Since the water becomes stagnant and deoxygenated, the tadpoles develop enormous external gills. They may stay within the nursery pool until they metamorphose, but usually a rise in water level releases them into the main pond where they have more opportunities to find food (or to become food for others).

ABOVE In the dish backed tree frog, the female carries her eggs in a circular depression on her back. The tadpoles do not hatch until their hind legs have developed.
RIGHT Female marsupial frogs carry their tadpoles in pouches on their backs, giving their bodies a curiously swollen appearance.

BELOW One species of tree frog from South America builds a "nursery pool," ringed by a mud wall. Its eggs are laid and fertilized in the pool (A), and the resulting tadpoles are able to develop in safety from marauding predators (B). When they can fend for themselves, the young frogs escape over the nursery walls (C).

Marsupial tree frogs

The tree frogs of South America include the marsupial frog, one of a number of species in which the female is equipped with a brood pouch. Outside the breeding season, this pouch looks like a small slit running lengthways along the animal's spine. When the female lays her eggs, the male fertilizes them and they slide into the pouch, which can hold up to 200 eggs. When these have developed into tadpoles, the female prepares to release them into water. Selecting one of the tiny pools that form among the leaves of plants, she separates the two sides of her pouch with one of her hind toes and ejects the tadpoles into the pool, where they complete their development into adult frogs. (In other species of the family, the female keeps the tadpoles in her pouch until they metamorphose, and the tiny, full-grown frogs hop out.)

Courting colors

The leptodactylid family of Central and South America is the largest family in the order of frogs and toads. It contains over 700 species, many of which vary a great deal in both appearance and behavior. For example, some spend their whole lives underwater while others live entirely on land. Some are active during the day; others are nocturnal.

One of the most common species is the South American bullfrog, found throughout much of the continent. It resembles the North American bullfrog in appearance and habits. It grows to about 8 in. long, and in some areas the local people collect and roast the frogs whole. During the mating season, the South American bullfrog adopts bright breeding colors. Its legs become orange or red—a dramatic

A   B   C

contrast to the greenish brown of its body. The male also develops a horny spur on its thumb that enables it to grip the female when they mate. The female deposits her foam-covered eggs on land, and the larvae begin their development within the frothy mass.

The robber frog genus is the largest in the leptodactylid family, and indeed in the whole frog order, with 400 species comprising about 10 percent of all known frogs. Some species live in trees and have developed all the characteristic tree frog adaptations, including adhesive disks on their toes. However, most of the genus are ground dwellers, inhabiting humid woodlands. They lay their eggs on or in the ground, and the embryos complete their development and change into young frogs while still inside the egg cases.

LEFT The red-eyed tree frog of Central America is one of several tree frogs that have opposable thumbs. The animal can press its thumbs firmly against its other fingers, allowing it to take a strong grip on leaves and branches when moving through the trees of its rain forest home.

The Puerto Rican live-bearing frog produces live young that hatch from their eggs in the oviduct. The species is one of only five live-bearing species in the order. The others belong to the true toad family.

A number of leptodactylids, including the four-eyed toad of Chile and Argentina, have evolved a dramatic defense tactic based on a bizarre color scheme. Under normal conditions, they resemble ordinary, medium-sized frogs with spotted brown, green or gray coloring and warty skins. On the lower part of their backs, however, they have two black patches that cover large skin glands. When threatened, the frog turns its back on its attacker and raises its rump, so that its body roughly resembles a face with two large black eyes. It is often enough to startle the predator, enabling the frog to escape. Like the South American bullfrog, the four-eyed toad lays its eggs in foam, depositing them in small, damp hollows that are sheltered but do not contain water. The eggs lie dormant until the rains come. Then, when the hollows fill with water, the tadpoles hatch and develop into tiny frogs.

FROGS AND TOADS
CLASSIFICATION: 8

The gold frog family

The family Brachycephalidae contains only two species, both from southeast Brazil. The best known of these is the gold frog or saddleback toad, *Brachycephalus ephippium*.

True tree frogs

The true tree frogs belong to the family Hylidae, a large family with 637 species grouped in 37 genera. They are found in the Americas, Europe, Central and eastern Asia and Australasia. They include many species of the genus *Hyla*, such as the European tree frog, *H. arborea*, which occurs over much of Europe and has a wide distribution across Asia as far east as Japan; *H. faber* of southern Brazil and Argentina; and the Pacific tree frog, *H. regilla*, and canyon tree frog, *H. arenicolor*, both of North America. White's tree frog, *Litoria caerulea*, lives in Australia. The marsupial frog, *Gastrotheca marsupiata*, is found in

northern South America, and the dish backed tree frog, *Fritziana goeldii*, lives in Brazil. The cricket frogs of the genus *Acris* occur in North America.

Leptodactylid frogs

The family Leptodactylidae is the biggest in the order Anura, with a total of 722 species in 51 genera. They are restricted to the New World, however, with most species in Central and South America, and a few reaching the southern USA. They include the South American bullfrog, *Leptodactylus pentadactylus*, of much of South America; the robber frogs of the genus *Eleutherodactylus*, which occur over most of the family's range, and include the Puerto Rican live-bearing frog, *E. jasperi*; the four-eyed toad, *Pleurodema bibroni*, of Chile and Argentina; the ornate horned frog, *Ceratophrys ornata*, of eastern South America; the Brazilian horned toad, *C. cornuta*, of Brazil; and the Lake Titicaca frog, *Telmatobius culeus*, of the high Andes.

THE EUROPEAN TREE FROG
— SINGING IN THE RAIN —

The European tree frog is well known throughout Europe for its brilliant colors and loud, rhythmic "keck-keck-keck" call. It is a small, plump and robust frog, rarely longer than two inches, with a smooth, glossy skin, flattened body and long, slender legs. Like most of the true tree frogs, it has loose skin on its belly that acts like a rubber sucker, enabling it to adhere to leaves and smooth bark. It also has adhesive disks on its toes, giving it a remarkable grip—it can climb a vertical sheet of glass with ease, and has no difficulty clinging to foliage in a high wind.

The European tree frog is generally bright green, usually with a dark stripe running from the eye down each side of the body—but its coloration varies, depending on the animal's state of health, the food it has eaten, its nervous condition and its surroundings. After shedding its skin, which it does every two weeks or so, it becomes a delicate ash gray. Among the tree frog's many other color variations, some are pale green with intense green spots. Those that live in stony or rocky areas are o[f] grayish brown with brown spots. So[me] have such deep pigmentation that the[y] are almost black; others, lacking the yellow pigment that contributes to green, are bright blue.

Whether gray or green, the Europe[an] tree frog is well camouflaged among [the] trees, bushes and grasses where it normally lives and feeds. It preys mainly on spiders and insects— especially crawling types such as bee[tles] and caterpillars, as well as flying insects such as butterflies. It catches them on the wing by leaping in the a[ir] and snapping them up in mid-jump. [It] then lands on another branch or leaf, easily sticking to it with its loose bell[y] skin and adhesive toe disks.

Powerful voices

In summer, the frogs gather near water to breed, and on rainy nights t[he] males sing to attract mates. They sou[nd] the "keck" note six to ten times, repeating it after a short pause. With their powerful vocal apparatus—a swollen throat sac that inflates to a considerable size—they are capable o[f] generating the loudest croak of any European frog. Since frogs are noisie[r] when rain is falling or imminent, the weather can be forecast from their son[g].

The male's croaking is an essentia[l] part of the breeding cycle, so a loud, continuous noise that makes the croak[ing] inaudible can seriously affect their breeding. In one case, a population o[f] tree frogs died out after a motorway w[as] built near their habitat. The pools an[d] vegetation were unaffected by the construction, but because the traffic noise blocked out the males' croaking, the females were not attracted to the breeding sites.

FAR LEFT Disk-shaped adhesive pads on its toes give the European tree frog a secure grip on smooth rush stems. The European tree frog and its relative, the stripeless tree frog, are the only European amphibians that habitually climb, and often occur high off the ground in trees and bushes. By day, European tree frogs usually stay inactive, crouched down with their limbs tucked beneath them to conserve moisture. But at night they emerge to hunt for insects and spiders. They are good swimmers, and sometimes hunt in the water for small fish.

ABOVE By launching themselves into the air, using their powerful hind limbs, European tree frogs can snap up flying insects with great agility. The length of the tree frog's slender limbs varies from one part of its range to another, with animals from southern Europe tending to have the longest legs.

RIGHT A blackberry provides an adequate perch for a tiny, immature frog. Even when adult, the European tree frog seldom grows to more than two inches in length.

ABOVE Most of the robber frogs of the New World lay their eggs out of water, on the ground or in vegetation, and without a protective mass of bubbles surrounding them. The young complete their development inside the eggs, passing through a tadpole-like stage before hatching out as adults.

Members of the family known as wide-mouthed toads have broad bodies and gaping mouths that are sometimes wider than half the length of the head and body combined. They have huge appetites and do not hesitate to bite if an intruder disturbs them.

Several species of leptodactylids, such as the ornate horned frog, are brightly colored with streaks of green and pale brown that blend in with the undergrowth and debris of the forest floor. They often burrow down into moss or fallen leaves and lie in wait with only their eyes showing. They prey on small rodents, birds, lizards and other frogs. When a victim comes close enough, the horned frog leaps into action, grasping its prey with its enormous mouth and swallowing it whole.

The Brazilian horned toad is another large species, measuring up to 8 in. in length and almost as wide. It has two long "horns" above its eyes that disguise its outline as it lies in ambush and give it a striking appearance.

Several aquatic species live in the high Andes. The most remarkable is the Lake Titicaca frog, found in the relatively shallow waters of one of the highest lakes in the world. At this altitude, the oxygen level in the air is very low, so the frog obtains most of its oxygen from the water, absorbing it through its skin. Its skin hangs down in baggy folds that greatly increase the skin's surface area, making the frog look much larger than it really is. It is such an efficient adaptation that the Lake Titicaca frog can spend its entire life underwater if necessary.

Mouth brooders

The breeding habits adopted by the slender, green or brown mouth-brooding frogs that live in the Andean foothills of south Chile and south Argentina must be among the most unusual of all the frogs and toads.

The best-known species is Darwin's frog, a small green or brown frog with a pointed snout. The male normally has a high-pitched, whistle-like call, but once

the breeding season begins, he is forced to stay silent since he uses his vocal sac as a predator-proof refuge for the developing tadpoles.

Darwin's frog is well-known for its unusual form of parental care. The female lays 20-30 eggs in clusters on damp ground. The males are attracted to the eggs, and gather around, waiting for them to hatch. When the tadpoles begin to move inside their protective jelly, each male takes several eggs in his mouth and stows them in his vocal sac, which inflates to such an extent that it compresses his internal organs. Despite this, he retains the tadpoles for three weeks until they complete their development. During this period, while they metamorphose into small froglets, they are thought to feed on substances secreted from inside the yolk sac. Then, when they reach about 0.4 inch in length, the male spits them out and they begin their independent lives.

Ghost frogs

Ghost frogs consist of four rare species from South Africa, including the Table Mountain ghost frog, which is only about 2.5 in. in length. They live near fast-flowing mountain streams in damp crevices under stones. The skin on their bellies is so white and thin that their abdominal organs and muscles show through. Tiny hooks cover the skin, enabling the frogs to climb over slippery rocks. One species has sharp spines on its skin, is partly tree-dwelling, and leaps after flies.

Ghost frog tadpoles have large, flattened heads and an enormous suction disk around the mouth with which they cling to underwater rocks. The Table Mountain ghost frog lays about 30 yolk-rich eggs on land, and the wedge-shaped larvae develop in mountain streams.

The myobatrachid family of frogs consists of about a hundred species, all from Australia, New Guinea and Tasmania. Although varied in appearance and habits, they all have toes that are never more than half webbed, small or absent toe disks, a small tongue and usually no teeth. Some have striking yellow, red, blue, black and white markings, and their bodies range from small, toad-like burrowing forms to large, powerful-limbed ones.

Highly adaptable, they live in environments that range from arid deserts to cold, moist mountains. Among the smallest—rarely more than one inch in length—are the 10 species of pseudophryne frogs. One of these, Bibron's toadlet,

ABOVE **The South American bullfrog is a large, bulky frog, reaching 8 in. in length, that is sometimes** hunted as a source of food. During the breeding season the animal's limbs turn orange-red in color.

FROGS AND TOADS CLASSIFICATION: 9

Mouth-brooding frogs and ghost frogs

The mouth-brooding frogs of the family Rhinodermatidae are found in southern Argentina and Chile in the foothills of the Andes. There are only two species, the most well known of which is Darwin's frog, *Rhinoderma darwini*. The four species of ghost frogs make up the family Heleophrynidae from South Africa. All grouped in the same genus, they include the Table Mountain ghost frog, *Heleophryne rosei*.

Myobatrachid frogs and glass frogs

The family Myobatrachidae consists of about 100 species in 20 genera, all confined to Australia and New Guinea. They include the humming frog, *Neobatrachus pelobatoides*, and the western banjo frog, *Limnodynastes dorsalis*, both of southwest Australia; and the desert shovelfoot, *Notaden nichollsi*, from the arid interior of Australia. The glass frogs of the family Centrolenidae occur in Central America, northern South America and southern Brazil. There are 64 species in two genera, including, *Centrolenella Tvireovittata*, from the cloud forests of Central America.

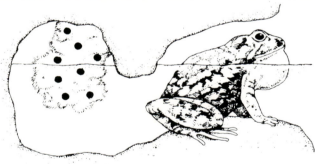

ABOVE The ornate horned frog of tropical America is a large, strong and aggressive frog. It has a huge mouth that it uses to catch and devour prey including birds, small mammals and other frogs. It lies in ambush in the undergrowth, concealed by its intricate camouflage, and snaps up any edible creature that strays too near. If disturbed, it will readily attack large animals, including humans that try to handle it.
LEFT The western banjo frog of Australia lays its eggs in a foam nest that floats on the water in a sheltered spot. The frog takes its name from the male's distinctive call, which has a sound similar to that of a locally made type of banjo.

lays its eggs in damp crevices under stones. Breeding takes place at any time during the six or seven months of the year when there is enough rain to keep the ground wet. However, the tadpoles must complete their metamorphosis in water, so if there is a drought after the female has laid her eggs, the eggs remain unhatched for several months until conditions improve. The western banjo frog, which derives its name from the call of the male, lays eggs in foam nests that float on the water between plants. The desert shovelfoot has adapted to survive in the dry interior of Australia by sharing the humid nests of the bulldog ant.

The glass frogs are small, bright green, tree-dwelling frogs that live near streams in the rain forests and high, mist-shrouded forests of tropical Central and South America. The females lay their eggs on the undersides of broad leaves that overhang the water, and the males of at least one species guard the eggs during their development.

Transparent skin

Glass frogs take their name from their skin, which is so transparent on their bellies—and sometimes also on their limbs—that their internal organs and bones are often plainly visible. Most have tiny eyes, set almost on the top of their wide, blunt heads. Glass frogs are secretive, elusive creatures, and little is known of their behavior.

MEDIA CENTER
EDEN PRAIRIE HIGH SCHOOL
17185 VALLEY VIEW ROAD
EDEN PRAIRIE, MN 55346

REFERENCE--NOT TO BE
TAKEN FROM THIS ROOM